PHILOS(

CRIME, AND

CRIMINOLOGY

CRITICAL
PERSPECTIVES
IN CRIMINOLOGY

SERIES EDITOR
Bruce A. Arrigo,
University of North Carolina,
Charlotte

Philosophy, Crime, and Criminology

Edited by

Bruce A. Arrigo and

Christopher R. Williams

UNIVERSITY OF ILLINOIS PRESS

URBANA AND CHICAGO

Library of Congress Cataloging-in-Publication Data
Philosophy, crime, and criminology / edited by
Bruce A. Arrigo and Christopher R. Williams.
p.   cm. — (Critical perspectives in criminology)
Includes bibliographical references and index.
ISBN-13: 978-0-252-03051-2 (cloth : alk. paper)
ISBN-10: 0-252-03051-6 (cloth : alk. paper)
ISBN-13: 978-0-252-07289-5 (pbk. : alk. paper)
ISBN-10: 0-252-07289-8 (pbk. : alk. paper)
1. Criminology.
2. Philosophy.
3. Crime—Philosophy.
I. Arrigo, Bruce A.
II. Williams, Christopher R., 1972–
III. Series.
HV6025.P494   2006
364—dc22   2005017094

For W. Byron Groves:
Although we did not know you, Casey,
your lessons are timeless, your wisdom
is profound, and your spirit is with us
always

CONTENTS

Part Three: Ethics and Crime

Part Four: Aesthetics and Crime

PHILOSOPHY, CRIME, AND CRIMINOLOGY

INTRODUCTION

Philosophy, Crime, and Theoretical Criminology

**CHRISTOPHER R. WILLIAMS
AND BRUCE A. ARRIGO**

Historically, philosophers have written very little about the subject of crime. Similarly, criminologists have written very little about the subject of philosophy. In both cases, the linkages between philosophy and crime have been left implicit—either in the more general metaphysical, ethical, and legal writings of philosophers, or the theoretical speculations of criminologists. However, to be sure, law and justice have been particularly significant concerns throughout the history of philosophy (e.g., Solomon & Murphy, 1990; Friedrich, 1963). From Plato, through Aquinas and Augustine, to Kant, Bentham, and Beccaria, many of the most important philosophical minds have confronted the complexities of social obligation, social offense, social control, and societal responses to crime directly and deeply. Yet hardly any of these same philosophers saw fit to address, in any systematic or comprehensive fashion, the behavior that makes necessary and possible recurrent debates on issues such as the meaning of justice, the proper reach of the criminal law, and the ethical underpinnings of criminal punishment.

Indeed, crime, it seems, has never been regarded as a suitably philosophical issue. Admittedly, at various historical junctures, the subject of criminal behavior has been taken up by legal philosophy, medical philosophy, theology, and, as a subset of immoral conduct, by ethics. This notwithstanding, crime per se has been and remains conspicuously absent from the sorts of general ontological, epistemological, ethical, and aesthetical analyses that might suggest new perspectives and alternative directions for its general comprehension and, by consequence, for its specific applications in law and justice studies.

At the same time, the discipline of philosophy and its corresponding intellectual subdivisions (i.e., ontology, epistemology, ethics, and aesthetics) have never been properly regarded as criminological concerns—save, perhaps, the ethical dilemmas and quandaries that emerge as issues of professional or practical interest within legal, law enforcement, and correctional circles. Regrettably, as criminology has evolved into an increasingly interdisciplinary and independent field with its own scholars and practitioners, the role of philosophical speculation, argument, analysis, and critique in matters of criminological import has withered into veritable nonexistence. Even in pedagogical formulations, criminology and philosophy are mostly regarded as distinct, and perhaps unrelated, subjects. For example, in colleges and universities around the world they typically represent separate departments, housed in different colleges, and often occupying space in entirely distinct physical quarters. Criminologists rarely interact with philosophers and vice versa. Criminology departments do not often—if ever—offer courses whose clear objective is to entertain and expose the connections between what criminology does and what philosophy is. Moreover, in many criminology programs, students may earn their degree without ever having taken a course in philosophy. At best, they are introduced to philosophical issues only by way of an occasional footnote or two in books and courses on theoretical criminology. Even then, such footnotes infrequently appear (see, however, Einstadter & Henry, 1995).

Yet criminology is fundamentally wedded to philosophy in countless ways, and the crossroads of criminology and philosophy are ripe for exposition and assimilation by scholars in both camps. This very sentiment was the basis for creating the present volume. As such, many of the implicit historical associations between crime and philosophy, as well as relevant philosophical concepts and arguments, represent topical foci for the chapters that follow. We hasten to add, however, that the philosophy-criminology union entertained in this book is not intended to be exhaustive. Rather than offering a comprehensive portrait of a philosophical criminology, we have instead chosen to concentrate on selected points of intersection with the promise that access to further critical junctures will most assuredly follow in subsequent works. Thus, rather than attempting to "fill" a gap in the literature, our primary interest is indexical; that is, we hope to "point out" such a gap, evocatively contributing to a more thorough and enlightened consideration of this underexamined relationship.

In the interest of an introduction, the remainder of this chapter pursues several goals. First, we address the historical development of the concept and study of crime as it has progressed from antiquity, through the Middle Ages, into modernity and, more recently, postmodernity. Admittedly, our historical treatment is modest, omitting several shifts in the evolution of the philosophy of crime. However, our intention is to provide merely a sense of the ways in which philosophy has addressed the issue of crime and, further, how such conceptions have been subjected to broader intellectual speculation and social transformation. Second, we offer some suggestions as to how a *philosophical criminology* or the introduction of philosophy into criminological analysis might occur. In other words, we address the specific value that philosophy ostensibly holds for the study of crime. In doing do, we briefly address each of the four core areas of philosophy (i.e., metaphysics or ontology, epistemology, ethics, and aesthetics), attending to their potential relevance for studies of crime. Given that the chapters in this volume flesh out many of these intersections and potentialities, our primary aim is to expose the reader to the contours of these philosophical subdivisions, providing in each instance an overview of and reference to several constitutive concerns. We conclude the introductory chapter with a synopsis of the book's organization and the substantive chapters representing this volume.

Crime in Philosophy

Many students and scholars alike often fail to recognize just how recent the temporal separation actually is between philosophy and criminology, the social sciences, and science more generally. We forget or, perhaps, never consider that only several centuries ago, the boundaries between what are now considered to be the physical and social sciences and philosophy were not so clearly demarcated (for a discussion of these boundaries, see, e.g., Benton & Craib, 2001). For nearly two thousand years, social science and philosophy were one and the same. The psychologists, sociologists, and criminologists of antiquity and the Middle Ages were *philosophers* associated with psychology, sociology, and criminology only by way of the sorts of questions they entertained. It was only during subsequent historical periods that these sorts of questions became affiliated with specialized academic disciplines (Rosenberg, 1988).

In fact the relationship between philosophy and crime is one that dates to antiquity. The essential questions of criminology—what crime is, why certain people engage in criminal behavior, how systems of justice should respond to lawbreakers—are questions that, until relatively recently, were examined almost exclusively by philosophers (though not, as previously noted, in any systematic fashion). In fact, the very notions of crime, law, and justice that we continue to wrestle with today—and upon which the discipline and practice of criminology are based—are firmly rooted in a philosophical tradition that extends as far back as Plato, through Kant, Bentham, Beccaria, and Marx, and into the theoretical variants of more recent scholars who have adopted, adapted, and incorporated philosophical critique into their criminological commentaries (e.g., Arrigo, 1999; DiCristina, 1995; Henry & Milovanovic, 1996; Newman, Lynch, & Galaty, 1993).

Though most books on criminology or criminological theory begin their historical descriptions with the insights of Cesare de Beccaria (1764/1963), crime, law, and justice were at least implicit topics of concern throughout the two-thousand-plus years of Western philosophy that preceded him. Rarely, however, have criminologists extended serious attention to such contributions (cf. Beirne, 1993; Foucault, 1977). In part, this lack of consideration may reflect the relative absence of anything resembling a complete and intellectually noteworthy philosophy of crime prior to the 1700s. While theories of law and justice were central concerns throughout antiquity, the concept of crime per se emerged only as a topic of inquiry ancillary to them. Nevertheless, philosophical considerations of crime can be traced at least to Plato, thereafter becoming a subject of theological concern throughout the Middle Ages, subsequently entering the cause-effect discourse of modernity through the legal ponderings of Beccaria and Bentham and the scientific discourse of the early biological positivists, and, finally, succumbing to the antifoundational and deracinating agenda of postmodernity.

We should keep in mind that, while crime may be a "social fact," the particular realities of crime are relative to time and place. Consequently, whatever implicit or explicit speculations might be derived from the likes of Plato or Kant, crime in ancient Greece or 18th-century Germany was dramatically different from what we find today in the Western world. Typifying the latter are issues of crime's hyperreality and the mass-mediated character of its existence (e.g., Arrigo, 1996). Such ontological considerations would have been unimaginable just a few short decades ago. Similarly, other contemporary realities such as the incidence of crime and of other social problems (e.g., drugs, racial conflict), technological advances in weaponry and other tools of the criminal trade, and the automobile as a means of transportation are criminological considerations unique to the 20th and 21st centuries. While many of the philosophical issues relevant to criminology are transhistorical and transcultural (e.g., free will vs. determinism; the nature of causality), others are not. Thus our philosophical criminology must be one that both draws from the perennial debates in philosophy while remaining cognizant of time and place.

Crime as Vice: Crime in the Origins of Philosophy

Law and justice were prominent concerns of ancient Greek and Roman philosophers, often figuring into broader moral and political debates (e.g., Friedrich, 1963). Theories of crime, while not often postulated as such, can be inferred from the general ethical and legal philosophies of many thinkers from antiquity. To be sure, crime was an integral component of theories pertaining to law and justice. For example, one could not have postulated a view of punishment without crime serving as a basis for such a theory (e.g., de Beccaria, 1764/1963; Foucault, 1977). Consequently, we can look to theories of law and punishment for some indication of how crime and criminal behavior were conceptualized.

At various points throughout the philosophy of Plato, we find some of the earliest efforts to explain crime. Not surprisingly, Plato weaves— mostly by implication—his theory of crime into his more general moral psychology. Following Mackenzie (1981), we can surmise three different analyses of criminality for Plato: (1) crime as ignorance; (2) crime as psychological disorder; and (3) crime as disease. In each case, criminality is understood to be a characterological deficit. Characterological deficits, in turn, were subsumed under the broader category of vice rather than virtue. For Plato—and the ancient Greeks more commonly—the moral person is virtuous. By contrast, the immoral person—including the criminal—is vicious. For purposes of this section of the book's introduction, Plato's understanding of crime as ignorance and crime as psychological disorder requires some further elucidation.

In the first analysis, vice is a state of the soul whereby the soul is defined as ignorant. More precisely, virtue is knowledge, while vice is ignorance. Plato understood all evil in this manner: "all wicked men are, in all respects, unwillingly wicked" (1988, p. 369). The individual who knows what is right, good, and just will necessarily pursue what is right, good, and just. This, then, is the essence of Plato's moral philosophy and, inferentially, his theory of crime: all people aim at that which they believe to be good. People, however, can be mistaken about what is actually good and, consequently, can remain in a state of ignorance and vice. As such, ignorance is both necessary for crime and it is sufficient for crime (Mackenzie, 1981).

In other places, Plato seems to link crime (i.e., vice) to the appetitive "part" of the soul. In the *Republic,* he sets forth his tripartite psychology wherein the soul consists of a relationship between rational, spirited, and appetitive aspects (for an introduction, see Pappas, 1995). The vicious soul is characterized by psychological disorder or conflict. Not only is knowledge essential to virtue, but order and control are essential as well. For the virtuous person, the rational part of the soul has mastery and control over the desirous or appetitive component. In vicious souls, reason loses this mastery and either inflated desires or perverted spirit compel vile action (Mackenzie, 1981, p. 171). In book 9 of the *Republic,* Plato offers a more specific analysis of the criminal disposition, pointing to three causes of vice: anger, pleasure, and ignorance. Anger and pleasure both compel a person toward wrongdoing, whereas ignorance reflects a lack of knowledge and a consequent lack of rational power over the emotions (Mackenzie, 1981, p. 174).

Given that virtue ethics characterized the thinking of ancient Greek and Roman philosophers, we can rightfully assume that crime was regarded as a form of vice or immoral behavior. However, the conceptualization of "crime as vice" was a historically informed and thereby historically specific phenomenon. Interestingly, nowhere is the historical nature of theories pertaining to crime and criminality more apparent than in the dramatic reformulations and ideological changes wrought by theology that followed the Greco-Roman era. This period is known as the Middle Ages.

Crime as Sin: The Middle Ages

The defining feature of the Middle Ages in general is the profound influence of theology on human conceptualizations of the world (e.g., Solomon & Higgins, 1996; Hyman & Walsh, 1983). Philosophical inquiry was largely replaced by theological speculation. Theoretical insights pertaining to law, crime, and justice were no different. The Middle Ages witnessed the demise of the Greek-inspired "crime as vice" philosophy and the emergence of the theologically inspired "crime as sin" framework. This was the dominant perspective on crime throughout the Middle Ages; that is, from the end of antiquity until the 17th and 18th centuries (Pfohl, 1994). In many practical respects, the notions of "vice" and "sin" are similar. The vices of antiquity and the sins of the Middle Ages described many of the same tendencies and behaviors. The locus of the transition from vice to sin was metaphysical. That is to say, while vice was understood by the likes of Plato to be human ignorance and the absence of virtue, the same behaviors became recast in the Middle Ages as transgressions against God and, consequently, sins issuing from human weakness (rather than ignorance) and lack of faith (rather than reason). In other respects, conceptualizations of crime in the Middle Ages display considerable parallels to subsequent criminologies; namely, the classical notion of freedom of choice and the positivist notion of deterministic causality (Pfohl, 1994; Einstadter & Henry, 1995; Vold, Bernard, & Snipes, 2001).

Throughout the Middle Ages, both the human world and social life were understood to be characterized by a continual struggle in which the forces of good and evil were pitted against one another. Indeed, following Pfohl (1994), the human world was conceptualized as a "battleground" wherein the power of good and evil played out their inherent hostilities. Manifest evil was a result of demonic or evil forces asserting their influence over the course of such eternal struggles. The "cause" of evil (and crime) was supernatural in nature. Thus, human beings were regarded as caught within the interplay of good and evil, torn between competing forces, and susceptible to the latter. From the theological perspective, individuals were "drawn into" evil and its various manifestations, a phenomenon often equated with succumbing to sin's dark and sinister allure.

More specifically, human beings could be drawn into evil in one of two ways: by giving in to temptation or by being involuntarily possessed by demonic forces (Pfohl, 1994). The former possibility assumed an element of free will; that is, people had the power to resist such forces but chose to acquiesce out of weakness. For Plato, these same powers of reason were what made human beings distinct and, consequently, able to pursue the good through virtue. The Platonic soul provided individuals with the capacity for virtue by way of reason and rationality. The conception of human nature throughout the Middle Ages was different only in one important respect—the "soul" was linked more directly to supernatural metaphysical sources. For example, according to St. Thomas Aquinas, the soul was a gift from God, implanting within humans a likeness to His ultimate reason (e.g., Dilman, 1999; Kenny, 1980). Therefore, sinful transgressions reflected a failure to responsibly use God-given powers of reason and choice. Ultimately, they were understood as sins against God himself. Crime-as-evil occurred because "human appetites toward worldly pleasures were enticed by the Devil to overcome our conscience embodied in our God-given soul" (Einstadter & Henry, 1995, pp. 34–35).

Human nature, then, was one of suggestibility and vulnerability yet with a corresponding power to resist the temptations of sin. Metaphysically speaking, human beings were vulnerable to evil forces and susceptible to succumb to such forces in the absence of strength or resolve to resist them. The evil to which people were susceptible assumed multiple forms. Most notably, these included the seven "deadly sins" or "wicked pleasures" (Solomon, 2001) of gluttony, pride, sloth, greed, anger, lust, and envy. They represented forms of the devil. Consequently, giving into lust or anger was equated with giving in to demonic forces or evil more generally. Interestingly, this line of thinking is not that far removed from Platonic conceptions of crime as vice: both regarded human life as a purposive pursuit of the good; both recognized crime or wrongdoing as evil; and both understood the immediate sources of evil similarly (e.g., anger, lust). In addition to ignorance, Plato specifically drew attention to anger and pleasure as sources of vice and crime, describing anger as an "innate impulse, unruly and difficult to fight as it is, caus[ing] a good deal of havoc by its irrational force" (1988, p. 373). With respect to pleasure, Plato asserted, "We say Pleasure wields her power on the basis of an opposite kind of force; she achieves whatever her will desires by persuasive deceit that is irresistibly compelling" (ibid.). For Plato, then, the vicious person was overcome by anger, unable to control (i.e., resist;

have power over) the vicious impulses. The difference, of course, lies in the ultimate source of evil.

Whereas Plato's vice was moral psychology, the sins of the Middle Ages found their source in the realm of the supernatural. Accordingly, in the latter instance, human beings were afforded some choice or element of reason that allowed them to resist evil. In this respect, then, the theologically based explanations of the Middle Ages were a forerunner to later classical ideas about free will and rational choice. The supernatural powers of evil were understood to be seductive, implying a countervailing power within human beings to oppose such temptations. Indeed, while all people were subject to enticement, the faithful could resist, especially with the help of family, law, and, ultimately, God (Pfohl, 1994). However, of philosophical—specifically metaphysical—importance in the Middle Ages was the distinction made between temptation as a source of evil and possession as a source of evil. The notion of possession, namely, that a person could be involuntarily consumed by demonic forces, implies a degree of determinism previously absent from discussions about human behavior. In short, once a person was possessed, the individual was no longer responsible for her or his choices. In contrast, temptation resulted from human weakness: that loss of faith embodied in carnal or other wicked pleasures.

Crime as Rational Hedonism: The Emergence of Modernity

The next significant philosophical shift in thinking about crime, law, and justice did not occur until the 17th and 18th centuries, emerging from the general intellectual climate of the Enlightenment and finding criminological cohesion in the legal philosophies of Beccaria (1764/1963) and Bentham (1996). Commonly understood as the beginning of modern criminology, mid-18th-century classicism offered a perspective of human nature and behavior that was largely free of theological influence, establishing instead the locus of crime in individual reason and thought. Rather than placing human nature and behavior within the narrowly construed confines of divine determination or in relation to the eternal struggle between the forces of good and evil, classical conceptions were firmly rooted in the principle of rationality, emphasizing personal responsibility, free choice, and hedonistic calculation.

The utilitarian logic of classicism marked a metaphysical departure from the theologically inspired metaphysics of the Middle Ages. Whereas the demonologies of this period were inspired by beliefs in supernatural forces, the 18th century witnessed the emergence of a rational frame-work within which criminals engaged in planful decisions to act with the intention of maximizing pleasure and/or minimizing pain. Unlike the "crime as sin" framework offered by demonology, 18th-century classicism understood human beings to be under the influence of nothing other than the capacities of intellect and choice. The "Age of Reason" brought with it both a revised metaphysics emphasizing the nature of human beings as rational animals and a revised epistemology emphasizing the role of reason in knowledge about crime and criminals.

Not unlike the conception of human nature offered by Plato, virtue in classicism was equated with the success of the individual in controlling appetites by way of reason and will. Crime was not a matter of other-worldly influence, nor was it afforded the considerably more humanistic dimension of ignorance. Rather, crime was a failure to use innate reason to make informed and calculated choices to bring about the best results. Human beings were understood as "independent, free-thinking, rational decision-makers who control[led] their own destiny by defining self-interest" (Einstadter & Henry, 1995, p. 47). However, following Hobbes (1985), human nature was characterized as hedonistic and self-interested, motivating people to pursue pleasure and personal gain at the expense of social concerns. Bentham's (1996) felicity calculus incorporates each of these elements: human beings rationally calculate the potential pleasures of a certain action against the potential pains associated with that action and, ultimately, act so as to produce the most pleasure with the least corresponding degree of pain. Thus, human beings are free-willed, capable of independent choice; rational and capable of calculating self-interest; hedonistic, motivated by the pursuit of pleasure and the avoidance of pain; and generally free to determine their own destinies. This assumption of freedom, in conjunction with the assumption of pure rationality, distinguishes the classical tradition in many ways from both its ancient and theological predecessors.

Overall, then, the classical paradigm emerged within and from the more global Enlightenment paradigm that emphasized the role of reason, freedom, and self-determination in human knowledge and behavior. The criminal of the classical era was not understood as tempted or possessed in a theological sense, or ignorant in a Platonic sense. Rather, the criminal was no different than the non-criminal, aside from the path to pleasure that he or she chose. All people were by nature self-interested and, therefore, were likely to turn to criminality. As all individuals were equally rational, hedonistic, and free, the defining feature of the criminal was his or her calculation that crime would yield more rewards than would conformity.

Positivism: Philosophy and the Origins of Criminology

The last major shift in criminological thinking emerged concomitantly with the birth of positivism in the sciences. Of philosophical importance, this transition carried with it a focus on causation and determinism, thus marking a modification from metaphysical to physical explanations. Over the course of nearly two thousand years, the concept of crime was varyingly positioned within the context of vice, sin, rational choice, and now a causal effect or consequence of scientifically identifiable determining forces. In this regard, positivism represented the shift from metaphysics to physics or science itself. Given that the formal origins of criminology proper emerged alongside positivism, this particular transition should be regarded as doubly significant: positivism signifies the birth of a new scientific paradigm and it represents the direction upon which contemporary criminology was founded and mostly continues to unfold.

The origin of the social sciences as specialized disciplines did not materialize in any identifiable form until the positivist turn in the 18th and 19th centuries. Social philosopher Auguste Comte (1957, 1988)—usually credited as both the father of positivism and sociology—argued that the methods of the natural sciences (e.g., physics, astronomy) could be applied, in principle, to the social world. Following his observations, sociology, psychology, anthropology, and later criminology emerged as disciplines in their own right. Interestingly, criminology did not exist as a differentiated field until a little over a century ago. Indeed, it was not until 1885 that legal philosopher Raffaele Garofalo (1968) coined the term "criminology" when referring to the study of law, crime, and justice. Prior to its emergence as a specialized discipline, criminological issues were the pursuits of philosophers and, more specifically, several different subfields within philosophy. Thus while philosophers such as Cesare Beccaria and Jeremy Bentham examined legal issues (e.g., punishment), biological positivists such as Cesare Lombroso and Enrico Ferri investigated criminal issues (e.g., phrenology). Indeed, Lombroso and Ferri sought to locate the cause of crime in human biological functioning (e.g., Lombroso, 1889, 1912; Ferri, 1900).

Criminology, then, was born under the influence of positivism. By virtue of its origin, criminology emerged as a *science*. More specifically, criminology was presented as an empirical science, considerably removed from the speculative insights of philosophy. The subject matter of criminology, as well as the methods criminologists used to investigate the social world, were intended to be distinct and, thus, separate from those employed by philosophers. While philosophy was exploratory in nature, consisting of the rational, conceptual, and theoretical analysis of mostly unobservable phenomena, criminology was empirical in nature, consisting of the concrete, objective, and scientific analysis of mostly observable phenomena. In this respect, criminology concerned itself with discovering empirical facts about lawmaking and lawbreaking through the use of scientific methods adopted from the natural sciences. Nowhere is the scientific orientation of criminology more apparent than in Edwin Sutherland's now classic description of criminology as a discipline whose "objective . . . is the development of a body of general and verified principles . . . regarding the process of law, crime, and treatment or prevention" (1924, p. 5). With aims, principles, and methods borrowed from the natural sciences, criminology separated itself from the basic questions that arguably formed the core of its subject matter.

Postmodernism: Philosophical Resistance to Modern Criminology

While perhaps not a major transition in the same sense or on the same scale as the theological transformation of the Middle Ages or the paradigm shifts of classical and positivist criminology, postmodernism represents a significant and recent departure in the philosophy of the social sciences. Postmodernism emerged in the social sciences during the 1980s and took hold in criminology during the 1990s (e.g., Henry & Milovanovic, 1996). Fueled, in part, by a number of alternative intellectual approaches (e.g., symbolic interactionism, labeling theory, phenomenology, and social constructionism) that developed during the mid-20th century, postmodernism questioned conventional, positivist wisdom about truth, reason, knowledge, and progress. Indeed, as philosophical critique, postmodernism rejected the framework and corresponding assumptions of modern science in particular and the modern worldview in general, arguing that they failed to more fully (and honestly) account for the discontinuities, irregularities, and contradictions of social life (e.g., Arrigo, Milovanovic, & Schehr, 2005). Specifically, postmodern metaphysics and epistemology provided theoretical tinder for those discontented with the modern emphasis on determinism, linear causality, absolutism, order, stasis, and other foundational assumptions that had theretofore permeated theory and research in the social sciences (Best & Kellner, 1997; Rosenau, 1992). These were the trappings of positivism; the taken-for-granted icons of science that neglected or dismissed other dimensions of the human condition (Arrigo, 1995; Milovanovic, 2003).

Postmodernism, while resisting easy definition, served and continues to serve as a complex and sophisticated challenge to a number of the fundamental assumptions of modernity. In many respects, the arguments of postmodernism borrow from or take up more traditional criticisms offered by forms of epistemological skepticism and varieties of metaphysical antirealist arguments. With roots in Socrates and Pyrrho of Elis, epistemological skepticism is constituted by a tradition of varying epistemic (knowledge-related) antagonisms, contesting the limits or extent of human knowledge. Many skeptics and postmodernists have challenged the notion that human beings *do* have knowledge—or, at least, particular types of knowledge or levels of certainty (Best & Kellner, 1997). What is resisted and debunked here is the absolute certainty that comes with claims to knowing a particular truth, thesis, form, or unity. In this respect, postmodernism defies and dispels the modern confidence in objectivity, particularly as it appears under the guise of science (e.g., Crotty, 1998). Instead, for the postmodernist, claims to objectivity and certainty are best understood as serving to establish or maintain oppressive power relations (Milovanovic, 1997). Indeed, assertions of impartial and neutral knowledge merely endeavor to disguise the reality (the power and authority) underlying claims to knowledge, truth, and progress (Arrigo, Milovanovic, & Schehr, 2005).

In its disavowal of absolute or categorical knowledge, postmodernism is sometimes affiliated with relativism, denying the existence of any total truth and claiming, instead, that things are true for someone or some group under specified conditions, rather than simply being completely true (e.g., Moser, Mulder, & Trout, 1998, *on relativism and truth*). In its most common form as found within the social sciences, relativism suggests that realities are either subjective or socially constructed and, consequently, relative to those individuals living them. In the absence of categorical truth, science loses its status as that which has unique access to objective, pristine reality. In other words, if objective, impartial, and certain reality no longer fundamentally anchors human experience, then science, as a method of inquiry into such realities or truths, can no longer claim authoritative status. Thus, according to postmodernists, by demystifying the assumption of fixed, certain realities, the supposed benefit of science—namely, its promise to uncover the truths of the world by way of its methods and techniques—is considerably undone (e.g., Best & Kellner, 1997).

Given the philosophical insights identified above, postmodernism challenges the claims made by individuals, groups, institutions, communities, and societies wherein particular perspectives are said to be the basis for absolute truth, knowledge, identity, meaning, and so forth. Instead, postmodernism reveals the ways in which unspoken values and implicit assumptions underscore all claims to understanding and meaning while, in the process, dismissing alternative ways of thinking, feeling, acting, and being (Arrigo, 1995). As a general proposition, modernism is accused of privileging certain sources of knowledge such as science and scientific inquiry over other potential sources of knowledge. The standards of science—linear thinking, syllogistic reasoning, objectivity, cause-effect logic—are assumptions that, when challenged, reveal inconsistencies, anomalies, contradictions, and irregularities. This is why postmodernists are quick to indicate that science is a useful perspective on the knowledge process; however, it is not *the* path to knowing social phenomena.

One of the more substantial features of postmodernism is its insistence that realities are linguistically mediated. In other words, the construction of knowledge and reality is framed, shaped, and given content through communication, whether written or spoken. Given that discourse structures thought nonneutrally—that is, in ways that already and always imply a certain orientation to people, events, and behavior—our thoughts, conversations, and stories concerning crime and criminals are mediated by the linguistic structures we employ to communicate (Arrigo, Milovanovic, & Schehr, 2005). These structures include such things as our use of certain words, phrases, or combination of both, the inflection and intonation in our voices, extraverbal cues (e.g., ummm, uh-huh), pauses, and even silences. Consequently, our understanding of or knowledge about crime, law, and justice are given expressive form (become realities) when constructed within linguistic systems (e.g., the language of the law or *legalese*). The meaning of these narratives is derived from how we convey the thoughts that we think as communicated from within the language system and/or structures we employ. Importantly, because the knowledge we have concerning these realities is textured by what we say and by how we say it, knowledge about crime, law, and justice is linked to the power language wields over us; that is, the power to define, interpret, and reinterpret social reality (Milovanovic, 1997). Many postmodern criminologists have offered detailed critiques explaining where and how criminological subjects (e.g., prisoners, lawyers, the mentally ill) consequently become silenced and are co-opted (e.g., Williams & Arrigo, 2002; Arrigo, 2002; Henry & Milovanovic, 1999; Milovanovic, 2003). In this scripted process, the knowledge and experiences of these subjects are muted or otherwise reconfigured wherein their identities are made compatible with the language system in use. Observations such as these have led some affirmative postmodern criminologists to define crime as the power to reduce or repress a person's humanity such that a person is rendered powerless (through language) to make a difference (e.g., Henry & Milovanovic, 1996).

Philosophy in Criminology: Charting a Philosophy of Crime

Given our summary comments in the previous section, we note that since its modern inception criminology has not been a discipline of systematic philosophical debate, analysis, or critique. Moreover, scholars and practitioners of crime have failed to recognize their role as potentially contributing to the broader ontological, epistemological, ethical, and aesthetical questions that philosophy more directly confronts. In both instances, the rise of science and, in particular, positivist science ushered in the decline of philosophical speculation and inquiry in matters of crime and justice. We find these circumstances to be a source of considerable intellectual concern. Indeed, we take the position that criminology and philosophy should not and, in fact, cannot be separated if the former is to achieve its stated or even unstated objectives. To be clear, the discipline's continuing efforts to understand law, to control and predict crime, and to make justice necessitates that criminology, in some meaningful way, align itself to philosophical concepts, issues, and arguments. Regrettably, because of the union between criminology and positive science, criminology proper has mostly failed to contemplate let alone critically examine its conceptual underpinnings, that is, the philosophical cornerstones that support its purpose and potential. This book was conceived as a much needed, though preliminary, attempt to address the sort of possibilities that philosophy embodies for criminology. In this respect, then, this volume represents an initial foray into the sorts of speculative matters that, in our opinion, criminology has appreciably and woefully neglected. Despite the increasing breadth of scholarship in crime and justice studies, philosophical considerations are only occasionally interjected that pose the fundamental questions impacting criminology from within or that force reflection upon contentious matters offering the discipline potential guidance from without.

The relevance of philosophy to criminological pursuits is manifold. In order to understand both the relevance of philosophy to criminology and the relationship that exists between the two, it is useful to identify the purpose and definition of philosophy. Blackburn (1994) describes the field as "the study of the most general and abstract features of the world and categories with which we think: mind, matter, reason, proof, truth, etc." Thus philosophy wrestles with concepts and categories through which the world is approached and, more specifically, the elements constituting it are studied. Importantly, these are concepts and categories about which we make assumptions and from which we proceed into more specific analyses. For example, reason is a requisite feature of law, justice, and various explanations of criminal behavior. Accordingly, it is essential that investigations concerning law, crime, and justice include some significant reflection about the very concept of reason itself. Interestingly, while legal philosophers have debated the philosophical underpinnings of such notions as reason for centuries, criminologists have rarely followed suit. However, reason is more than just a legal notion. It is also a fundamental aspect of being human, relevant to how we conceive of self, others, and one's place in society, how we go about attaining knowledge of the world we inhabit, how we understand the choices and actions of others, and how we make distinctions such as right and wrong.

In this regard, then, when we investigate people and society philosophically, "the concepts with which we approach [these phenomena] themselves become the topic of enquiry" (Blackburn, 1994, p. 4). Indeed, concepts such as "crime," "law," "justice," "reason," "fairness," "due process," and the like are not simply to be measured scientifically; rather, they are to be subjected to philosophical clarification and analysis. Thus, a philosophical criminology is less interested in crime rates than in how crime rates presuppose certain definitions about crime and how measurements of crime contain certain theoretical and methodological presuppositions.

As a practical matter, however, the study of crime does not include, let alone emphasize, this particular orientation. For example, consider the Federal Bureau of Investigation's Uniform Crime Reports. The UCR attempts to provide standardized definitions of certain crimes; that is, definitions that link all instances of rape, murder, and so on by drawing attention to that which underlies each such occurrence, thereby making the reality of rape or murder a definitive, categorical ontological reality. However, these efforts presuppose that identified crimes have an objective nature—that rape is rape, for example, by virtue of something inherent in the act that is observable and, in some sense, measurable. This assumption of objectivity is reinforced by the necessity that rape be a *verifiable* reality. Consistent with the tenets of logical positivism and the framework endorsed by modern science, knowledge claims have meaning only by way of their verification. In the context of the UCR, measurements of criminal incidence depend upon both legal criteria and police verification that the criteria correspond to offender behavior and, only secondarily, to victim experience. Presumably, victims can be mistaken in light of their limited access to knowledge of the event.

Almost by definition, then, philosophy uniquely redirects the investigatory focus to the concepts that are inescapable in criminology, concepts that do not lend themselves to exact measurement or precise empirical analysis. Again, following Blackburn's definition of philosophy, a philosophy of criminology would seek "not so much to solve historical, physical, or legal questions, as to study the concepts that structure such thinking, and to lay bare their foundations and presuppositions" (1994). In this respect, we might view a philosophical criminology as a *self-conscious* criminology. Philosophy, continues Blackburn, "is what happens when a practice becomes self-conscious" (ibid.). Criminology, in the accepted and commonly practiced sense, might best be understood as the "raw material" within which a philosophical criminology seeks to gain access, to inquire, and to know. Indeed, a philosophy of crime, law, and justice would endeavor to clarify, explain, interpret, and/or critique such raw materials.

Given the above observations, philosophy's (potential) role in criminology might be viewed as twofold. First, philosophy serves as a foundation for criminological thought, research, and knowledge. In this capacity, criminology rests upon philosophy and, consequently, relies upon it for criminology's most basic premises, assumptions, theories, and methods. Second, philosophy serves not so much as a foundation but as an "underlaborer" (Benton & Craib, 2001). Philosophy becomes the crucible for comprehension, providing guidance and support from without for the work that criminology does from within. This guidance and support may assume many forms. For example, philosophy and philosophical inquiry may expose the prejudices and unquestioned assumptions upon which criminology proper too often rests. In this instance, philosophy can help position criminological knowledge within a macrological context of *human* thought, charting the course of criminological *verstehen* on the epistemological map.

Thus far, our efforts regarding the establishment of a philosophical criminology have mostly examined the broad contours of this endeavor. However, we also note that such an undertaking would assume very specific manifestations. Indeed, there are countless ways to conceptualize a philosophy of crime or criminology. In part, this is because philosophy is a discipline unparalleled in the depth and breadth of its subject matter. At its most obvious and fundamental level, a philosophical criminology would analyze various aspects of law, crime, and justice through the various subdivisions of philosophy. In this respect, we might regard a philosophical criminology as the epistemological, ontological (or metaphysical), ethical, and aesthetical assessment of crime. Analytically speaking, this approach to the study of crime would entail coming to terms with the various conceptual issues, problems, and complexities underlying theoretical criminology itself and, to a lesser extent, the practical aspects of criminology proper.

Criminologists, knowingly or not, are inevitably involved with philosophical concerns. For example, inquiries into the *cause* of crime entail metaphysical and epistemological assumptions about causation and the possibility of knowledge and certainty (e.g., DiCristina, 1995). When lawmakers define crime and when criminologists examine criminal behavior, they make ontological commitments to certain views of reality and to certain interpretations of the human condition. Those same definitions and investigatory models are firmly rooted in morality—and a selective one at that. As criminologists determine what issues to confront (and how to confront them), their choices become *selective* representations of the field. However, that which is selected is done so based on presupposed ontological realities. The choice of research topics alone involves moral considerations in that certain subjects are selected at the expense of other—presumably less significant though equally worthwhile—topics.

As such, a philosophical criminology would differ from criminology per se in how the identified subject matter was taken up and investigated. To illustrate, consider how both would assess theoretical efforts in criminology. A philosophically animated criminology would provide a critical examination of the competing theories of crime and criminality, with particular attention to the validity of the philosophical assumptions and presuppositions that underlie them. Criminology proper (positive criminology) would engage in empirical inquiries, lending support (or not) to the explanatory and predictive capabilities of a particular theory. Thus, rather than unreflectively embarking on new or additional studies of crime and criminality, employing the conventional methodologies of the discipline, a philosophical criminology would analyze the epistemological, ontological, ethical, and aesthetical aspects of the methodologies themselves used for purposes of advancing criminological science. As such, a philosophical criminology does not entail a drastic change in *what* criminology does, only in *how* it is approached, analyzed, and manufactured.

To be sure, the inquiries constituting the terrain of philosophical criminology are inherently and deliberately reflective and critical. Many of these inquiries promise no certain answer. Several others beg responses that are themselves probing questions and troubling concerns. However, the purpose of philosophy and, by extension, philosophical criminology is not so much to find solutions as much as it is to simply question. What is criminology? What is crime? What is their relationship to justice? What are researchers doing when they study crime and justice? What are people doing when they engage in criminal behavior? What methods should we use to study crime and justice? Can we ever attain knowledge of crime and justice? What status can and should we ascribe to our research findings? What role does morality play in criminology? Each of these is a question that, by inference, juxtaposes criminology alongside philosophy and, more specifically, the various subdivisions within philosophy. In the next section, we briefly describe each of these subfields, given their wholesale importance to the various chapters of this book.

Criminology and the Questions of Philosophy

If a philosophical criminology is best understood as the epistemology, ontology, ethics, and aesthetics of crime, we can access what such an endeavor might look like by attending more exactingly to the kinds of issues entertained by these subdivisions. Contemporary philosophy is often divided into a number of interrelated branches: ontology/metaphysics, epistemology, ethics/moral philosophy, aesthetics, logic, and their application to other cognate areas (e.g., philosophy of law, science, religion). We note that in each case these branches are not exhaustive nor are they mutually exclusive. For example, ethical concerns are intimately wedded to ontological concerns (i.e., existence and being) and epistemological concerns (i.e., what we can know), just as epistemological matters presuppose a certain metaphysical reality. Our focus in this book is on the four commonly recognized branches of philosophy: ontology (or metaphysics), epistemology, ethics, and aesthetics.

Ontology

The term "metaphysics" has been varyingly employed and defined throughout the history of philosophy. Consequently, when we speak of metaphysics, we are referring to a timeless category of questioning that resists easy explanation. The term was originally employed as a reference to the writings of Aristotle that came after the *Physics* in his compiled works (Hamlyn, 1984). Aristotle's own characterization of metaphysical pursuits was that of the science of Being qua Being; that is, Being as such. The Aristotelian tradition of metaphysics is closer to *ontology* (*onta* = being; *logos* = study of), or the study of being. Generally speaking, metaphysics and ontology are concerned with questions of reality and, in particular, the "things" of existence that lie beyond physics or outside the realm of physical, that is, scientific investigation. Thus, the traditional questions of metaphysics and ontology are, at the same time, the "big" questions that have perplexed civilization since antiquity and, presumably, for as long as people have been self-conscious and reflective. In this respect, metaphysical pursuits are the most basic problems of existence, fundamental in the sense that nearly everything else depends on them (Taylor, 1974). For example, consider the following questions:

> What is real?
> What is the difference between appearance and reality?
> What does it mean to "exist"?
> What is the purpose of human existence?

Queries such as these are vastly different from those one might find in the social sciences. The social sciences concern themselves with questions that can be answered through exploration and discovery; however, philosophical pursuits of the metaphysical variety offer little in the way of supposed certainty or even substantial probabilities. For this reason, perhaps, many social scientists (criminologists included) fail to ponder these most fundamental of issues—at least in the context of their scholarly undertakings. In Richard Taylor's words, "Except for rare, reflective souls, people go through life just taking for granted those questions of existence, purpose, and meaning that the metaphysician finds most puzzling" (1974, p. 1). Indeed, most social scientists tend to neglect or dismiss the most vexing questions of existence, purpose, and meaning. Interestingly, the answers to these timeless queries *should* mark the beginning of our scholarly endeavors but, instead, most often stand merely as unreflective assumptions from which our work proceeds. Regrettably, the questions of metaphysics and ontology often loom in the background rather than the foreground of social scientific and criminological inquiry.

While metaphysics addresses a multitude of themes relevant to the social sciences, subsequent chapters in this text implicate ontological concerns more specifically. That is to say, we adopt the Aristotelian tradition of inquiry, focusing on "Being *qua* Being and the properties inherent in it [by] virtue of its own nature." Unlike the sciences, Aristotle argues, metaphysics does not "divide off some portion of [Being] and study the attribute[s] of this portion." Rather, metaphysics as ontology is interested in "first principles and most ultimate causes . . . the elements of Being not incidentally, but *qua* Being" (Aristotle, 1933, p. 147).

Not surprisingly, the theories, hypotheses, and methods embraced by the social sciences contain implicit assumptions of an ontological nature. To speak of a philosopher's ontology is to make explicit the kinds of things that he or she presumes to exist. Similarly, to speak of a criminologist's ontology means to make evident the sorts of things that the investigator assumes exists within her or his conceptual and analytical framework. With respect to theoretical undertakings, ontology asks what factors or forces must be present, that is, real, in order for the theory to be true. Prevailing theoretical explanations of crime and criminal behavior presuppose a particular, although often unexamined, understanding of the reality of crime and human behavior. In contrast, a more critical and philosophical approach directly confronts and deliberately exposes the specific assumptions about the reality of crime and human behavior that most criminological theories neglect.

For example, we previously noted that one of the distinctive features of the social sciences is their positivistic approach to various matters of practical interest. However, scientific investigations into the character of phenomena must commence with assumptions about the nature of those phenomena firmly underfoot. A key distinction in philosophy and, by implication, in the social sciences has been the difference between *realism* and *antirealism*—the latter being inclusive of intellectual positions such as idealism, linguistic idealism, and conceptualism. Realists argue that a "real" world exists independent of our conscious experience of it. The kinds of things that exist have a reality of their own, as opposed to a reality that is either imposed upon them by human consciousness or that requires some degree of interaction with human consciousness. Realists assume that an objective and knowable reality exists outside of persons naming that reality as such. Consequently, ontological realism has important epistemological (knowledge-related) implications. Ontological realism is often linked to the epistemological position that we can *know* what this independently existing reality is if we use the proper research strategies and tools.

Antirealism, in contrast, holds that phenomena (the world "out there") do not exist separate from our human consciousness of them. Rather than being independent in the nature of their existences, these things that we take to exist are products of our minds, our language, and/or our conceptual schemes. Thus, what we presume is real, to exist, or to be are convenient shorthands, conventional stand-ins for the awesome complexity of the social world. In this respect, then, they are also quite relative. A related subset of ideas that has become increasingly popular—particularly in postmodern circles—is *linguistic idealism*. Linguistic idealism argues more specifically that human beings create reality through the employment of mind-dependent linguistic (language-based) and social categories. What is real and the nature of what is real for human beings largely depends upon the language we use to describe those things and the linguistic categories by which we understand them.

There are significant differences to consider in relation to the ontological status of various *types* of things. For example, while it may be reasonable to take a realist perspective on the physical world, not all meaningful reality is physical in nature. The existence of neurotransmitters in the brain may be quite real and, in fact, they may exist regardless of whether we are aware of them. Similarly, it is not too substantial a leap of faith to assume that there are a variety of physical elements constituting our physical surroundings. The existence and nature of these elements endures regardless of whether we know anything about them, what we believe or want their reality to be, or how we go about studying, analyzing, and critiquing them. However, the nature of physical facts is qualitatively different than their social counterparts. Thus, one may be a realist with respect to the physical world yet an antirealist with respect to the social world.

To illustrate, consider the existence of beauty and the nature of morality. While aesthetic realists maintain that there is some independent standard by which this or that phenomena is either more or less beautiful, this line of reasoning is difficult to adopt in a social world where standards of beauty vary dramatically, given such factors as history, culture, and even individual perception. In the case of beauty, then, we may be justified in arguing that it is bound to human perceptions and social conceptions, notwithstanding realist sensibilities. Similarly, it may be difficult to adhere to a realist view of morality. This approach purports the existence of objective, universal standards of right and wrong, good and evil. Yet the existence of profound historical, cross-cultural, and intracultural differences in conceptions of morality represent compelling evidence, suggesting that it is inexorably wedded to human consciousness. It follows, then, that where morality is (increasingly) linked to definitions of crime, we might be equally suspicious of these taken-for-granted interpretations regarding the nature of criminal behavior.

In summary, ontology investigates what sorts of things are real and what the nature of their reality is. In the context of the social sciences, ontological assumptions form the basis of our conceptions and explanations of individual and collective behavior. The task of a philosophical criminology is to explicate the assumptions that lie beneath, around, or through these manifold characterizations. From our perspective, the difference between what criminology takes to be real and the ontological nature of that reality the discipline calls into question will have profound implications for how we understand crime and for how we promote justice in society and in our lives.

Epistemology

Epistemology refers to the theory of knowledge (*episteme* = knowledge; *logos* = theory of) or the philosophical study of knowledge itself. Broadly speaking, the theory of knowledge is interested in the (1) nature or conditions of knowledge; (2) sources of knowledge; and (3) scope or limits of human knowledge. Epistemological and epistemic concerns focus on what knowledge is, how we attain it, and what status we can ascribe to it (i.e., the legitimacy of knowledge claims). Similar to questions of ontology, epistemological queries are conceptual rather than scientific:

What is knowledge, and what does it mean to "know" something?
What sorts of things, if any, do we actually have knowledge of?
Must we be certain to claim that we have knowledge, or are we jus-
    tified in claiming knowledge based on probability?
How does knowledge differ from opinion, and, given the distinc-
    tion, how do we differentiate knowledge from opinion?
If we can know what knowledge consists of, how do we acquire it?
Is truth, as a necessary component of knowledge, necessarily rela-
    tive?

Questions such as these draw attention to the more general concept of
knowledge itself that informs specific domains or disciplines, including
criminology, rather than to specific forms of knowledge found in criminology. In explaining what knowledge is and how we attain it, epistemology confronts the role of criminological *verstehen* in our broader comprehension of the world. In other words, if criminology operates under
the assumption that it advances our knowledge of society, of social phenomena, and of human behavior, epistemology asks us to consider *how*
criminology advances these understandings.

In relation to the theory of knowledge, criminology is a specific
domain of knowing. Importantly, as Moser, Mulder, and Trout (1998)
suggest, all existing and potential domains of knowing are domains of
knowledge. Put differently, they are all instances of the general category of knowledge. Biology, history, film studies, and criminology all
represent specific knowledge domains with distinct subject matters and
with seemingly differing conceptions of what knowledge is and how it is
accessed or acquired. However, epistemologically speaking, each of these
disciplines—notwithstanding their relative independence—is involved
in the same pursuit: knowledge acquisition. Thus, the questions of epistemology are not specific to criminology or any other discipline; rather,
they are weighty matters that underlie *all* human pursuits of knowledge
and understanding. In this regard, then, criminology is intimately linked
to all other existing and potential domains of knowledge. For example,
examining the general category of knowledge allows us to consider what
unites criminology to film studies and, perhaps, more fundamentally,
how awareness and pursuit of these similarities can further the way in
which each discipline understands its role in the more general epistemic
scheme of things. Indeed, if we do not understand the general domain of
knowledge, we cannot adequately comprehend specific manifestations

of it, namely, scientific knowledge, literary knowledge, mathematical knowledge, or criminological knowledge (ibid.).

When engaged in discipline-specific knowledge pursuits (i.e., knowledge about crime, law, and justice), there will always be an epistemological stance and some epistemic assumptions inherent in any theoretical perspective or investigative endeavor. For example, criminological theories offer explanations of crime and criminal behavior. In this respect, they are instances of *explanatory* knowledge. In short, they answer the why and how questions of criminology rather than providing *descriptive* knowledge. The latter indicates whether some phenomenon is or is not the case. Explanatory knowledge can either explain how something like crime functions, or it can offer causal explanations as to why something like crime exists or operates as it does. The latter sorts of theories rely additionally on metaphysical assumptions about the nature of causation and determinism, exposing them to further philosophical criticism and debate.

Epistemological assumptions weave themselves through theoretical perspectives into methodologies and the subsequent methods issuing from those methodologies. For example, if a criminologist operates from within an interactionist perspective, he or she is (knowingly or not) subscribing to an epistemology that holds that reality is not discovered but constructed and that we can only know this reality by studying the persons who have constructed it and to whom it is meaningful. Knowing reality requires that we understand what reality is to the particular person or collective investigated. Consequently, the interactionist tradition assumes a relativistic regard to truth; namely, that some things are *true for* someone or some group without meeting the standards required for something to simply *be* true (Moser, Mulder, & Trout, 1998). Since truth is an essential feature of the classic tripartite definition of knowledge (i.e., justified, true, belief), the nature of truth proposed or assumed by any given theoretical perspective is a key epistemological feature of that tradition. Further, because criminological research is founded on theoretical propositions, its various undertakings inherit the metaphysical and epistemological assumptions of those theories—including assumptions concerning the nature of truth and how to acquire it.

The epistemological foundation of Western science, and, consequently, that of criminology and the social sciences more specifically, has been that an objective truth exists. Moreover, with the appropriate methods of inquiry, the conviction is that we can attain accurate and more-or-less certain knowledge of that objective truth (see Natanson, 1963). This *correspondence* theory of truth dates to Aristotle and carries the assumption that for a statement to be true, it must correspond with reality. In this view, truth is not relative; rather, it emerges from how things actually are in the world—independent of human beliefs about how such things are. However, the problem with the correspondence view of truth is that it requires humans to have cognitive access to the world that is not mediated by other beliefs or assumptions (Moser, Mulder, & Trout, 1998). This cognitive access is the basis on which interactionists, constructionists, and subjectivists critique positivistic theories of crime.

As previously noted, criminology emerged alongside and mostly remains wedded to positivism in the natural sciences. The fundamental assumption of all positivistic theories of crime rests on its response to perhaps the most historically significant epistemological debate. The core of this debate considers the source(s) of knowledge—where knowledge comes from—and how we acquire it. Traditionally, the answers located the font of knowledge either in reason (rationalism) or experience (empiricism). The natural sciences, and positivism within the social sciences, have largely adopted the latter; that is, the basis of knowledge resides in human sensory experience and the application of the empirical method used to make sense of those experiences. Benton and Craib summarize the essential tenets of empiricism as follows: (1) Human beings are "blank slates," acquiring knowledge of the world only though our engagements with it; (2) genuine knowledge claims are testable through observation or experiment; (3) we cannot have knowledge of entities that cannot be observed; (4, 5) scientific explanations are demonstrations that phenomena are instances of scientific laws that are general, recurring patterns of experience; (6) knowing a law should enable us to predict future occurrences of that phenomenon; and (7) factual statements and value judgments necessarily should be (and usually are) distinguished (2001, p. 14).

In addition to empiricism as the only legitimate source of knowledge, positivism carries with it a number of additional epistemological assumptions, including

1. *Progress:* Scientific knowledge is closely linked to the idea of progress. Following Comte, the discovery of the laws of nature and society allows us to impose control on nature and society in the interest of social progress.

2. *Certainty:* Scientific knowledge is presumed to be accurate and certain and, in that respect, different from opinion, belief, knowledge from authority, and other nonscientific ways of knowing the world. Consequently, science is privileged over other ways of knowing and presumed to have privileged access to truth.

3. *Facts:* Scientific knowledge differs from other ways of knowing in that it purports to be founded on facts about the world. Knowledge is objective rather than subjective, as is the case with opinions, beliefs, feelings, and intuition. In their everyday lives, people impose subjective meaning on the world around them. Science, however, imposes no meanings; rather, it discovers meaning that is "out there" awaiting discovery.

4. *Quantification:* The properties of things that lead to knowledge of those things are properties that can be measured and, thus, quantified. Characteristics such as size, shape, number, position, and the like can be objectively measured and, thus, known. (Crotty, 1998, p. 53)

However, criminology has not fully acceded to the assumptions of positivism. Indeed, positivism (and empiricism) has been challenged by alternative epistemologies and methodologies, many of which have made their way into criminology (e.g., Arrigo, 1999). For example, constructionist epistemology allows for all knowledge and, therefore, all meaningful reality, to be contingent upon human practices. Meaningful reality and knowledge about it are constructed through the interaction between human subjects and their lived world. Moreover, this reality is developed and transmitted within a social context. In short, reality is what is real for the people living it; and knowledge of that reality is what is true for them. Rather than searching for universal, objective truths, constructivism allows for multiple truths reflective of multiple realities.

Closely linked to constructionist epistemology are a number of theoretical and methodological stances in the social sciences, including variations of interpretivism such as symbolic interactionism, hermeneutics, and phenomenology. Rather than assuming an objective social world, interpretivism approaches the social world and, consequently, knowledge of it through culturally derived and historically situated forces. In stark contrast to the positivist orientation, interpretivists place considerable importance on understanding constructed and variable realities as opposed to explaining objective and universal realities. For the positivist, the assumption is that knowledge—or more precisely certain knowledge—of the social world that accepts, embraces, and condones multiple realities and truths is simply not possible.

Ethics

Ethics, or moral philosophy, concerns itself with questions that pertain to human character, decision making, conduct, and the consequences of individual and group behavior. Generally speaking, these inquiries attempt to establish how we should be (with others) and what we should do (in particular situations). Historically, ethics has approached these sorts of questions from several points of departure: as meta-ethical examinations of ethical logic and argument; as normative examinations of human character, conduct, and consequence; and as applied examinations that link normative theories to specific, practical circumstances and issues (e.g., Brandt, 1959).

Meta-ethics investigates the meaning of ethical terms, the logic of ethical arguments, and poses questions about the nature and possibility of ethics itself. For example, are human beings free to make moral choices? Are there absolute and universal moral values? Is all behavior necessarily self-interested? By virtue of the kinds of questions it poses, much of meta-ethics is linked to broader metaphysical and epistemological concerns such as freedom and truth. Contrastingly, normative ethics consists of theories pertaining to good and evil character, right and wrong conduct, and good and bad consequences stemming from human behavior. Though normative ethical theories are numerous and disparate in many ways, each is interested in broad philosophical inquiries. For example, what is "goodness" and what is the "good" life? What does it mean to be a "virtuous" person? Are there moral duties and obligations? Are consequences all that matter? More generally, normative ethics is interested in what we should or ought to do and how we should or ought to live our lives. Finally, applied ethics answers practical ethical questions. These are ethical matters to which the answer implies some action or response. Applied ethics is concerned with what actions we should take with regard to various problems—including such things as institutional responses to crime. The "correct" action in any given scenario is ideally linked to the operative normative framework.

Perhaps most importantly, when assessing the ethical foundations of crime one must confront the moral philosophical nature by which crime itself is understood, whether the criminal act or event is historic or contemporary. From antiquity to the present day, crime has been conceptualized, to some degree, as a wrongful transgression or as an immoral act. That is to say, the link between politics, morality (or religion), and definitions of crime has always been an explicit, though contested, reality. In ancient Greece, crime was conceived as vice where the transgressor's disposition reflected the absence of virtue, as discussed above. Throughout the Middle Ages, crime was defined by the church. Consequently, heresy assumed many forms; however, what they all shared in common was a deviation from dominant moral sensibilities as dictated by the religious elite (see, e.g., Pfohl, 1994). More recently, nearly all categories of criminal behavior are defined in relation to prevailing ethical or moral precepts. Crimes against persons are violations of normative standards related to the treatment of others, as are many crimes against property. Crimes of public decency are explicitly grounded in conceptions of normativity. In each instance, what becomes apparent is the seamless unification of ethics and the very concept of crime.

Beyond the obvious link between ethics and crime, the foundations of criminological theory and research each carry certain moral assumptions and implications. All theoretical and analytical endeavors in the social sciences are either grounded in ethical assumptions or entail actions that have ethical and/or moral effects. For example, in the context of research on crime, law, and justice, we might question the role that moral values play in the construction, execution, and analysis of criminological research. In this context, we note that one of the basic tenets of positivism proper is that science is value free. As such, scientific endeavors to understand, predict, and control the world are informed only by facts discovered about the world (e.g., Crotty, 1998). However, sociologically speaking, science can be understood as always operating from within a dominant paradigm (Kuhn, 1970; Barnes, 1982). Consequently, observations are never value free; rather, they are always guided and informed by theories, models, hypotheses, and methods that, in turn, are always informed by politics, history, culture, and the like. Similarly, the choice of research topics often is guided by and the construction of research questions are typically informed by the researcher's preexisting beliefs and values regarding the subject matter. However, when personal experience operates as a basis for the choice of topics, it represents a source of potential bias. While many qualitative methodologies recognize, work with, and own these set of assumptions (e.g., ethnography, phenomenology), more traditional positivistic methodologies continue to operate on the assumption of value neutrality.

On a more conceptual and philosophical level, ethics informs one's commitment to a particular theoretical or intellectual perspective, and certain ethical precepts are implied by the theoretical or intellectual perspective in use. The attractiveness or relative worth of a theoretical perspective is often linked to the position it occupies on the political continuum. In many cases, the commitment of social scientists to a particular theory or set of theories is a political and moral commitment rather than an objectively based, scientific commitment. For example, theories implying some degree of determinism are considerably more liberal in both their explanations of criminal behavior and their implications for policy and practice. Most positivist theories tend to concede the influence of causal forces on human behavior; thus, crime is understood to be an imposed reality rather than a matter of unbridled choice. Moreover, when extending this line of analysis, we note that many theories of biological, psychological, and sociological determinism support the logic of rehabilitation rather than retribution as an appropriate response to crime. In contrast, theories emphasizing free will and personal responsibility have a conservative foundation. As such, they mostly appeal to those with more traditionally punitive political and moral sensibilities.

Relatedly, all theories of crime recommend or imply that certain courses of action should follow, given crime, criminals, and violations of law. These courses of action (e.g., prevention strategies, punitive practices, rehabilitative implications) are themselves subject to moral criticism. For example, certain biological theories involve such morally questionable techniques as genetic therapy, surgical procedures, and selective breeding. Moral criticisms are launched on the basis of intrusions upon or infringements of one's individual freedoms, liberty interests, and rights to self-determination. Contrastingly, many critical criminological theories either implicitly or explicitly call for dramatic social change, including the transition from capitalist to socialist forms of political and economic organization. These are theories that challenge the moral foundations upon which contemporary individualistic democracies are based (e.g., Arrigo, 2000).

Importantly, ethics need not be concerned only with traditional issues in criminology, such as police misconduct or institutional responses to crime. Broadly conceived, ethics focuses on an assessment of the value-oriented motivations that underlie the choices people make and the manifest behavioral forms of those choices. In this regard, then, ethics is not simply about human conduct and the consequences stemming from it. Moreover, ethics fundamentally examines the types of reasoning or forms of understanding that give rise to much of human behavior. Given that values and understanding reflect a particular worldview, experience, and/or social position, ethics need not be limited to normative conceptions of morality. Rather, ethics can inform and coordinate practices that challenge normativity and dominant views of morality, either on an individual or group level. For example, Martin Luther King Jr.'s insistence that people have a moral obligation to disobey unjust laws implies that criminal behavior can be, under specified conditions, *more ethical* than conformist behavior. Thus, in the context of criminal activity, ethics challenges us to consider what people are doing when engaged in this behavior—not simply where and how these actions fall in relation to normative structures of thinking, feeling, acting, and being.

Aesthetics

Philosophically speaking, contemporary aesthetics is understood to encompass two interrelated and topical concerns: the philosophy of art and the philosophy of aesthetic experience in relation to objects that are not art. Key questions of aesthetics include the following:

How do we come to value certain artistic forms over others?
What is the *role* of artistic or creative activity in the realm of
   human "being"?
Where does or should artistic production "fit into" human existence?

The philosophical questions that comprise the field of aesthetics developed from two historical concerns, first presented for analysis by Plato: the theory of beauty and the theory of art. The theory of art has remained within roughly the same boundaries as postulated by Plato, generally asking what constitutes art and what distinguishes works of art from natural and other objects. For Plato, the primary theoretical issue concerning art was its imitative nature. However, as imitation, art was viewed negatively in that it was deceptive, luring people away from truth (i.e., the Forms). In addition to being a misleading influence, art was also seen as antisocial and destructive by Plato. Within the framework of his tripartite constitution of the soul, art emerged from the passionate, desirous, and appetitive aspect of the soul. According to Plato's framework, and as subsequently appropriated by Freud, art was to something to be controlled (e.g., Lodge, 1953).

While not deviating from the imitative conceptualization of art per se, Aristotle perceived art as embodying a more positive function. Admittedly for Aristotle, art appealed to the emotions; however, it did not call forth the emotions in their destructive sense. Instead, art was *cathartic*, purging the emotions of its viewers (Else, 1967). Thus, art possessed a dramatically different psychological and social function for Aristotle: one that symbolized a positive rather than negative influence. The value and meaning of art continues to be fervently debated today, serving as a focus around which issues of, for example, television violence and pornography are hotly contested. Critics of pornography often point to its latent tendency to stimulate and arouse the more antisocial, primitive, and base instincts in humans, linking pornography to everything from pedophilia, to rape, to serial (lust) murder. In contrast, proponents of pornography argue that it offers users an alternative avenue by which these more primitive emotions and desires can be figuratively and privately (rather than literally and publicly) expressed, thus serving a pro-social function. In this assessment pornography is cathartic, providing a convenient and safe outlet for the appetitive part of the soul where it might otherwise emerge as aggression, violence, or some other destructive form.

Plato's art-as-imitation theory would go largely unchallenged until the 19th-century expressionists. Expressionism marked a dramatic turning point in the philosophy of art in that it ushered in an intellectual tradition that was artist-centered as opposed to object-centered. Prior to the 19th century, most theories of art concentrated on objects of art. Expressionism carried with it a newfound appreciation for art, emphasizing the way in which it expressed or typified emotion for the artist. As an intellectual movement, Expressionism is closely linked to Romanticism in philosophy and literature. At its core, Romanticism was a reaction against what its authors and practitioners saw as "the routine, oppressive, and materialist nature of modern industrial existence" (O'Malley & Mugford, 1994, p. 196). Human beings were "an infinite reservoir of possibilities constrained by social fetters" (ibid.). As a celebration of creativity and individuality, Romanticism understood modern social life to be a repressive instrument of containment and, in the context of human creativity, a challenge to human essence. Promoting a transcendence of these constraints en route to self-realization, Romanticism emerged as a harsh critic of science and empiricism—both of which served as distractions from that which was most human (e.g., Berlin, 1999).

Expressionism "generated a new role for the artist and a new interest in artistic creation" (Dickie, 1997, p. 49). The artist came to be seen as a "means of getting in touch with vital sources and of attaining a kind of knowledge that science could not give" (ibid.). With this new importance accorded the artist, as opposed to the objects of art, emerged a new appreciation for the emotional and expressive qualities of artistic creation and those of being human more generally. In short, art came to be understood as something that could affirmatively contribute to human existence against a backdrop of science, technology, and industrialization.

In the same broad sense in which Expressionism was both aesthetic and social criticism, Marx's account in the 19th century interpreted art as institutionalized idolatry and as bureaucratized ideology (see Vazquez, 1973). Importantly, Marx understood art to be a central, defining characteristic of being human. Indeed, the essential need to create, to express, and to enjoy is transhistorical, transcultural, and, in that sense, ontological. However, while Marx recognized that art was essential to being human, it was also subject to historical, cultural, political, and social constraints on its expression. For example, capitalism, as the recurring object of Marx's critical philosophy, ensures its continued existence by controlling the productive and, by extension, creative and expressive undertakings of its citizens. Under capitalist forms of socioeconomic organization, artistic talent is concentrated within a select few (i.e., the artists) while, for the masses, essential creative and expressive energies are redirected (or, in the tradition of Freud and Marcuse, sublimated) into labor and consumption (Marx & Engels, 1996, p. 109). What is problematic about this division is that the routinization of labor and the monogamization of cultural consumption means that creative, expressive needs are demonstrably not met, resulting in personal alienation and fostering counterexpressions of artistic license and production, including deviant forms.

During the 20th century, a number of other significant changes occurred in the broad field of aesthetics. Many philosophers (e.g., Kupfer, 1983) now understand art to be more than (if not other than) the traditional objects and experiences found within museums, galleries, and concert halls. Today, aesthetics permeates all aspects of everyday existence and, consequently, is imbued with moral, social, political, and personal significance. Work, play, and even sex are understood by some as embodiments of the aesthetic dimension of our humanity (ibid.). To this extent, then, aesthetics represents a lens through which we can investigate routine human activities, experiences, and relationships and the institutions that shape them all.

The contributions that aesthetics offer criminology remain largely uncharted; however, as a subdivision of philosophy it can evoke new understandings of human social behavior, the motives that inform them, and the ways in which culture and structure impact both. Indeed, aesthetics facilitates our appreciation for a number of human activities in crime and deviance that are not typically regarded as aesthetical in nature or form (e.g., Ferrell & Sanders, 1995; Ferrell & Websdale, 1999). For example, culture plays a unique role in defining what is beautiful, especially in the types and forms of things that we are expected to find desirable. What is deviant or criminal can be, in turn, a reflection and manifestation of that which is normally desirable. In discussing sexuality and advertising (the selling of sex), Huer argues that America has become a "pornographic society" in which we can no longer clearly demarcate perversion from mainstream beauty and sexuality: "No longer confined to the less desirable segments of the community, pornography is a pervasive element of our whole society" (1987, p. 11). However, the forms of perversion that constitute the deviant and criminal sexual realm are perhaps best understood as direct reflections of the pervasiveness of normative pornography lodged deep within Western society's cultural core. Thus, are we truly surprised to learn of pedophilia's robust existence in a society that sexualizes prepubescent girls and boys as part of its normal aesthetic functioning? Issues such as this are situated at the crossroads of aesthetics and criminology. As such, they represent protean realms of analysis, especially when viewed as part of the topography constituting the philosophy of crime.

Organization of the Book

Based on our cursory observations to this point, we note that this anthology represents a suggestive, and much needed, foray into the realm of philosophy and philosophical inquiry. We take the position that this orientation signifies a far-too-neglected basis for much of what passes as criminological *verstehen* in the academy today. Accordingly, mindful of the preceding assessment on crime and theoretical criminology, the text is divided into four sections containing two chapters each. Each section emphasizes one of the traditional subdivisions of philosophy: ontology, epistemology, ethics, and aesthetics. Initially, we had hoped to create a clearer distinction between chapters that examined the development of theory in crime versus those that applied theory in specific criminological contexts. We quickly recognized that this exercise was mostly artificial and, instead, endeavored to categorize the chapters based on their affinity for one of the four subdivisions of philosophy. While this classification system is largely contrived and somewhat arbitrary, it does create a useful pedagogical lens through which readers can filter the relevant philosophical material in question.

Moreover, in order to situate the chapters within their assigned section, a brief description of the section and the chapters within it is presented. This introduction represents a point of departure that initiates the philosophical portion of the text under consideration. The intention here is to identify where and how the two chapters work independently of one another and where and how they are linked together. In both of these instances, however, the relationship between philosophy and crime is brought into sharper focus.

Although clearly modest in its own right, *Philosophy, Crime, and Criminology* charts a bold and provocative direction in the study of theoretical criminology. Seeking wisdom and guidance from the forgotten discipline of philosophy proper, the chapters in this anthology revisit the insights of such luminaries as Baudrillard, Foucault, Deleuze, Rorty, Hume, Nietzsche, Popper, Sartre, de Beauvoir, Kant, and others to unearth how the timeless debates on causality, truth, meaning, freedom, being, knowledge, agency, and becoming substantially contribute to the philosophical basis of crime. Indeed, we submit that these weighty and complex matters are the very journey that criminology proper has yet to thoughtfully consider and fully investigate. Ultimately, however, readers (and reviewers) must decide if this anthology meaningfully contributes to the theoretical discourse on crime in ways that deepen and extend our appreciation for criminological *verstehen*. It is in this spirit of exploration and discovery that we invite all to partake of this text.

References

Aristotle. (1933). *Metaphysics: Books I–IX* (trans. H. Tredennick). Cambridge: Harvard University Press.

Arrigo, B. A. (1995). The peripheral core of law and criminology: On postmodern social theory and conceptual integration. *Justice Quarterly, 12*(3), 447–472.

———. (1996). Media madness as crime in the making: On O. J. Simpson, cultural icons, and hyper-reality. In G. Barak (ed.), *Representing O. J.: Murder, criminal justice, and mass culture* (pp. 123–136). New York: Harrow and Heston.

Arrigo, B. A. (Ed.). (1999). *Social justice/criminal justice: The maturation of critical theory in law, crime, and deviance.* Belmont, CA: Wadsworth.

———. (2000). Social justice and critical criminology: On integrating knowledge. *Contemporary Justice Review, 3*(1), 7–37.

———. (2002). *Punishing the mentally ill: A critical analysis of law and psychiatry.* Albany: State University of New York Press.

Arrigo, B. A., Milovanovic, D., & Schehr, R. C. (2005). *The French connection in criminology: Rediscovering crime, law, and social change.* Albany: State University of New York Press.

Barnes, B. (1982). *T. S. Kuhn and social science.* London: Macmillan.

Beccaria, C. (1764/1963). *On crimes and punishments* (trans. H. Paolucci). Indianapolis, IN: Bobbs-Merrill.

Beirne, P. (1993). *Inventing criminology.* Albany: State University of New York Press.

Bentham, J. (1996). *The principles of morals and legislation.* J. Burns & H. Hart (eds.). New York: Oxford University Press.

Benton, T., & Craib, I. (2001). *Philosophy of social science: The philosophical foundations of social thought.* New York: Palgrave.

Berlin, I. (1999). *The roots of romanticism.* Princeton, NJ: Princeton University Press.

Best, S., & Kellner, D. (1997). *The postmodern turn.* New York: Guilford.

Blackburn, S. (1994). *The Oxford dictionary of philosophy.* New York: Oxford University Press.

Brandt, R. (1959). *Ethical theory: The problems of normative and critical ethics.* Englewood Cliffs, NJ: Prentice Hall.

Comte, A. (1957). *A general view of positivism* (trans. J. Bridges). New York: Robert Speller and Sons.

———. (1988). *An introduction to positive philosophy.* F. Ferre (ed. and trans.). Indianapolis: Hackett.

Crotty, M. J. (1998). *Foundations of social research: Meaning and perspective in the research process.* Thousand Oaks, CA: Sage.

Dickie, G. (1997). *Introduction to aesthetics: An analytic approach.* New York: Oxford University Press.

DiCristina, B. (1995). *Method in criminology: A philosophical primer.* New York: Harrow and Heston.

Dilman, I. (1999). *Free will: An historical and philosophical introduction.* New York: Routledge.

Einstadter, W., & Henry, S. (1995). *Criminological theory: An analysis of its underlying assumptions.* Fort Worth, TX: Harcourt and Brace.

Else, G. (1967). *Aristotle's Poetics: The argument.* Cambridge: Harvard University Press.

Ferrell, J., & Sanders, C. (Eds.). (1995). *Cultural criminology.* Boston: Northeastern University Press.

Ferrell, J., & Websdale, N. (Eds.). (1999). *Making trouble: Cultural constructions of crime, deviance, and control.* New York: Aldine de Gruyter.

Ferri, E. (1900). *Criminal sociology.* New York: D. Appleton.

Foucault, M. (1977). *Discipline and punish.* New York: Pantheon.

Friedrich, C. (1963). *The philosophy of law in historical perspective* (2nd ed.). Chicago: University of Chicago Press.

Garofalo, R. (1968). *Criminology.* Montclair, NJ: Patterson Smith.

Hamlyn, D. (1984). *Metaphysics.* Cambridge: Cambridge University Press.

Henry, S., & Milovanovic, D. (1996). *Constitutive criminology: Beyond postmodernism.* London: Sage.

Henry, S., & Milovanovic, D. (Eds.). (1999). *Constitutive theory at work: Applications in crime and justice.* Albany: State University of New York Press.

Hobbes, T. (1985). *Leviathan.* New York: Penguin.

Huer, J. (1987). *Art, beauty, and pornography: A journal through American culture.* Buffalo, NY: Prometheus Books.

Hyman, A., & Walsh, J. (1983). *Philosophy in the Middle Ages* (2nd ed.). Indianapolis: Hackett.

Kenny, A. (1980). *Aquinas.* New York: Hill and Wang.

Kuhn, T. (1970). *The structure of scientific revolutions* (2nd ed.). Chicago: University of Chicago Press.

Kupfer, J. (1983). *Experience as art: Aesthetics in everyday life.* Albany: State University of New York Press.

Lodge, R. (1953). *Plato's theory of art.* London: Routledge and Kegan Paul.

Lombroso, C. (1889). *The criminal man* (4th ed.). Bocca: Torrino.

———. (1912). *Crime: Its causes and remedies.* Montclair, NJ: Patterson Smith.

Mackenzie, M. (1981). *Plato on punishment.* Berkeley: University of California Press.

Marx, K., & Engels, F. (1996). *The German ideology.* New York: International Publishers.

Milovanovic, D. (1997). *Postmodern criminology.* New York: Garland.

———. (2003). *Critical criminology at the edge: Postmodern perspectives, integration, and applications.* Westport, CT: Praeger.

Moser, P., Mulder, D., & Trout, J. (1998). *The theory of knowledge: A thematic introduction.* New York: Oxford University Press.

Natanson, M. (1963). *Philosophy of social sciences.* New York: Random House.

Newman, G., Lynch, M., & Galaty, D. (1993). *Discovering criminology: From W. Byron Groves.* New York: Harrow and Heston.

O'Malley, P., & Mugford, S. (1994). Crime, excitement, and modernity. In Gregg Barak (ed.). *Varieties of criminology: Readings from a dynamic discipline.* Westport, CT: Praeger.

Pappas, N. (1995). *Plato and the Republic.* New York: Routledge.

Pfohl, S. (1994). *Images of deviance and social control: A sociological history* (2nd ed.). New York: McGraw Hill.

Plato. (1988). *The Laws of Plato.*(trans. T. L. Pangle). Chicago: University of Chicago Press.

Rosenau, P. (1992). *Postmodernism and the social sciences: Insights, inroads, and intrusions.* Princeton, NJ: Princeton University Press.

Rosenberg, A. (1988). *The philosophy of social science.* Boulder, CO: Westview.

Solomon, R. (2001). *Wicked pleasures: Meditations on the seven deadly sins.* Boston: Rowman and Littlefield.

Solomon, R., & Higgins, K. (1996). *A short history of philosophy.* New York: Oxford University Press.

Solomon, R., & Murphy, M. (1990). *What is justice?: Classic and contemporary readings.* New York: Oxford University Press.

Sutherland, E. (1924). *Principles of criminology.* Philadelphia: Lippincott.

Taylor, R. (1974). *Metaphysics* (2nd ed.). Englewood Cliffs, NJ: Prentice Hall.

Vazquez, A. (1973). *Art and society: Essays on Marxist aesthetics* (trans. M. Riofrancos). New York: Monthly Review Press.

Vold, G. B., Bernard, T. J., & Snipes, J. B. (2001). *Theoretical criminology* (5th ed.). New York: Oxford University Press.

Williams, C. R., & Arrigo, B. A. (2002). *Law, psychology, and justice: Chaos theory and the new (dis)order.* Albany: State University of New York Press.

PART ONE

Ontology and Crime

By necessity, questions of ontology explore the nature of reality or existence. In relation to a philosophical criminology, what is examined is the social reality of crime. In this section, this question is posed both theoretically and pragmatically. Chapter 1 investigates the ontology of crime as linked to culture and mass-mediated representations of reality. The contemporary philosophical development of ontology is traced to Karl Marx, the Situationists, and Jean Baudrillard. The argument is made that in the postmodern era, people conspicuously consume media-generated images such as representations of crime that they take to be true, factual, and concrete. However, these images are simulations whose value stems from their "sign-exchange" meaning. Moreover, these meanings are based on other simulations that continuously morph reality, manufacturing a hyperreal, otherworldly state of existence. Thus, the distinction between reality and image, substance and illusion, authentic and counterfeit are obliterated. To ground the more philosophical analysis, the phenomenon of serial murder and the case of Aileen Wuornos are discussed in detail.

The nature of crime's reality is further investigated in chapter 2. Drawing on social constructionist approaches from de Beauvoir to Foucault, this chapter focuses on a contemporary paradox regarding public perceptions of three social problems: public harassment, school violence, and domestic violence. In theory, prescriptive conceptions of normalized masculinity (and masculinities) are fundamentally related to the genesis of these issues. Yet in practice, as this chapter demonstrates concretely, gender-related ideologies and their "everyday" pervasiveness have not been widely recognized to be at the root of these problems. Thus, while public harassment, school violence, and domestic violence are distinctive in some ways, they also are interrelated through the ongoing sway of normative masculinity(ies).

While the crimes assessed in these two chapters are certainly different, the philosophical lens of ontology draws attention to common core themes of criminological relevance. To what extent is it possible to locate the deeper, taken-for-granted structure of crime via philosophical inquiry? In what ways is crime an artifact of cultural forces (e.g., gender, the media)? How do images of murder and violence undo or reaffirm crime's social existence? Questions such as these implicate the profound role that ontology assumes when investigating the philosophical foundations of criminological *verstehen.*

ONE

The Ontology of Crime: On the Construction of the Real, the Image, and the Hyperreal

BRUCE A. ARRIGO

What is the nature of reality, existence, or Being? This is the ontological question that will be systematically examined in relation to crime and criminological theory in the discussion that follows. To situate the overall analysis, the chapter is divided into four sections.

Section 1 reviews the notion of ontology as linked to culture. One expression of culture is crime and, more broadly, criminological theory. This culture-crime-theory relationship is generally discussed, mindful of those mediating forces (e.g., politics, religion) and their corresponding effects (e.g., policies regarding criminal law, interpretations of criminal behavior) that come to typify social reality and criminological *verstehen*. Section 2 explores how representations of social reality are based on the "consumption" of cultural images. Contributions from Karl Marx, the Situationists (i.e., Guy Debord), and Jean Baudrillard are incorporated into the analysis. Major philosophical transitions in the ontological status of reality are identified. Section 3 applies these insights to the social ontology of crime and examines the phenomena of murder and serial homicide. The manner in which these offenses are founded on collapsing images of the real and the hyperreal are delineated. The highly publicized case of Aileen Wuornos is used to illustrate these matters. Section 4 discusses the conceptual and practical implications of the preceding analysis. Particular attention is directed toward criminological theorizing, the social reality of crime, and the cultural foundations and biases to which criminology proper is ontologically committed. Contributions from postmodern criminology and constitutive theory inform the analysis.

Culture, Crime, and Theory: Assessing the Relationship

Reliance on theory commits us to believe in a certain kind of reality. In this respect, theory becomes a prism through which we interpret and make sense of people, situations, and behavior. This reality, as expressed through and embodied in various cultural manifestations of ongoing interpersonal, institutional, and communal life, is what is meant by *social* ontology. Whether reflected through parenting skills, a child custody evaluation, or collective procreative practices, for example, social ontology presupposes a particular, often taken-for-granted, regard for the ontology of family and of family life.

Mindful of the relationship between theory per se and social ontology more generally, the philosophical issue here is one of accessing the nature of existence, reality, or Being as personified in the specific context of crime and criminological theorizing. Another way to state this is as follows: crime and theory pertaining to it are artifacts of culture; accordingly, what is the nature of criminological knowledge such that it already presumes a certain regard for the reality/existence of crime? This matter draws attention to the "type" or "level" of reality (Groves, 1993, p. 24) by and through which our understanding of crime is theoretically fashioned (see also Arrigo & Young, 1998).

At the outset, I note that the nature of criminological theory, as a tangible expression for or interpretation of the reality of crime, is linked to manifold forces. In brief, these include political, economic, biological, legal, psychological, theological, and sociological conditions with their corresponding effects. In the Western world, these conditions run the gamut from the privileging of capitalism and democracy, to the value assigned to physical health and psychiatric wellness, to the changing norms surrounding law, social control, and punishment. These illustrations are not exhaustive; rather, they remind us that theory about crime does not emerge in a vacuum. Instead, criminological *verstehen* is inexorably linked to and mediated by sundry forces that are themselves expressions of culture in a given and mostly self-referential historical period.

Although perhaps self-evident, this last point should not be underestimated. Consider, for example, theorizing about the insanity defense and definitions of crime in the wake of the attempted assassination of former president Ronald Reagan by John W. Hinckley. As Tighe insightfully observed, when Hinckley pled "not guilty by reason of insanity in answer to the indictment for his March 1981 attack . . . , he rejuvenated a movement which has become almost a tradition in the United States: that of reforming the insanity defense" (1983, p. 224; see also Steadman, McGreevey, Morrissey, Callahan, Robbins, and Cirincione, 1993).

What is interesting about this reformulation is the relationship between cultural dynamics (especially public outcry for policy alterations fueled by protracted media reporting and intense political wrangling), definitions of crime with respect to insanity and mental illness, and criminological theory pertaining to both (Arrigo, 1996a). Indeed, as I have explained elsewhere, "Hinckley's acquittal [produced] a massive reform [the Insanity Defense Reform Act of 1984], designed to limit the constitutional (especially due process) protections of insanity acquittees. . . . In the wake of this clamor for reform, some states (e.g., Montana, Utah) implemented legislation effectively abolishing the insanity doctrine as an affirmative defense in all criminal cases" (Arrigo, 2002, p. 130). In this illustration, cultural forces (the political maneuvering to restrict the constitutional rights of psychiatrically disordered defendants and the media frenzy surrounding the attempted presidential assassination) produced major federal policy changes in our treatment of mental illness and crime, expressed through theoretical reformulations for both. Not surprisingly, this same logic regarding the culture-crime-theory relationship is an unspoken but felt staple for much of what passes as sound research in the academy today (e.g., Altheide, 2002; Barak, 1994, 1996; Ferrell & Websdale, 1999).

If cultural representations of reality (e.g., the politically charged and media-manufactured depictions of mental illness in the wake of the attempted assassination of Reagan) delimit our understanding of crime and, by extension, criminological theory, then these representations and images are themselves the basis on which the ontology of crime takes on philosophical and practical significance. By representations and images, I mean those signs and sign systems of culture (Best & Kellner, 1997; Smith, 2001), whether written or spoken, that function as a shorthand for the reality on which they are premised. Some explanation here is warranted.

Images about crime, the criminal law, and criminal behavior abound (Surette, 1998). Whether reading about, listening to, or watching the police apprehend a suspect, the jury deliver a verdict in a criminal case, the imprisoned riot over confinement conditions, or juveniles undergo transfer to the adult system, a "text" about actors, events, and behaviors in the criminal justice system is continuously being constructed, deconstructed, and reconstructed (Arrigo, Milovanovic, & Schehr, 2005). This text is itself an assemblage of images where multiple (and often discordant) voices are brought together signifying something approximating a coherent narrative. In this way, print, television, and radio accounts about crime, criminals, and the criminal law have as much to do with the social ontology of crime as do such things as the author's conscious or unconscious intent; his or her selection of words or phrases used to convey meaning; the recipient's political and religious predilections; his or her conscious or unconscious interpretation of what was written or spoken; the unique standpoint or perspective of both the sender and receiver of the message; and the settings, costumes, and props employed in the story's unfolding. These dynamics make the meaning of crime a complex, multifaceted endeavor (Arrigo, 1995; Manning, 1999). Moreover, they redirect our attention to what the ontological status of crime is.

Each of the previously articulated elements in the interpretive process is an emblem of or sign for the reality it ostensibly represents (e.g., the existence, status, or value of crime). As a collection of sign meanings for the specific actor, event, or behavior in question, these facets of the crime text are always and already saturated in a cultural logic (e.g., political, economic, ideological) that communicates the reality of wrongdoing through this specialized and circumscribed lens. Consequently, these images, as culturally conceived, are a convenient, taken-for-granted stand-in for the reality of crime.

Given the preceding observations, the sign images of crime, as arti-facts of culture, are the source of criminological knowledge. Mindful of this chapter's purpose, the ontological question can be formulated more specifically as follows: what is the nature of criminological theory and knowledge, as mediated by culture, signs, and sign systems, such that they presuppose a certain regard for the existence of crime? Stated dif-ferently, the question is, how does culture manufacture criminological *verstehen* wherein the effect is the social ontology of crime? If culture names and defines the conditions that give rise to criminological theory and the existence of crime, then the manner in which culture and repre-sentations of it are produced, disseminated, and consumed in society are fundamental to understanding crime's reality. This issue draws critical attention to the relationship between culture, consumption, and social ontology and is the focus of the next section.

Culture, Consumption, and Social Ontology

It is difficult to identify the place at which an analysis of culture, con-sumption, and social ontology can best commence. However, it is use-ful to examine the work of Marx (1978), especially his critique of "labor power and the abstraction of the worker in the dialectical struggle of use-value versus exchange value" (Arrigo, 1996b, p. 124; Kellner, 1989).

For Marx, the capitalist mode of production signifies the triumph of objects (i.e., exchange-value) over subjects or workers and the inherent use-value of their labor. In this process, "the worker sinks to the level of a commodity and becomes indeed the most wretched of commodities" (Marx, 1978, p. 70). This is because the capitalist mode of production nur-tures "de-personalized" consumable products, representing a "triumph over [their] human producers" (Arrigo, 1996b, p. 124). This process signi-fies the inversion of the abstraction in a capitalist political economy; one that affirms the degradation of *being into having* (Marx, 1978, pp. 92–93). In other words, the disappearance of the commodity's intrinsic use-value or worth occurs when it is reduced to an artificial equivalent: money. In this transformation, people and their labor, as well as society and its prog-ress, are built around the elusive value assigned to commodities sold in the marketplace, reducing the qualitative, concrete uniqueness of people's labor to the quantitative, abstract logic of economic equivalence. However, lost in this exchange process is the subject's intrinsic, creative connection to his or her work as the source of personal identity, masked, distorted, or otherwise neutralized through a financial transaction.

What is of particular interest in Marx's critique is how the culture of consumption in a capitalist political economy operates such that the subject is alienated and exploited. For Marx, the ontology of material production displaces the subject's humanness, rendering the person (and his or her labor) a consumable commodity that when placed in the marketplace can be bought and sold based on an artificial, though shared, standard of monetary worth. The result is the disappearance of the subject's being and identity, giving rise to alienation from one's labor, from others, and, ultimately, from one's self. Belliotti aptly characterizes the ontological limits of the capitalist mode of production based on Marx's insights:

> In sum, capitalist social and economic institutions prevent the actualiza-
> tion of [one's] potential and thereby disconnect workers from [themselves]
> because they stifle workers' voice, creativity, and imagination; transform
> labor power itself into a commodity, . . . and fail to mediate the social
> aspect of labor by cooperation and solidarity. . . . In this fashion . . . capi-
> talism nurtures workers' desperation for material possessions, not their
> sense of creative expression. (Belliotti, 1995, p. 4)

Thus, following Marx (1978), the culture of consumption in a capitalist political economy subverts the human project of creative self-expression, embodied in what people produce. Indeed, labor power is transformed into depersonalized consumable goods. In this respect, then, the nature of ontology in a materialistic society operates principally "to facilitate and legitimate the underlying [political] economic structure of society," whether based on instrumental or structural approaches (Lynch, Micha-lowski, & Groves, 2001, p. 44).

Building upon Marx's observations, the logic of consumption in relation to culture and ontology also has been explored by the Situationists (e.g., Debord, 1983; Lukacs, 1971). In particular, the Situationists "applied Marx's notion of the commodity form, abstraction, and inversion to late twentieth century monopoly capitalism" (Arrigo, 1996b, p. 124). Unlike Marx, who focused on the logic of equivalence, competitive capitalism, and production, the Situationists examined the effect of advanced state-regulated capitalism (i.e., television and other media-based technologies) on consumption and conspicuous consumerism (Best, 1989, p. 28). For the Situationists, late capitalism and the mass-mediated reality through which it was manufactured, distributed, and consumed ushered in alternative types of abstraction and, consequently, new forms of oppression and alienation (Kellner, 1989). These matters are relevant to the chapter's focus on ontology and therefore warrant some further explanation.

Central to the Situationists' critique was the notion of the *spectacle*. The spectacle refers to a society in which people consume phenomena created by others rather than generating their own commodities or products. The spectacle thrives amid a culture in which television and other media-based technologies manufacture advertisements or other information about consumer products absent anyone's direct contact with them. For example, fast food, sleek cars, and stylish clothes are all consumer products. However, our fascination with them emerges from the images the media disseminates about them. Indeed, following the logic of advanced consumer capitalism, cheaper food, quicker cars, and chicer clothes are the emblems of normative social life.

However, the spectacle also desensitizes and sanitizes human consciousness. It "subverts the . . . subject's attention away from the task of living and being human, away from the concrete dimension of suffering, oppression, and violence" (Arrigo, 1996b, p. 125). Returning to the language of Marx (1978), the spectacle *culturalizes* use-value (Best, 1989). The spectacle signifies "the moment when the commodity attains the total consumption of social life" (Debord, 1983, p. 42). Monopoly capitalism and bureaucratically controlled consumerism (carefully manipulated by continuous media-generated images) elevate use-value to new levels of abstraction, given the consumerization of the spectacle (Kellner, 1989). Where Marx's critique argued that the commodity's fetishism resulted in the exploitation of the worker, the Situationists proposed that "the fetishism of the spectacle produce[d] new and heightened avenues through which hegemony and alienation appear[ed]" (Arrigo, 1996b, p. 125).

Thus, Marx's inversion of the abstraction, organized around the early, competitive capitalism of production and resulting in the degradation of being into having, gave way to the monopoly capitalism of the spectacle in which, according to the Situationists, we witnessed the transformation of *having into appearing* (Debord, 1983). Indeed, the concrete commodity is replaced with its manifold representations (i.e., consumer signs). Through the sophisticated and continuous manufacturing of the product's media-crafted image, the public identifies with the illusion, rather than the reality, of the commodity. The function of these representations is in their symbolic value. In a highly technologically advanced consumer society, the appearance of the commodity is more persuasive, is more meaningful, than is the commodity's actual use-value. Indeed, we purchase a brand of sneaker, watch a specific television show, or even vote for a particular politician not because one is better than its counterparts, but because the corporate-sponsored and smartly crafted images about these commodities tell us that their product is better than all other competitors. When form overtakes substance, when illusion supersedes reality, when the society of the spectacle replaces the society of the commodity, life is no longer lived directly, deeply, and actively (Arrigo, 1996b). What is abstracted is not simply the worker and his or her labor; rather, it is reality itself that is raised to the level of a concept or construct (Kellner, 1989). According to the Situationists, the ontological character of reality itself is subjected to abstraction.

If form and image displace substance and being, then advanced monopoly capitalism signifies that period during which "a total inversion of reality and illusion" occurs (Arrigo, 1996b, p. 126). This is a historical moment marked by image-objects rather than by objects themselves. Indeed, ontologically speaking, the existence of oppression, victimization, and marginalization would be traceable to the "intangible world of unreal images over the tangible world of real forces and relations of production" (Best, 1989, p. 32). For the Situationists, then, it was the *appearance* of existence that was real. That which had heretofore been defined as substance, authentic, or true represented no more than illusion, the artificial, and the tangible unreal (Debord, 1983).

The legacy of Marx's abstraction, taken to one extreme by the inversion of the image-object over the commodity as described by the Situationists, was elevated to new heights through the insights of Jean Baudrillard. As the spectacle overtook objects, Baudrillard pondered whether illusion was more real than reality. Stated differently, does an inversion of opposites (e.g., counterfactual over factual, counterfeit over authentic), as described by the Situationists, fully account for the social ontology of our existences today? In order to appropriately answer these questions, it is useful to examine Baudrillard's reconceptualizations regarding culture, consumption, and exchange-value.

Central to Baudrillard's (1968, 1970) early critique on the commodification of one's labor in a capitalist political economy (Marx) and the commodification of the spectacle in a mass-mediated consumer society (the Situationists) was his insistence that both have meaning through their "sign-exchange-value." In the previous section on culture, crime, and theory, I suggested that the sign images of crime, as artifacts of culture, were the source of criminological knowledge. However, little in the way of explaining the function of signs was provided. Before examining Baudrillard's contributions to the nature of ontology in contemporary society, some brief observations on the epistemology of signs and sign systems are in order.

The logic of signs comes from the philosophy of semiotics (e.g., Arrigo, Milovanovic, & Schehr, 2005; Smith, 2001). Semiotics is the study of language, including entire fields of communication (e.g., law, medicine, computers, art). Semioticians are interested in the words or phrases used to convey meaning about an event, person, or phenomenon, applied in a specific context or during a particular historical period. In order to investigate these matters, semioticians assert that all communication, whether written or spoken, is constituted by and is conveyed through signs. "Signs are objects, events, gestures, words/phrases signifying something more or something other than the objects, events, gestures, words/phrases themselves" (Arrigo, 1996b, p. 127). The following are examples:

> "His criminal behavior was cold, calculating, and much like that of a psychotic killer."
> "Janet's efforts at work are so efficient that I often think of her like a machine."
> "Obviously, students did not study. Their overall performance was pathetic!"
> "The war on drugs is a fight we must win."

In each of these instances, meaning is dependent on what is said and on how it is conveyed. In addition, however, the way in which the receiver of the message interprets these expressions and understands the intent of the author will depend, on large part, on the recipient's life experiences, emotional state, stock of knowledge, and so on that, consciously or otherwise, contribute to the overall meaning-making process. Semioticians further point out that signs are composed of signifiers and signifieds. The former are the specific words, phrases, gestures, or cues investigated. The latter are the contents assigned to the signifier. The signifier/signified relationship is what constitutes a sign. Thus, semioticians maintain that the written or spoken word is *encoded* and that accessing meaning entails the *decoding* of the word, phrase, gesture, cue, or other message. Expressions such as "psychotic killer," "like a machine," "performance," "pathetic," "war on drugs" all are saturated with various contents or are "multi-accentuated" (Volosinov, 1983). However, depending on circumstances (e.g., the status of the person speaking, the context in which the expression is uttered), particular interpretations will be given preferred standing over equally worthwhile others.

For Baudrillard (1972), sign-exchange-value referred to Marx's notion of abstraction but at the level of the symbolic. Indeed, "the commodity-form is eclipsed by the sign-form and subsequently bears no relationship to any reality whatever" (Baudrillard, 1983b, p. 11). This is because in a media-regulated consumer culture, "objects are abstracted at the level of semiotic exchange [absent any] relationship per se to the physical, material, objective universe. In this equation, the binary relationship between use-value and exchange-value is obliterated" (Arrigo, 1996b, p. 128). Whether we are inclined to purchase milk, toothpaste, a computer, or even a home, the value that these commodities possess is mediated by the effusive culture of technologically manufactured image-objects. These image-objects themselves circulate in the marketplace of signs, anchored, although only temporarily, in the dominant sign meanings assigned to them in a capitalist political economy. This process reoccurs through stylish print, radio, and television media campaigns and advertising strategies. For example, the changing culture of consumption surrounding cigarette smoking, cosmetics, breakfast cereals, drug use, hairstyles, travel, vacationing, religious preoccupations, college education, and every other facet of social life is subjected to the media-crafted logic of the sign. This is a level of abstraction in which "the exchange of material products under the law of general equivalence [is replaced] with the operationalization of all exchanges under the law of the code" (Best, 1989, p. 35), that is, the law of the sign.

Baudrillard's (1976) analysis on sign-exchange-value led him to ponder whether there was anything behind the appearance of the image-object to retrieve. In other words, Baudrillard questioned whether the inversion of form over substance and the privileging of illusion over reality simply cloaked the ontological character of our existences and, as such, affirmed the presence of an authentic, factual reality awaiting discovery and valorization. In response, Baudrillard (1983a, 1983b) rejected such dichotomizations. In the digitized information age of conspicuous consumerism, in the cybernetically sustained world of simulation, "there is no longer a real to be recovered behind the illusion [and, thus,] there is no illusion either" (Best, 1989, p. 37).

For Baudrillard (1983a), sign-exchange-value "ravages and absorbs the real" (Arrigo, 1996b, p. 129). Anchored in the discourse of technology and the logic of the media-manufactured symbol, the foundations of the factual, of the authentic, are consumed and digested. However, these foundations are themselves artificial, mere representations of an intangible, unreal existence. Thus, reality and illusion are not polar opposites; rather, they are pseudo states of being, *hyperreal* states of existence, that collapse and collide only to emerge and disappear amid a mass-mediated culture of evolving sign meanings. These meanings are *simulations*— "miniaturized models of reality, imitation units of authenticity" (Baudrillard, 1983b, pp. 20–25)—that are devoured in an ultramodern culture of technologically induced conspicuous consumption (Pfohl, 1993). For Baudrillard, this state of affairs marks the transition from *appearing to simulacra;* the quixotic and hypnotic moments when image-objects are replaced with and interpreted for their sign-exchange-value in a capitalist culture. Thus, the physical world of time, space, form, and consciousness is territorialized and vanquished by their ambulant representations, floating symbolic meanings that constitute an artificial, virtual reality that is itself foundationless.

To be sure, Baudrillard's semiotic and cultural critique raises disturbing questions about the nature of ontology in contemporary society. The conflation of the authentic and the counterfeit, the collapsing of the concrete and the intangible, radicalized through sign-exchange-value, means that the experiences we partake of, the people with whom we interact, and the behaviors in which we engage are themselves a part of an illusory non-world, a simulated reality (Kellner, 1989; Smith, 2001). "This is not the same as a fantasy, an hallucination, a fabrication, or a dream. Instead, this is the moment in which form and substance collide forging an ambiguous, non-real state that is simultaneously fictionalized and authenticized" (Arrigo, 1996b, p. 130). Thus, culture, consumption, and social ontology in today's mass-mediated society produce a hyperreal state where pseudo sign forms, in all their incompleteness, endure. For Baudrillard, this *is* the status of our existences: fragile and fragmented, illusory and unreal, vapid and virtual.

The Hyperreality of Crime: On Murder and Serial Homicide

Table 1.1 presents the major transitions in the relationship among culture, consumption, and social ontology as discussed in the previous section. In particular, the philosophy of Marx, the Situationists, and Baudrillard are summarily depicted, mindful of (1) what each argues is consumed; (2) what each (explicitly or otherwise) identifies as the nature of reality; and (3) what each indicates are the socio-cultural effects of their analysis, given their respective positions on the consumption-ontology association.

In part, the significance of table 1.1 stems from the various implications of Baudrillard's thesis, especially in relation to the ontological status of crime. In today's conspicuously consuming sign culture, the nature of criminological theory commits us to a certain kind of reality. Images of offenders, victims, punishment, law, policing, and the like pervade our consciousness and are expressed through language linked to the logic of simulacra and simulations. These representations signify an evolving reality about the social, political, economic, and other conditions that give rise to crime and its meaning, and it is through this sign-exchange-value process that criminological knowledge is manufactured and the social ontology of crime is established. But what are these representations? What meanings are temporarily anchored and given preferred status in our collective criminological psyches?

To some extent, researchers have examined these questions, choosing to investigate how the media constructs crime and justice images (Surette, 1998), how it fashions fear and a climate of crisis (Altheide, 2002), and how reality television programming is a simulated form of crime entertainment (Fishman & Cavender, 1998). However, none of these works accounts for the philosophical foundations of crime in a

Table 1.1. Major Transitions in Culture, Consumption, and Social Ontology

Theorist	What is consumed	Nature of reality	Sociocultural effect
K. Marx	objects; labor power; depersonalized commodities	transformation of being into having	legitimization of the political economy; status quo
Situationists (G. Debord)	image-objects; the spectacle; representations	transformation of having into appearing	illusion over reality; counterfeit over authentic
J. Baudrillard	media-manufactured signs; simulations; semiotic meanings	transformation of appearing into simulacra	hyperreality; obliteration of reality-appearance dichotomy; ontology as foundationless

mass-mediated culture. Thus, crime's ontological status is presumed to "really" exist, exposed to distortion and confusion by the stylish and sundry representations of it. However, this interpretation overlooks, ignores, or dismisses the disturbing conclusions reached by Baudrillard. To address these shortcomings in the extant research, one protean example concerning the construction of crime is examined in the remainder of this section: the ontology of murder and serial homicide.

The Hyperreality of Murder and Serial Homicide

Research on extreme violence is not new. One topical illustration found within the criminological and victimological research is murder and, more specifically, multiple homicide (e.g., Egger, 2002; Hickey, 2002; Jenkins, 1994; Levin & Fox, 1985; Shipley & Arrigo, 2004). What is perhaps most fascinating about the phenomenon of murder is its social construction, that is, the way in which images about it, anchored in political, ideological, and, thus, cultural representations, mythologize its place in society and in our everyday, taken-for-granted lives. Slotkin makes this point in his assessment of how certain expressions (e.g., "mind hunter," "psychotic killer," "going postal") evoke circumscribed images whose meaning-making power is both symbolic and transformative:

> Over time, through frequent retellings and deployments as a source of interpretive metaphors, the original mythic story is increasingly conventionalized and abstracted until it is reduced to a deeply encoded and resonant set of symbols, "icons," "keywords," or historical clichés. In this form, myth becomes a basic constituent of linguistic meaning and of the processes of both personal and social "remembering." Each of these mythic icons is in effect a poetic construction of tremendous economy and compression and a mnemonic device capable of evoking a complex system of historical associations by a single image or phrase. (Slotkin, 1992, pp. 5–6)

Today, as investigators contemplate the meaning of murder and serial homicide, its dominant socially constructed image is built around the intersecting forces of law enforcement intervention, news media reporting, and popular culture depictions (Egger, 2002; Jenkins, 1994). Consequently, the public interprets the serial killer and this form of criminal behavior as that of "a roaming lone white male predator; as an emerging, rapidly increasing new type of crime; and as an interjurisdictional crime needing federal law enforcement expertise and resources" (Surette,

1998, p. 14). To substantiate and fuel the significance of this construction, serial homicide has been linked to other social problems, not the least of which include "missing children, pedophilia, sexism, racism, and homosexuality by various groups of claims makers" (ibid.).

However, for purposes of this argument, the mythic images that emerge around murder and multiple homicide are not, in and of themselves, particularly significant. Ontologically speaking, this would simply draw attention to the appearance of the phenomenon as more authentic than its reality, a position consistent with the logic of the spectacle as articulated by the Situationists. Instead, what is at issue is how these representations, steeped in a mass-mediated and hyperreal culture of evolving sign meanings and simulations, are as foundationless as the supposed reality on which they are based. What is at stake is the obliteration of the reality-appearance dichotomy altogether. In this context, then, both the symbolic and transformative simulacra for murder and serial homicide, as depicted within contemporary society, need to be semiotically decoded.

One recent and compelling illustration of Baudrillard's thesis in relation to the phenomenon of murder and multiple homicide comes from the tragic life and eventual execution of Aileen Wuornos. Her story is noteworthy because she came to personify, at least from the consuming public's perspective, one of the deepest and darkest of criminal minds imaginable: a profoundly tortured and tormented offender (e.g., Ahern, 2001; Russell, 1992). In the end, "Aileen was punished for her serial killings. [This is because she became] the source and product of violence: rejected/detached, unlovable/unloving, and predatory/psychopathic" (Shipley & Arrigo, 2004, p. 156). At the same time, however, the severe emotional trauma Aileen Wuornos ostensibly experienced, linked to her troubled, dysfunctional, and violent childhood, helped produce a woman of awesome callousness and deceit, recklessness and rage (Kennedy, 1992). In order to examine the manufacturing of these various images and how they inform the social ontology of murder and serial homicide in a mass-mediated sign-exchange-value consumer culture, some background material on Aileen Wuornos and her life story are in order.

The Case of Aileen Wuornos

Aileen Wuornos was born on February 29, 1956. Aileen and her brother Keith believed that Lauri and Britta Wuornos (their maternal grandparents) were their parents until they were 11 and 12, respectively. There were five Wuornos children in total, or so Aileen believed. Diane (the daughter of Lauri and Britta) already had left the home as Aileen was growing up. She was rarely spoken of and was estranged from her parents. Barry (Lauri and Britta's son) was 12 years older than Aileen and was undoubtedly his father's favorite. He moved out of the house when Aileen was only a toddler. Lori (a second daughter of Lauri and Britta Wuornos) was only two and a half years older than Aileen and was raised with Aileen and Keith. Lori was spared much of the abuse that Aileen and Keith suffered. Aileen and Keith were often mistaken as twins and were a mere 11 months apart. Both Aileen and Keith experienced severe bouts of victimization at the hands of Lauri Wuornos, their grandfather (Ahern, 2001; Kennedy, 1992).

Aileen described sadistic abuse committed by her grandfather. She recounted numerous beatings with a leather strap on her bare buttocks (Ahern, 2001). Aileen spoke of being beaten on consecutive days while her skin was still raw from prior assaults. Her grandfather often told her she was "evil, wicked, worthless [and that she] should have never been born. She wasn't worthy of the air she breathed" (Russell, 1992, p. 11).

Britta, Aileen's grandmother, was complacent and did little to stop Lauri from abusing Aileen and Keith. Britta was an alcoholic, and the disease would claim her life when Aileen was 15 years old. She was described as quiet and introverted but with a kind demeanor. Britta was characterized as emotionally frail and nervous, despite her sturdy physical appearance. Lori maintained that she and her mother did not have mother-daughter conversations (e.g., she started her period without knowing what it was). Aileen would later say that she idealized her mother (grandmother). Britta and Lauri had a distant, affectionless relationship. Except for their once-a-year family vacation, they did little with one another. They exhibited no physical affection toward one another or toward their (grand)children.

At the age of 11, Aileen was told that Barry and Lori were her uncle and aunt, not her siblings. She was also told that the eldest child, Diane, was actually her mother. Diane had abandoned Aileen and Keith as babies, and Lauri and Britta had adopted them. Aileen and her brother were informed that their mother had remarried and had two other children, which served to further alienate them from their grandparents (Russell, 1992).

Lauri forbade Diane to date, so he was particularly incensed when she began a relationship with Leo Pitman, the local "hood." Leo Pitman was Aileen and Keith's biological father. He was raised by his grandparents

and was known to be abusive to his grandmother. He was frequently tru-
ant from school, had poor grades, and engaged in petty criminal behavior
(Kennedy, 1992). He was moody and had a violent, explosive temper. Leo
and Diane divorced before Aileen was born. Eventually, Leo Pitman was
convicted of kidnapping and raping a seven-year-old girl. He committed
suicide while serving a life sentence for this crime.

Diane attempted to be a single mother for about a year. She was 15
at the time. During this period, friends described her as a good mother.
A man Diane briefly dated recalled going to see her around lunchtime
on one occasion and hearing loud crying babies as he climbed the stairs.
Entering her home, he saw Diane asleep on the couch. While she was in
the same room as her children, she was unresponsive to the wailing of
her babies. He woke Diane up, and she claimed to have been drunk and
unable to hear them. Diane's downstairs neighbor later complained that
she let her children cry all morning. Much to her friends' dismay, Diane
left one day to go out for dinner and never returned. There was no phone
call or explanation. The two children were left with Diane's roommate,
Marge. Aileen was approximately six months old at the time. Marge kept
the kids for almost a week and finally called Lauri and Britta to come
and take the children with them. They took their grandchildren in and
raised them as their own for a number of years. Diane went to Texas,
never clarifying why she left. When Diane was 18, she made a second
attempt to reunite with her family; however, fractious relations with her
parents rendered this attempt unsuccessful. When Aileen was two and
Keith three, Diane left the children with a babysitter and did not return.
Once again, her parents picked up the children and Diane was gone for
good (Ahern, 2001).

During her (pre)adolescent years, Aileen was described as incorrigible,
possessing a fighting temper. Her angry outbursts were unpredictable and
frequently unprovoked. As might be expected, Aileen did not socialize
well with peers. She performed sexual acts with boys for cigarettes and
loose change. Indeed, as Russell observed, "this little girl learned how
to disassociate herself from her body; to blank off emotions" (1992, p.
13). People in her community labeled Aileen a "whore" and a "slut,"
and she resigned herself to the role of social outcast. Until high school,
almost all agreed that Aileen was without friends (Ahern, 2001). She and
her brother Keith had a strange bond in which they were quite protec-
tive of each other but would constantly fight while at home. Friends of

Keith claim to have witnessed incest between the brother and the sister. In addition, Aileen claimed that her grandfather had sex with her. However, these reports were never substantiated.

During her teenage years, Aileen shoplifted and had frequent run-ins with the police. She was thrown out of parties for being vulgar, drunk, and instigating fights. Just after her 15th birthday, Aileen gave birth. Several rumors circulated that the father was Keith (her brother), Lauri (her grandfather), a neighbor boy, or an older man in the community. The baby was immediately given up for adoption at the request of her grandfather. Shortly thereafter, Aileen dropped out of school and was displaced from her grandparents' home (Ahern, 2001).

During this tumultuous time, Aileen lost her grandmother, Britta, to liver failure. Lauri blamed Aileen for the death of his wife. Soon thereafter, Aileen began a cross-country journey that took her to Florida when she was 16 (Court TV, 1999). Within five years of Britta's death, Aileen's brother Keith died of throat cancer. She blamed herself for his death.

As a young adult, Aileen continued to frequent bars, carouse, and philander. At the age of 20, she married a man 50 years her senior. During this time, she drank heavily, stayed out all night, and spent a lot of money (Kennedy, 1992). The marriage lasted a month, as Aileen's husband filed for a divorce and a restraining order against her for beating him with his own cane (Russell, 1992). Subsequent heterosexual and homosexual relationships also ended acrimoniously. Following her divorce, Aileen was repeatedly arrested. Her offenses included such things as assault and battery, disorderly conduct, driving under the influence, and two arrests for weapons offenses. Aileen had a variety of additional criminal charges under a number of pseudonyms (Ahern, 2001).

Aileen moved around routinely and sometimes lived with Lori and her husband. She did not have any regular employment and never helped with household chores. She continued to be argumentative and threatening, particularly to men (including Lori's husband). She bragged openly about how she survived on the road. For example, she convinced a minister and his family who lived in a different town to take her in and help her. She stayed for a few days and then left after burglarizing their residence. She also would boast about all of the truck drivers that would pick her up for sex.

On May 20, 1981, Aileen held up a convenience store for $35 and two packs of cigarettes. She was charged with robbery with a deadly weapon.

Aileen was sentenced to three years imprisonment in Florida. Following her release in 1984, Aileen experienced her first homosexual relationship, although it was short-lived. When Aileen spoke to her sister, Lori, she would talk of men, always focusing on violence or on being used. Around this time, her criminal behavior also escalated. She was arrested for forging two bad checks, totaling $5,595. She never showed up for her court hearing. In 1985, she was stopped in a stolen vehicle. According to Aileen, she was prostituting herself sometimes 25 to 30 times a day (Kennedy, 1992).

At around this time, Aileen met Tyria (Ty) Moore. Their romantic relationship lasted four and a half years, from when Aileen first committed murder almost until she was arrested. Throughout their association, prostitution, deceit, transience (they moved from hotel to hotel), excessive drinking, violence, jealousy, and grandiosity were a part of Aileen's daily life (Ahern, 2001). For example, Aileen had a fascination with fame and often said that someday there would be a book written about her. She told Cammie Greene (one of Ty's closest friends) that she and Ty were going to be like Bonnie and Clyde and that they would be doing society a favor (Russell, 1992).

Now in her thirties, Aileen Wuornos was extremely overweight and looked very haggard (Ahern, 2001). She was not able to attract the same type of man that she had in the past, and this was very demoralizing to her (Court TV, 1999). During this period, Aileen met Richard Mallory, a 51–year-old man from Clearwater, Florida, who owned his own electronics repair shop. Mallory had been divorced for many years and admittedly loved spending time in gentlemen's clubs procuring the services of prostitutes in his free time. He had no history of attacking the many women he encountered during the nearly 20 years prior to his murder. Despite this, Aileen alleged that he raped her. This allegation was inconsistent with the forensic evidence from the crime scene and his body. Aileen made the same claim for each of the other six victims she killed.

In each of these instances, Aileen would linger on the Florida highway until someone stopped and offered to drive her to a particular destination. While in the car, Aileen would openly admit that she was a prostitute and that she needed help making money. Alcohol, marijuana, and other stimulants were frequently used during these exchanges. While the victim parked the car in a secluded area, Aileen would peel off her clothes and discuss prices. Some hugging and kissing occurred until Aileen encouraged her companions to undress. Then, while these men took off their clothing, Aileen exited the car, taking her belongings with her. When the victims sensed danger, Aileen would shoot and kill them. Typically, she would scream at her companions, alleging, "I knew you were going to rape me!" (Russell, 1992, p. 149). She would fire again and again while watching her victims die. Aileen would then put her clothes back on, take the money and/or personal effects from her dead companions, drive their automobiles to a desolate location, and drink her last beer before returning to her lover, Tyria Moore.

After being taken into police custody, Aileen Wuornos gave various renditions of her crimes. For example, once she indicated that the murders were the result of anger when her companions refused to have sex with her (Court TV, 1999). In other instance, Aileen reported that she would fight with her victims about sex and that when they became abusive, demanding that she have intercourse with them, she endeavored to protect herself from being raped (Ahern, 2001). Despite the assorted versions, Aileen was convicted of predatory and serial homicide. She was put to death by lethal injection at Broward Correctional Institution in Pembroke Pines, Florida, on October 9, 2002.

Consuming the Signs of Aileen Wuornos:
On Murder, Serial Homicide, and Social Ontology

The life narrative of Aileen Wuornos is provocative and revealing on many fronts. To narrow the focus to this discussion, however, her story is compelling because of what it tells us about the ontology of murder and multiple killing in a mass-mediated, hyperreal culture. In order to address this matter, some commentary on the interdependent effects of language, image, and consumption are warranted. At issue is the utility and relevance of Baudrillard's thesis and the media's (re)presentation of Aileen Wuornos the person, the victim, the offender, the psychopath.

As previously suggested, Wuornos came to symbolize a tragic figure of some mythic dimensions, which rendered her both the source and product of violence. She was rejected/detached, unlovable/unloving, predatory/psychopathic. Each of these dichotomous characterizations was fueled by media accounts that endeavored to tell the public who this murderess "really" was.

For example, in an interview with Court TV following her arrest, trial, conviction, and sentence, Wuornos remarked, "It took me 17 years to finally kill somebody . . . to have the heart to do it, a rapist or anybody. But I finally got really stone cold and said you know, enough is enough" (1999). Comments such as this, popularized through print, radio, and television/cable reporting (e.g., CNN, C-Span, NBC, Fox News, Court TV), helped to transform Aileen Wuornos into a conspicuous commodity—but as a consumer product to be devoured and vanquished. The media skillfully manufactured, both visually and linguistically, a string of hypnotic and alternating images with their corresponding semiotic effects: the child who was neglected and abandoned (i.e., victimized); the adolescent who was rebellious and defiant (i.e., delinquent); the woman who was manipulative, promiscuous, and without conscience (i.e., mentally ill); the offender who was remorseless, contemptuous, and who would kill again and again (i.e., a serial murderer).

Through these dramatic characterizations, portrayed repeatedly in various news reports, the media endeavored to choreograph, to craft, to authenticate the identity of Aileen Wuornos. However, these accounts were mere image-objects, thoroughly seductive and smartly designed sign appearances that functioned as substitutes for the real, tangible figure of a woman responsible for the deaths of seven men. Adding to the fictionalized reports were the in-court proceedings themselves. Stylized images captured on film and disseminated to a listening and viewing audience further communicated the alternating message that Aileen was a victim, a villain, an antihero, and an outcast (Shipley & Arrigo, 2004). Background reporting on Aileen's sexual escapades and self-destructive drug behavior, especially as linked to family members and lovers, appealed to the public's prurient fascination for the phenomenon that Wuornos came to symbolize. Indeed, as subplots to the criminal trial and the gruesome deaths for which she was accused, these events—mediated by language and representation, form and imitation—further elevated the status of Aileen Wuornos to mythical, hyperreal proportions.

Yet the public still craved more: more information, images, sound bites, and meanings, semiotically abstracting the identity of Aileen Wuornos and, at the same time, the ontology of murder and serial homicide. At the center of this consumption was a woman whose childhood and adolescence was marked by continuous physical, emotional, and sexual abuse. However, these images, also designed to sate a consuming public's appetite for additional details about Aileen's traumatic personal history, were nothing more than contrivances and illusions. There was no reality behind these media-generated representations to consume because the physical, material, tactile person Aileen Wuornos was not reducible to or located within these digitally enhanced depictions. Elsewhere, I have assessed Baudrillard's thesis concerning the implosion of meaning, simulation, and hyperreality, explaining how the reality-appearance duality semiotically extinguishes itself given the logic of technologically induced conspicuous consumerism:

> [W]hen there no longer is a real to recover behind illusion, when there no longer is a tangible concrete universe to retrieve in the wake of an intangible, abstract contrivance, then there is no illusion either. As the foundation upon which the commodity [Aileen Wuornos] was packaged and positioned, the public devoured and ravaged a plethora of images generated and produced by the media. (Arrigo, 1996b, p. 132)

The mass-mediated reporting of Aileen Wuornos—the person, the victim, the offender, the psychopath—as both source and product of violence, resulted in conspicuous sign-exchange-value consumerism. The images of Aileen were culturalized and devoured. But in this activity of territorializing imitations and simulations, reality also was swallowed up and digested. Again, this is because there was no "real" person to retrieve. Instead, there were only images of a woman based on carefully crafted sound bites and visual depictions that changed depending on the message being conveyed (e.g., Wuornos as rejected/detached, unlovable/unloving, predatory/psychopathic). Consequently, these (re)presentations signified nothing more than commutating signs—that is, simulacra—that reproduced Aileen Wuornos repeatedly, incessantly. These were floating signifiers/signifieds (e.g., words and expressions, characterizations and meanings) bearing no relationship to any authentic, stable reality known to the viewing and listening public.

Cases like those of Aileen Wuornos obliterate form and substance as distinct categories and collapse the counterfeit and the authentic as separate realms. As such, they transform the social ontology of murder and serial homicide into one that is radically relativized and subjectivized. Special reports, news documentaries, true-crime novels, nightly talk-show features, journalistic commentaries, in-depth interviews, and even recent films such as *Monster* established a pseudo world of meaning in which the social construction of homicide and serial killing was abstracted beyond recognition. This was the fragmented, unreal, and vapid existence that Aileen Wuornos personified.

As a culture, we have likened multiple murders and the offenders who commit them to satanic killers and other cultists (e.g., Charles Manson), to cannibalistic and ritualistic killers (e.g., Jeffrey Dahmer), and now to mentally unbalanced and predatory female stalkers (e.g., Aileen Wuornos) (Jenkins, 1994; Shipley & Arrigo, 2004; Surette, 1998). Moreover, the public is anesthetized in this simulated and cybernetic process of sustained consumable imagery such that its capacity to reflect and cogitate is not simply undone but is altogether eliminated. Lost in this process of media-manufactured reality, especially in the face of murder and serial homicide, is our ability to distinguish "between right and wrong, good and evil, justice and injustice, crime and virtue, truth and fabrication, reality and appearance" (Arrigo, 1996b, p. 132).

The postmodern world in which we find ourselves reminds us that harm is real and that pain is deep. Yet our much-needed ability to confront such devastation directly and intimately is undermined in a mass-mediated culture of hyperreality. To be sure, this realization is as problematic for the social ontology of murder as it is for the social ontology of crime. To address this matter, the next section speculatively considers both the conceptual and practical implications of the language-image-consumption relationship. In particular, the significance of hyperreality, in relation to the social ontology of crime, criminological knowledge, and mass-mediated culture is examined, mindful of the constitutive postmodern agenda in crime and justice studies.

The Implications of Hyperreality for the Social Ontology of Crime

The case of Aileen Wuornos was popularized and, to some extent, morosely glamorized (Ahern, 2001; Kennedy, 1992) through various news media reports. Metaphysically speaking, this sensationalism is relevant to the extent that it helped fashion a portrait of the homicide offender: one steeped in sound bites, camera angles, video clips, mood music, and other media techniques that dramatically crafted and authenticated, although temporarily and partially, the life and times of a person some would label the first female serial murderer (Russell, 1992; Shipley & Arrigo, 2004). But it was this hyperreal and simulated depiction of a woman, continuously (re)presented and stylized as villain and victim, predator and psychopath, unlovable and unloving, that established her identity as fragmented, incomplete, and abstract. More significant is that the public's insatiable fascination for her criminal behavior, and the media's willingness to disseminate more and more consumable images about her conduct, rendered the ontological status of murder and multiple homicide increasingly fragile, disjointed, and relative. It is at this juncture that Baudrillard's thesis regarding language, image, and consumption squarely confronts the social ontology of crime, theory, and culture.

One way to assess this relationship is to draw upon the insights of postmodern theory and constitutive criminology (Arrigo, Milovanovic, & Schehr, 2005; Henry & Milovanovic, 1996). The question is, how can the consumable, media-driven images invoked and manufactured through crime discourse (e.g., murder, serial homicide) be deconstructed for what they signify (i.e., technologies of control, societal fear and suspicion, individual pathology) and reconstructed for what they might represent (i.e., languages of possibility, collective healing and redemption, personal competencies), thereby establishing a replacement form of criminological *verstehen?* Consistent with the position of affirmative postmodernist thought, this query acknowledges the provisional, positional, and relational dimensions of human existence and ongoing social interaction (Arrigo, 2003; Best & Kellner, 1997). Accordingly, the foregoing analysis suggests some possible ways to rethink the ontology of crime in a mass communication culture of sign-exchange-value consumption.

Postmodern Theory, Constitutive Criminology, and the Ontology of Crime

By now it is axiomatic that the "linguistic turn" in social theory represents a dramatic change in our approach to and understanding of various facets of institutional life. As Best and Kellner observe, the legacy of postmodernism "in theory, the arts, and the sciences [represents] a major paradigm shift and, some would argue, an epochal transformation from a modern to a postmodern world" (1997, p. viii). This is a period marked by contingency, indeterminacy, perspectivity, discontinuity, and hermeneutics (Arrigo, 2003). In relation to crime, postmodernism reminds us that how we talk about such things as punishment, policing, law, criminal responsibility, social control, and so forth symbolizes artifacts of culture and dominant discourses mobilized to exercise dominion over those who think, act, feel, and know differently (Arrigo, 1995). Lanier and Henry make a similar observation.

> Put simply, postmodernist theory alerts us not only to the socially constructed (and thus somewhat arbitrary) nature of societies' rules, norms, and values, and therefore to what is called crime, but also to the total society as a source of crime.... A postmodernist definition of crime

involves a much wider range of harms than a legal or even a sociological definition, in that it includes harms created by the routine practices of our society's institutions, such as work, bureaucracy, government, law, [the media], and family . . . Furthermore, unlike [other] theories, which identify a causal force, whether this be at the level of individual, family, institutions, community, culture, or social structure, postmodernism sees the "cause" of crime in the interplay of all of these elements as expressed through prevailing ways of describing our world, called *discourses*. (1998, pp. 278–279)

Related to postmodern theory is constitutive criminology. Central to the constitutive argument is the coproduction of crime mediated by discourse. In this context, human subjects create the world they inhabit but also are shaped by the institutional and organizational dimensions of civic life they develop and continuously rebuild (Henry & Milovanovic, 1996). Thus, the meaning of crime emerges from the dialectic of agency and structure, in which the "naming" of reality (e.g., murder, serial homicide), unconsciously or otherwise, can strip people of their humanity. This is "the power to deny others their ability to make a difference" (ibid., p. 116). Lanier and Henry aptly summarize the constitutive criminological viewpoint as follows:

Constitutive criminology redefines crime as the harm resulting from humans investing energy in harm-producing relations of power. Humans suffering such "crimes" are in relations of inequality. . . . What is human is to make a difference to the world, to act on it, to interact with others, and together to transform [the] environment and ourselves. If this process is prevented, we become less than human; we are harmed. (1998, p. 283)

One area where the application of both postmodern theory and constitutive criminology is particularly salient is the "reality construction" (Surette, 1998, pp. 4–15) so prominently featured in the media. In this scripted process, the identity of a person is reduced and repressed consistent with certain narrative techniques and linguistic ploys that are repeatedly disseminated to and consumed by the public. Moreover, in this symbolic and transformative staging, the person in question is mythologized; the story that unfolds is subjectivized, and the reality that is manufactured is authenticized (Smith, 2001). Thus, the hyperreality of crime prevails! However, in order to explore this process further, mindful of the affirmative contributions postmodern theory and constitutive criminology can offer both conceptually and pragmatically, a return to the case of Aileen Wuornos is warranted. At issue here is the deconstruction of the harm (i.e., crime) the media discursively perpetrated against her and the reconstruction of the possibility that she more completely embodied. Both of these activities draw critical attention to the image-language-consumption relationship, as well as to the crime-theory-culture link integral to this chapter's overall metaphysical thesis. As such, the activities of deconstruction and reconstruction represent provocative directions in rethinking the social ontology of crime.

Applications in Postmodern Theory and Constitutive Criminology There are four strains of postmodern constitutive analysis relevant to a reassessment of the case of Aileen Wuornos. These include the phenomena of (1) the decentered subject, (2) the recovering subject, (3) the social structure as deconstructive/reconstructive, and (4) newsmaking criminology. Each of these conceptualizations will be linked to the media's reality crafting in the instance of Wuornos, to the phenomena of murder and serial homicide and, to a broader extent, to the social ontology of crime.

1. *The decentered subject.* Reference to the decentered or divided subject implicates the work of Jacques Lacan (1977). Lacan argued that identity (i.e., who we are) and meaning (i.e., what we know) are inextricably bound to and conveyed through language and language systems (e.g., medicine, law, journalism). However, when we speak (or write), Lacan noted that discourse typically functions as a "stand-in" for the person. In other words, for Lacan, the "real" identity and the "real" meaning are masked in jargon (e.g., legalese): concealing, silencing, and, to some significant degree, oppressing the person's genuine thoughts and feelings. Lacan's position resonates with semiotics as discussed previously, in which the role that language plays in communicating hidden messages and implicit values that need to be decoded was explained. Thus, if language is already encoded (anchored in unspoken but felt assumptions), then the discourse in use unconsciously structures and arranges the thoughts that we think, rendering the person who communicates more unstable than stable, more disunified than unified, more decentered than centered. In short, the fullness of the person is incompletely conveyed through language, especially when dominant discourses (e.g., law, science) are in effect.

The media's reality construction of Aileen Wuornos relied upon "experts" (e.g., lawyers, psychiatrists, criminologists, police officers) to establish a linguistically coherent, sound-bite sensitive, and publicly consumable narrative that reduced and repressed her humanity. Both expressions of harm are indicators of power disparities in human relating. Crimes of reduction "occur when offended parties experience a loss of some quality relative to their present standing" (Lanier & Henry, 1998, p. 283). Crimes of repression "occur when people experience a limit, or restriction, preventing them from achieving a desired position or standing" (ibid.).

To the extent that the media continuously reduced Wuornos's identity to her murderous and psychopathological conduct, she became an object of maudlin fascination. She was transformed into an entity, a thing, a curious phenomenon "objectified into non-personhood" (Shipley & Arrigo, 2004, pp. 148–149). In this respect, her dignity as a person was taken from her. To the extent that the media routinely manufactured the image that Wuornos was rejected/detached, predatory/psychopathic, unlovable/unloving, she was relegated to the status of a highly marketable and thoroughly consumable commodity. In this respect, her capacity to be other or more than sign-exchange-values was repressed. Indeed, in her case, the appearance-realty dichotomy was obliterated: all that remained were an array of pseudo sign forms simultaneously fictionalizing and authenticating her existence, generalizing and abstracting the crime (and, therefore, its ontological status) for which she was executed.

2. *The recovering subject.* The notion of a recovering subject draws critical attention to the role of human agency in the construction of identity and meaning. In other words, social structural forces (e.g., the media, the criminal justice and mental health systems) help fashion reality, always and already mediated by language. However, "[s]ocial agents are knowing agents who, even when they are subjected to determinisms, contribute to producing the efficacy of that which determines them in so far as they structure what determines them" (Bourdieu & Wacquant, 1992, pp. 167–168). Thus, people are active producers, through language, in the relationships they experience, in the projects they take up, in the world they inhabit.

Recovering subjects do not necessarily recognize where and how they help author their lives and those of others. However, "[h]uman agency is connected to the structures that it makes, as are the human agents to each other in making those structures" (Henry & Milovanovic, 1996, p. 39). In this dialectic, discourse, and the awesome power that it wields, is essential to recognizing and reclaiming one's place as coarchitect in human affairs and civic life. In order to liberate oneself from being decentered, the recovering subject must resist those organizing parameters of meaning, often imposed upon the individual by structural and institutional forces, and promote alternative vocabularies of sense making. These *replacement discourses* substitute "an inchoate life narrative [with] a congruent one, and . . . transform [the] meanings that previously blocked the person's story with new ones" (Omer & Strenger, 1992, p. 253).

As a divided subject manufactured by the media, Aileen Wuornos contributed to her predicament, her own demise. For example, at the hearing to waive her remaining appeals for execution, Wuornos exclaimed, "I killed those men, cold as ice. And I'd do it again, too. . . . There's no chance in keeping me alive or anything, because I'd kill again. I have hate crawling through my system" (Zarella, 2002). Statements such as these, chilling and eerie as they were, further fueled the media's depiction of and the public's prurient interest in a murderess that came to symbolize a cold-blooded and calculated serial killer. However, in the instance of Aileen Wuornos, the logic of replacement discourses would directly challenge and repudiate the complicity of the mental health and criminal justice systems that neglected to treat and help her when both had ample opportunities to do so. As Shipley and Arrigo explain:

> Aileen Wuornos was a product of her own machinations, forged in the crucible of parental neglect and abuse, and was a recipient of institutional malaise, ensconced in the politics of criminal justice and mental health abandonment and indifference. Although she was most assuredly responsible for her criminal behaviors, the systems in place to help Aileen failed her with impunity. In this way, the cycle of violence into which she plummeted was complete. Her personal victimization as a child was externalized in adolescence and adulthood, resulting in the death of seven men. Unable to secure much-needed assistance for her unfathomable torment, Aileen was punished [executed] for her serial killings. (2004, p. 156)

3. *Social structure as deconstructive/reconstructive.* The divided subject can be recovered through discourse, especially when relying on

replacement discourses that more completely convey the subject's humanity. However, it is unrealistic to expect human agents to retrieve their voice or to restore their identity without acknowledging the role that institutional or organizational forces play in coshaping the reality that people live. Indeed, both structure and agency "are mutually implicated in any production of knowledge" (Henry & Milovanovic, 1996, p. 65). Consistent with postmodernism, then, what is pivotal is the manner in which reality is spoken (and thus embodied) by various systems that define and construct reality.

One example of how social structural forces linguistically shape the world we inhabit is with the phenomenon of capital punishment. In response to the impending execution of Aileen Wuornos, Circuit Judge C. McFerrin Smith observed, "The loss of any human life is sad. [However,] the public will be indifferent because [Wuornos] did so many terrible acts. She earned the public's indifference" (Frederick, 2002). What is so shocking about this statement is that the meaning of Wuornos's death was linked to how the *legal system* interpreted her life, her criminal behavior, and how the system's *agents* (Judge Smith) gauged the public's response to both. Indifference signified a justification for why Wuornos no longer mattered and why her execution was acceptable. I note, too, that comments such as this contributed to the narrative that was being constructed for, disseminated to, and consumed by the public. It was a text built around a coordinated language system (i.e., the jargon of legal justification), producing circumscribed meanings about the value of Aileen Wuornos's life and death taken to be de facto reality.

Interestingly, by deconstructing the social structural forces at work that contribute to reality construction, it is also possible to identify them as mere summary (and therefore incomplete) representations. What matters is the investment people place in such spoken meanings and the behavior organized and mobilized around their presumed legitimacy. Again, this is where the media's role becomes paramount as it has the power to select and emphasize certain images, particular interpretations, and to make them appear concrete, while dismissing or forestalling equally worthwhile others. And herein lies the possibility for reconstruction. To the extent that such harmful images can be exposed for what they are and destabilized before they become solidified in the minds of audiences, it might be possible to reverse the alienating and marginalizing reality construction that occurs and, in its place, construct an alternative, more complete text about people, their relationships, and their ongoing human social interaction.

4. *News-making criminology.* One practical outlet for implementing each of the three previously articulated strains of postmodern constitutive thought is news-making criminology. News-making criminology refers to the "conscious efforts and activities of criminologists to interpret, influence, or shape the presentation of 'newsworthy' items about crime and justice" (Barak, 1994, p. xiii). This is a deliberate effort in which criminology can (and should) "confront the production of news crime by placing [its] own *journalistic spin* on crime and justice [rather than to] confine [its] expertise to facilitating the production of newsworthy crime stories" (ibid., p. xiv). As a practical endeavor, news-making criminology proposes to reorient the public to the ideological and cultural dynamics at work in which law is legitimated, crime is produced, and justice is (or is not) rendered.

Thus, mindful of Baudrillard's thesis regarding language, image, and consumption, news-making criminology reinterprets the way in which criminological *verstehen* is culturalized. By identifying, through the deployment of mass-mediated communication, where and how human agents and social structures coproduce a consumable, virtual reality, the person can be recovered and the institutional forces of which one is a part can be reconstructed. This is the affirmative postmodern constitutive agenda. Admittedly, in this process of renaming and reimaging phenomena (e.g., murder, serial homicide), the social ontology of crime remains fictionalized and fragmented. However, the replacement discourses by which popular representations of offenders are debunked and alternative ones assembled establish, both in theory and in practice, the reconstitution of life narratives that more fully validate the becoming self in society.

The mythos surrounding Aileen Wuornos, manufactured by ultramodern mass communication technologies and venues, inundated the public with consumable simulations. Wuornos came to symbolize, through words, sounds, and images, the embodiment of tormented evil, and, because of the power of discourse, was transformed into a disposable object of social indifference. She was both the source and product of violence: rejected/detached, predatory/psychopathic, unlovable/unloved. News-making criminology is one vehicle that draws attention to how such reality construction (re)occurs, and how more affirmative renderings of human subjects and the structures of suffering they endure can be rearticulated. In this context, criminological *verstehen* is reconceptualized and the social ontology of crime endures: an artifact of image, language, and consumption in the postmodern hyperreal world we all provisionally, relationally, positionally inhabit.

Conclusions

The media-manufactured, consumable sign culture in which we live produces hyperreality: representations based on representations *ad infinitum*. This is a historical period in which simulations and simulacra abound, and the appearance-reality dichotomy is obliterated. The social ontology of our existences, then, is reduced to images that are as foundationless as the supposed reality on which they are based.

In a mass-mediated world of digitized information and technologically driven communication, the ontological status of crime is similarly ephemeral. However, given increasing relativism, abstraction, and subjectivism, the question that remains is where and how words, sounds, and images can be disseminated and consumed so that they convey, more fully, the humanness of the person who offends. This chapter endeavored to philosophically chart the stages of intellectual development that have taken us to the precipice of the ultramodern and the semiotic. Although seemingly pessimistic and nihilistic, future criminologists must actively deconstruct and reconstruct the culturalization of crime theory and criminological *verstehen*. Although these efforts will produce (affirmative) fictions of their own, the reclamation of the subject's identity, exposed repeatedly and subtly to both harms of reduction and repression, may very well be achieved. In the final analysis, it is this very act of liberation that restores the humanity of us all.

References

Ahern, A. (2001). A biography of Aileen Wuornos. Court TV (online). http://www. courttv.com/onair/shows/mugshots/indepth/wuornos. html.

Altheide, D. L. (2002). *Creating fear: News and the construction of crisis.* New York: Aldine de Gruyter.

Arrigo, B. A. (1995). The peripheral core of law and criminology: On postmodern social theory and conceptual integration. *Justice Quarterly, 12*(3), 447–472.

———. (1996a). *The contours of psychiatric justice: A postmodern critique of mental illness, criminal insanity, and the law.* New York: Garland.

———. (1996b). Media madness as crime in the making: On O. J. Simpson, consumerism, and hyper-reality. In G. Barak (ed.), *Representing O. J.: Murder, criminal justice, and mass culture* (pp. 123–135). New York: Harrow and Heston.

———. (2002). *Punishing the mentally ill: A critical analysis of law and psychiatry.* Albany: State University of New York Press.

———. (2003). Postmodern justice and critical criminology: Positional, relational, provisional science. In M. D. Schwartz and S. Hatty (eds.), *Controversies in crime and justice: Critical criminology* (pp. 43–55). Cincinnati, OH: Anderson.

Arrigo, B. A., Milovanovic, D., & Schehr, R. C. (2005). *The french connection in criminology: Rediscovering crime, law, and social change.* Albany: State University of New York Press.

Arrigo, B. A., & Young, T. R. (1998). Theories of crime and crimes of theorists: On the topological construction of criminological reality. *Theory and Psychology: An International Journal, 8*(2), 219–252.

Barak, G. (Ed.). (1994). *Media, process, and the social construction of crime: Studies in newsmaking criminology.* New York: Garland.

———. (1996). *Representing O. J.: Murder, criminal justice, and mass culture.* Guilderland, NY: Harrow and Heston.

Baudrillard, J. (1968). *Le system des objets.* Paris: Denoel-Gonthier.

———. (1970). *Le societé de consummation.* Paris: Gallimard.

———. (1972). *For a critique of the political economy of the sign.* St Louis: Telos Press.

———. (1976). *L'exchange symbolique et la mort.* Paris: Gallimard.

———. (1983a). *In the shadow of the silent majorities.* New York: Semiotext(e).

———. (1983b). *Simulations.* New York: Semiotext(e).

Belliotti, R. (1995). The legacy of Marxist jurisprudence. In D. Caudill & S. Gold (eds.), *Radical philosophy of law: Contemporary challenges to mainstream legal theory and practice* (pp. 3–32). Atlantic Heights, NJ: Humanities Press.

Best, S. (1989). The commodification of reality and the reality of commodification: Jean Baudrillard and post-modernism. *Current Perspectives in Social Theory, 9,* 23–50.

Best, S., & Kellner, D. (1997). *The postmodern turn.* New York: Guilford.

Bourdieu, P., & Wacquant, L.J.D. (1992). *An invitation to reflexive sociology.* Chicago: University of Chicago Press.

Court TV. (1999). Mugshots: Aileen Wuornos.

Debord, G. (1983). *Society of the spectacle.* Detroit: Red and Black.

Egger, S. A. (2002). *The killers among us: An examination of serial murder and its investigation* (2nd ed.). Upper Saddle River, NJ: Prentice Hall.

Ferrell, J., & Websdale, N. (Eds.). (1999). *Making trouble: Cultural constructions of crime, deviance, and control.* New York: Aldine de Gruyter.

Fishman, M., & Cavender, G. (1998). *Entertaining crime: Television reality programs.* New York: Aldine de Gruyter.

Frederick, H. (2002). Convicted serial killer Aileen Wuornos granted death wish. *News-Journal* online: Special reports. http://njcnt1.news-jrnl.com/cgi-bin/.pl.

Groves, W. B. (1993). Criminology and ontology. In G. R. Newman, M. J. Lynch, & D. H. Galaty (eds.), *Discovering criminology: From W. Byron Groves* (pp. 23–36). New York: Harrow and Heston.

Henry, S., & Milovanovic, D. (1996). *Constitutive criminology: Beyond postmodernism.* London: Sage.

Hickey, E. (2002). *Serial killers and their victims* (3rd ed.). Pacific Grove, CA: Brooks/Cole.

Jenkins, P. (1994). *Using murder: The social construction of serial homicide.* New York: Aldine de Gruyter.

Kellner, D. (1989). *Jean Baudrillard: From Marxism to postmodernism and beyond.* Cambridge: Polity Press.

Kennedy, D. (1992). *On a killing day.* Chicago: Bonus Books.

Lacan, J. (1977). *Ecrits: A selection* (trans. S. Sherida). New York: Norton.

Lanier, M. M., & Henry, S. (1998). *Essential criminology.* Boulder, CO: Westview Press.

Levin, J., & Fox, J. A. (1985). *Mass murder: America's growing menace.* New York: Plenum.

Lukacs, G. (1971). *History and class consciousness.* Cambridge: MIT Press.

Lynch, M. J., Michalowski, R., & Groves, W. B. (2001). *The new primer in radical criminology: Critical perspectives on crime, power, and identity.* Monsey, NY: Criminal Justice Press.

Manning, P. K. (1999). Semiotics and justice: "Justice," *Justice,* and JUSTICE. In B. A. Arrigo (ed.), *Social justice/criminal justice: The maturation of critical theory in law, crime, and deviance* (pp. 131–149). Belmont, CA: Wadsworth.

Marx, K. (1978). *The Marx-Engels reader* (2nd ed., R. C. Tucker, ed.). New York: Norton.

Omer, H., & Strenger, C. (1992). The pluralist revolution: From one true meaning to an infinity of constructed ones. *Psychotherapy, 29,* 23–261.

Pfohl, S. (1993). Twilight of the parasites: Ultra modern capital and the new world order. *Social Problems, 40,* 125–151.

Russell, S. (1992). *Damsel of death.* London, England: BCA.

Shipley, S. L., & Arrigo, B. A. (2004). *The female homicide offender: Serial murder and the case of Aileen Wuornos.* Upper Saddle River, NJ: Prentice Hall.

Slotkin, R. (1992). *Gunfighter nation.* New York: Antheneum.

Smith, M. W. (2001). *Reading simulacra: Fatal theories for postmodernity.* Albany: State University of New York Press.

Steadman, H. J., McGreevy, M. A., Morrissey, J. P., Callahan, L. A., Robbins, P. C.,

& Cirincione, C. (1993). *Before and after Hinckley: Evaluating insanity defense reform.* New York: Guilford Press.

Surette, R. (1998). *Media, crime, and criminal justice: Images and realities* (2nd ed.). Belmont, CA: West/Wadsworth.

Tighe, J. A. (1983). Francis Wharton and the nineteenth-century insanity defense: The origins of a reform tradition. *American Journal of Legal History, 27,* 224–253.

Volosinov, V. (1983). *Marxism and the philosophy of language.* New York: Cambridge University Press.

Zarella, J. (2002). Wuornos's last words: I'll be back. CNN.com law center. http://www.cnn.com/2002/LAW/10/09/wuornos.execution/.

TWO

Normalized Masculinity: The Ontology of Violence Rooted in Everyday Life

JESSIE KLEIN AND
LYNN S. CHANCER

By 2004, insights generated from the feminist movement of the 1960s and 1970s have profoundly shaken the academy and permeated the interdisciplinary field of criminology; far less clear, though, is that the gendered structures of everyday life have been analogously transformed. Certainly within the academy generally, and regarding criminology specifically, gender's ramifications are now understood to necessarily encompass the study of men (and "masculinities") as well as women (and "femininities"). Meaningful for criminologists, too, is that formerly male-dominated subjects like gangs have now expanded to include feminist scholars and the querying of women's involvement (or lack thereof). Concerns about victimization suffered by women have spawned seemingly countless academic and policy studies about rape, battering, and sexual harassment in and outside the United States.

Less certain, though, is whether similar significant changes have registered in the social world that generates the behaviors sociologists and criminologists, of more and less feminist bent, eventually study. For the argument can be made that connections between normalized masculinity/masculinities and assaultive-to-criminal behaviors that women still disproportionately suffer have not yet been made visible, and acted upon, within social institutions outside the academy—from the criminal justice system to the media, the educational system, and within traditionally oriented families.

For the most part, policy responses—criminal, education, or otherwise—tend to respond to the most obvious manifestations of criminal-to-assaultive behaviors discussed here (and yet even in the extreme, certain forms of violence are not addressed at this level as extrapolated below). What we are trying to show is that normalized masculinity is operative in everyday dynamics, and it is the escalation of these "normal" behaviors that are then labeled as deviant and addressed with specifically targeted policies.

Ontologically, then, we address, instead, a network of power relations that permeate every aspect of social life. Transformation, then, cannot be executed solely through the institutions of laws and regulations that address the most extreme "deviant" behaviors—rather we focus on the ontological foundation of normalized masculinity; in the words of Michel Foucault, "Despair and time eat away the bonds of iron and steel, but they are powerless against the habitual union of ideas, they can only tighten it still more; and on the soft fibres of the brain is founded the unshakeable base of the soundest of Empires" (1991, p. 62). This is the empire we seek to shake. Therefore, normalized masculinity(ies) are analyzed; Robert W. Connell's framework of hegemonic, subordinate, and marginalized masculinities helps expose the ideological structures underlying specific assaultive-to-criminal behaviors by showing the incipient aspects of these actions in the normalized masculinities of everyday life. To explore this contention more systematically, this article proceeds in three parts.

In part 1, we document three types of assaultive-to-criminalized behaviors—public harassment, school violence cases, and domestic violence—where gender, and in particular "normalized" expectations of masculinity/masculinities—was at once implicated in explaining each problem and overlooked in cultural responses. Part 2 then explores, more theoretically, the sources of such blindness: despite considerable progress in academic understanding, why has the role of gender in perpetuating social problems like public harassment and school and domestic violence been by comparison relatively ignored? Finally, part 3 suggests how the fundamental influence of gendered expectations of masculinity(ies) on socially harmful behaviors that range from public harassment through school violence and domestic violence can be brought into clearer public relief, both in and outside the academy.

Before proceeding, it should be noted that we draw on several other overlapping theoretical traditions in making the ensuing analysis. Though feminist theorists from de Beauvoir to Butler have differed in many respects, what their perspectives have in common are sweeping indictments of gender-based dichotomies between the "masculine" and "feminine" as both socially constructed and humanly restrictive. Yet these fundamental dualisms continue to be widespread, imposed "consensually" through precisely the kind of ideological hegemony that Antonio Gramsci attributed in the Marxist tradition to class position and R. W. Connell later discussed in the context of "hegemonic" and other forms of imposed but normalized masculinities. In addition, this discussion also taps the work of feminists like Jessica Benjamin and Nancy Chodorow who have stirred Freudian-based psychoanalytic insights about the unconscious into their analyses of gender-based social troubles. Thus, as argued in *Sadomasochism in Everyday Life* (Chancer, 1992), "push/pull" dynamics played out through domestic violence often suggest unconscious rebellion against the supposedly superior situation of diverse masculinities. Analogously, in the paragraphs below, we analyze school violence cases as also entailing socialized reactions against the injunctions of the widespread but sometimes unbearable injunctions of gender.

Different-and-Similar Kinds of Omissions

We chose public harassment, school violence cases, and domestic violence as examples because each instance poses a slightly different situation wherein the pertinence of gender-related "norms" to social problems has not been fully perceived outside, and in the case of school violence even inside, the academy. First, in the case of public harassment, a "socially injurious" type of behavior as defined by sociologist Carol Brooks Gardner (1995) has hardly been recognized qua social problem at all; this is what makes this first instance intriguing. Thus, we are starting with a demonstrably gendered social problem that nonetheless has not been perceived by the criminal justice system and beyond as meriting serious and sometimes "criminal" sanctions. Second, in the case of school violence cases, no one questions that awful crimes occurred—that is, homicides. Yet, as we show, the important and arguably "obvious" role of gender in the genesis of these forms of violence was not apprehended in most early media accounts of them. Moreover, in this second case, even serious academic accounts of the relationship between expectations of normalized masculinity and school violence cases have yet to appear. Third, and in one important respect contrasting with the two cases above, domestic violence has frequently been associated with gender-based and feminist perspectives outside and inside the academy. However, we contend that this type of violence tends to be interpreted in the larger culture more as "deviant" than as manifesting a deeply embedded social problem that connects "everyday" with extreme manifestations of "boys will be boys" behaviors.

Overall, then, these "cases" diverge insofar as they highlight three different social manifestations of overlooking gender in spite of its apparent centrality to all of them. One problem is currently not defined as criminal (public harassment); another is defined as criminal but not necessarily as gender-related (school violence); the third tends to be defined as criminal and gender-related, but not necessarily as "caused" by the by-products of "normalized" masculinity taken to an extreme (domestic violence). Then, too, each case highlights a distinctively different "place" where the problem is occurring and being ignored. In the case of public harassment, as Brooks Gardner writes, women (and, to some extent, men as well) find themselves bothered in public places. Unlike the "private" realms of domesticity where other kinds of sexual politics are played out, this form of harassment takes place, for example, on subways, on streets, or in malls. Moreover, it is the criminal justice system that seems particularly implicated in the persistence of social blindness and (mis)identification. School violence cases have occurred, by definition of course, in schools. Yet documented below is that the media played a crucial interpretive role in failing to apprehend gender's significance in these cases, highlighting other possible explanations of violence instead. It ignored the role of families and schools that overlooked or failed to censure children's behavior that was potentially injurious to girls and boys in discriminatorily gendered ways. Just as obviously, domestic violence cases have indeed taken place in the "privacy" of homes, residences, and apartments.

Nonetheless, two commonalities linking public harassment, school, and domestic violence cases are equally noteworthy. For one thing, public harassment, school violence, and domestic violence cases all manifest, albeit differently, long-term consequences of culturally pervasive "boys will be boys" attitudes that still often minimize and/or condone aggressive-to-violent statements and behaviors on the part of men and boys toward girls (and sometimes toward other boys and men as well).

Moreover, while on one level the three problems occur in different social sites and appear to implicate particular institutions (for example, the criminal justice system or the media) more than others, on another, these distinctions are superficial. For public harassment is not only overlooked by the criminal justice system: in addition, media articles have accorded this problem "low profile" treatment (if covered at all), and families and schools may also be partly at fault. Analogously, not only the media is involved with overlooking possible relationships between school violence and normalized masculinity: in addition "boys will be boys" attitudes persist among many educators, frequently in families, and among criminal justice practitioners as well. Finally, while families and schools still perpetuate gendered stereotypes, the criminal justice system has also long been criticized for failing to treat domestic violence with sufficient seriousness and resources. Thus, a second commonality that connects public harassment, school violence, and domestic violence as social problems is that all three manifest culturally pervasive attitudes that are at once specific and widespread. We turn now to documenting each of these social problems in greater detail.

Public Harassment

In *Passing By*, Carol Brooks Gardner purposely distinguishes this term from "sexual harassment"; the latter has been more commonly and successfully targeted by feminists and is usually defined as occurring between superordinates and subordinates at work and at educational institutions. Unlike public harassment, sexual harassment has been accorded media and popular attention, partly due to the highly publicized efforts of well-known legal scholar Catherine MacKinnon. But whether noticed or not, according to Brooks Gardner, this "other" kind of harassment is among a general set of troubles to which all citizens are subject. I call these actions public harassment, that is, that group of abuses, harryings, and annoyances characteristic of public places and uniquely facilitated by communication in public. Public harassment includes pinching, slapping, hitting, shouted remarks, vulgarity, insults, sly innuendo, ogling, and stalking. Public harassment is on a continuum of possible events, beginning when customary civility among strangers is abrogated and ending with the transition to violent crime: assault, rape, or murder. (1995, p. 4)

Note, then, that public harassment takes place when people are engaged in a range of activities that occur in the open, in everyday life. Brooks Gardner details incidents where women are doing something as simple as walking when they find themselves either the object of catcalls or, more ominously, trailed "to their places of work or to their homes" (p. 130). She describes situations in which women are groped when going to work on public transportation on, say, particularly crowded subways or buses; on the more serious end of this example, several parties recounted having been "stabbed with pencils and pens and with what they believed were sticks and pins" (p. 134). Rarely, though, did more frightening instances result in any kind of criminal sanction or even individual or community action (such as censuring the harassing party's actions). From the criminal justice system's point of view, if women are "only" followed—even if frightened to the point of panic—no action can be taken unless such acts of public harassment result in "actual" (as opposed to imagined) assault. Moreover, in cases where women may only have been followed once, stalking—that, in legal terms, presumes patterned rather than isolated behavior—cannot even be charged or proved.

Yet, according to a survey of women and men that Brooks Gardner conducted in a middle-sized midwestern city, public harassment incidents of various kinds are exceedingly common. This finding was borne out when, after using Brooks Gardner's book in "Sociology of Family" and "Social Problems" courses taught by one of this chapter's authors several times at both Barnard/Columbia and at Fordham University, the overwhelming majority of women students said they related to examples presented in *Passing By*. Indeed, this reading regularly sparked conversation in more than only an "academic" sense. Especially memorable is the following story vividly described by a student regarding her experiences on a New York City train. This student was sitting next to a young woman who was being aggressively spoken to, or at, by a man standing above her on the subway car; the young woman was clearly becoming more and more uncomfortable and upset. When the student intervened to help the young woman by saying, "Leave her alone," this man reached out and slapped her hard across the face before running off the train as it entered a station. Yet other people on the train didn't try to stop the man; instead, another person astoundingly told the student to "calm down—the man was 'just' flirting." Interestingly, too, when rereading the obviously evocative *Passing By* in a café while preparing to teach, one of this chapter's authors also noticed a man staring at her more and more intensely. "What's the book about?" he said to her and then slid his hand along her leg, ironically—or quite purposefully, perhaps, from his point of view—reenacting the very phenomenon to which *Passing By* calls attention.

But if public harassment commonly occurs, is it indeed related to the prerogatives of masculinity? Brooks Gardner found that compared to women, men disproportionately engage in public harassment; students' experiences confirmed this observation. Interestingly, though, she found that men too were sometimes victimized by such harassment; one important example is gay men who may find themselves mocked in public places in ways certainly comparable to women's victimization in this regard. That public harassment is therefore disproportionately committed by men, though, will not come as a surprise to anyone familiar with the now extensive and interdisciplinary literature that documents "normal" masculinity involving prerogatives that the "first sex," to use de Beauvoir's phrase, grew comfortable exercising over the "second." To trail women to work or by subway, make comments or catcalls, grope women in crowded places—and/or, for that matter, to do this to some men—is unimaginable unless one experiences a sense of social power, indeed, social "permission."

Of course this is not to say that—as we will argue later—the enculturated characteristics of masculinity do not regularly bring disadvantages, and severe psychological limitations, to those pressured by gendered dictates to "act like a man" in more-and-less aggressive ways. (Indeed this is exactly what we will be saying.) But it does suggest that, to the extent that gender has historically skewed human traits into clusters of "masculine" and "feminine" practices, it is not surprising that persons socialized into the former are more likely to engage in "publicly harassing" behaviors than those socialized into the latter. Moreover, Connell's point, explained in greater detail below, that "masculinity" itself is internally differentiated by men's class, race, and sexual orientation, applies here as well. Men who have been "marginalized" by race and class discrimination may, in some instances, compensate for these social mistreatments through public harassment that expresses "machismo" forms of entitlement; likewise men in Connell's "complicit" category may sit, as sometimes do construction workers, making comments about women who walk by. Relevant, too, are men in the dominant or "hegemonic" category of Connell's classificatory system who may make demeaning comments in public aimed at "subordinated," that is, gay or bisexual, men.

But if public harassment is common, and its relationship to normalized masculinity(ies) relatively easy to trace, why has it been overlooked as a social problem requiring cultural work to change? Brooks Gardner writes that "we as a society have neglected public harassment, especially the heterosexually romanticized public harassment that women experience from men" (p. 9). She also observes, "For change to come about, basic changes must be made in interpersonal relationships between women and men, as well as in the use we make of the core character of public-place interaction and communication" (p. 238). Perhaps, then, the reason public harassment itself has been overlooked relates not just to problematic by-products of socially dictated masculinity(ies) but to the very pervasiveness of these dictates and the problems thereafter produced. In other words, public harassment may be dismissed from our everyday cultural consciousness precisely because the attitudes it manifests are taken to be "ordinary."

Returning to anecdote, in another "Social Problems" course at Columbia, students' reactions to *Passing By* were striking in the following respect as well. Whereas most of the female students related to Brooks Gardner's descriptions of being harassed rather than harassing, one male student—who happened to be an acclaimed football player on campus—related to the position of a victim. According to this football player, women frequently "harassed" him as well by making comments about how "gorgeous" he was and by expressing interest in sleeping with him. Interestingly, though, this young man's "public" recounting of his experiences led to laughter in the classroom, definitely including his own, whereas young women's accounts were tinged with fear. Thus, public harassment may be ignored for two reasons: one, already presented, is that it taps deeply embedded "boys will be boys" attitudes that remain taken for granted in the culture at large. But second, and in addition, efforts to publicize the problem may lead to "technical reversals"—that is, to statements that "men experience this too"—that, although in one respect are accurate, defuse the seriousness of the problem by stripping it of social context. For the condoning of "boys will be boys" behaviors and the fear this engenders in women who have experienced public harassment cannot be understood apart from the history of traditionally gendered interactions that this social problem reflects. But, before exploring gendered explanations in further detail, let us turn to a second problem related to normalized masculinity(ies) that is also both pervasive and largely ignored within American culture.

School Violence Cases

Clearly differentiating school violence cases from incidents of public harassment is that, in the former, no one doubts that crimes occurred whereas, in the latter, a threat of crime and violence can be felt, but they are not necessarily defined as such. However, in common with public harassment, the importance of normalized masculinity expectations in school violence's genesis is again widely overlooked. This omission is evident from the fact that the overwhelming majority of media accounts about school violence—ranging in seriousness from premeditated single-person homicides to larger-scale killings like that at Columbine High School in Littleton, Colorado—did not focus on the relevance of gender. Yet after looking at five school violence cases that occurred in the United States between 1997 and 1999 in greater detail, including the Columbine case, it is apparent that not only were all the perpetrators young men but that their targets were girls who rejected them and/or other boys who called them gay. Adding to the astounding fact that this shared feature could be overlooked is that crime reports released by the U.S. Department of Justice continue to show young males committing a disproportionately large number of homicides compared to young women. For example, in 1996, men committed 12,000 homicides in the United States in comparison to women's commission of 1,331 (Angel, 1999).

But instead of exploring this gender differential further—or at least placing it high among a combination of factors to be investigated—most journalistic accounts focused only on three factors: the need for gun control in American society, violence in the media itself, and the behavior of parents. In addition, following Columbine, "bullying" was a frequently cited journalistic factor, though in a way that again did not seriously treat this problem's relationship with gender. But, more specifically, how, as compared to the role of gender, did these popularly cited factors behind school violence fail to provide sufficient explanation? Let's start with guns. Even though lack of gun control in the United States may be a mitigating factor, as filmmaker Michael Moore effectively showed in his Oscar-winning *Bowling for Columbine* (wherein, again, the possible relevance of gender was not at all explored), school violence also occurs in countries with tight gun control laws. For instance, several horrific school shootings have taken place in Germany, a country with very strict gun control laws. Furthermore, research shows that even if stricter gun control laws lead to decreased use of guns and thus fewer deaths, nonfatal injuries would likely increase (Spitzer, 1995; Spina, 2000). But while decreasing the numbers of deaths that result from school violence is clearly important, so is determining what generates cultures of violence within school settings, a basic question that gun control laws alone fail to address. This is because, whether lax or strict, gun control laws have nothing to do with why boys turned to these weapons.

The second explanation of school violence often cited in media accounts was that the perpetrators were influenced by popular culture, specifically, by the violent character of video games, music, and movies. However, the relationship between media violence and "real" violence continues to be controversial; virtually no researchers believe a firm cause-and-effect connection has been established (Cline, 1974). Indeed, thus far, none of the claims against video manufacturers and entertainment studios that have been filed on behalf of victims' families, claiming that media violence incited these boys to kill, have been upheld in state or federal courts (Savastana, 2003).

But even if media depictions provided the theatrics of the violence and guns the weapons, again, how can one explain why only young boys perpetrated school violence that turned out to be homicidal? Certainly girls are exposed to the same videos, music, movies, television shows; even if they are not watched as often by girls as boys, this differential in turn begs gender-related explanation. Moreover, violent images produced in the United States are distributed widely around the world, yet school shootings do not occur elsewhere as frequently as in the United States (Savastana, 2003). In and of itself, then, this explanation appears inadequate.

The third explanation frequently presented in media accounts was parental neglect, predominantly on the part of single and working parents, that eventually culminated in children exhibiting violent behaviors and engaging in school shootings (e.g., Friedman, 1999; Applebome,

1998). Yet statistics do not show any correlation between single working parents and school shootings, since a third of the perpetrators came from two-parent traditional families with a stay-at-home parent. Many of the boys who killed or wounded most people victimized in school violence cases of the late 1990s were raised in traditional nuclear families.

In addition to denouncing single and working parents, though, researchers criticized perpetrators' parents for missing the "warning signs" (Savastana, 2003). However, it is clear that even if parents did miss some cues, so did teachers, students, neighbors, clergy, and other members of the communities in which the young men who shot their fellow students lived. For instance, the police failed to act on reports filed against Eric Harris for maintaining a Web site that openly threatened students in Littleton, Colorado; they also did not respond to specific complaints of a neighbor whose son was directly threatened. At school, other teachers and students did not respond to concerns about repeated threats and violent imagery and rhetoric even though each of the student killers gave some form of warning, often in a piece of writing intended for use in school (Savastana, 2003). Rather than indict parents, then, the cultural acceptance of the boys' obsession with violence needs to be understood. What allowed so many members of these communities to ignore the warning signs? One definite possibility is that many educators, neighbors, friends, and parents adopted a "boys will be boys" attitude that led them to mistakenly believe aggressive statements had no deeper meaning. Again it may have been the very "normalcy" of such remarks "in everyday life" that explains why myriad parties—including but not limited to parents—did little to prevent words from turning into actions.

A fourth explanation—retaliatory responses against school bullies—became popular after the deadliest massacre to date, in Columbine High School in Colorado; students who were regularly teased and beaten up took revenge on their more popular peers who bullied them. Again, however, the specific role of gender in this phenomenon has not been emphasized.

Bullies are overwhelmingly male (Hall, 1999; Talbott, 2002), and targets of bullies tend to be boys who are perceived to be gay (Tomsho, 2003), boys who threaten the bully's perceived "proprietary rights" to an individual girl, and girls, who also endure different forms of sexual harassment and dating violence (Carlson, 2003). In five of the shootings between 1996 and 2002, young boys targeted and shot girls who had rejected them—a horrific result of dating violence similar to domestic violence (Carlson, 2003). In three other cases, boys "protected" their girlfriends by shooting other boys who seemed to threaten their relationship. In 11 cases, boy perpetrators targeted more popular boys who attacked their masculinity, often by calling them gay (Klein & Chancer, 2000).

Teasing, gay-bashing, dating violence, and sexual harassment are often so commonplace in schools they are considered normal behaviors (Ambert, 1994; Tonso, 2002; McGuffey & Rich, 1999). Because such teasing is considered a normal expression among youth, this initial harassment is not flagged as problematic, and the devastating consequences continue to escalate. Gay harassment and dating violence are not perceived as significant problems among youth, and beliefs that such teasing (that can lead to assaults) is normal has inadvertently, at best, made horrific forms of violence commonplace at schools. When bullying does receive attention in schools, the specific role of gender is almost entirely absent, and so the roots of such violence remain unchallenged and entrenched.

Domestic Violence

Domestic violence differs from the social problems analyzed above in being both well-recognized and frequently discussed in terms of gender-based dichotomies between men and women. But, in this instance, routinely overlooked is another aspect: popular depictions of domestic violence usually characterize this third social problem as "extreme" behavior, thereby ignoring the extent to which this type of violence exists on a continuum of "normal" to extreme manifestations of masculinity. For instance, most popular cultural representations of domestic violence—say, Farrah Fawcett's performance in *The Burning Bed* (1988, directed by Robert Greenwald) or Julia Robert's portrayal of a battered woman in *Sleeping with the Enemy* (1991, directed by Joseph Ruben)—portray the batterer as homicidal and/or psychotic. In so doing, such depictions concomitantly individualize the problem and abstract it from the life of communities wherein domestic violence relationships are embedded and (in one sense) "enabled." Therefore, the "fault" for domestic violence is rarely perceived as residing even at all in wider social relationships—for example, possibly in tolerating aggressive behavior in boys that may begin early in life—but only in the "deviant" batterer himself (occasionally herself) and sometimes in the victim who has not left the situation.

Instead, though, the following argument can be made. Perhaps domestic violence is best conceived as both distinctive and as intimately connected with a wider range of normalized masculine behaviors that may or may not end up in violence. For example, drawing on popular culture yet again, a psychological literature appeared in the 1980s and 1990s that prominently featured titles like *Men Who Hate Women and the Women Who Love Them*, *Women Who Love Too Much* and *Love Addiction*. While this literature did not mention domestic violence per se, frequently mentioned were (usually heterosexual) relationships in which women felt they had to "walk on eggshells" lest they say anything that offended—often leading to verbal abuse from—their partners. From this body of literature, too, then, one can conclude that a range of condoned behaviors that involve expressing aggressive feelings toward women are linked with, though not strictly speaking equatable with, domestic violence.

Yet by viewing domestic violence in the dominant culture only as actualized violence, it becomes relatively easy to deflect attention—as can happen with "deviantized" phenomena in general—from this problem's relationship, qua extraordinary sexism, with "ordinary" sexism. This has policy implications as well: unless a connection between "less" and "more" problematic forms of aggressive violence toward women is borne in mind, criminal justice programs, policies, and analyses designed to deal with the post facto extremity of battering can multiply while far-reaching attempts to transform cultural attitudes and unjust social structures will not necessarily be labeled key anti–domestic violence measures themselves. Moreover, by not making such connections, the overlooking of behaviors like public harassment becomes easier to understand: this, too, is seen as relatively innocuous when only acts of actual violence are treated, by the culture writ large, as meriting intervention. Therefore, an essential component of redressing domestic violence—at least from the standpoint of prevention—may involve, paradoxically enough, aiming beyond and not necessarily only at reforming battering per se. Yet the fact that domestic violence's relationship with normalized masculinity—and, as Connell writes, masculinities—is overlooked means that such wider social connections are not sufficiently perceived.

The Problem of Normalized Masculinity(ies) in Theory and Practice

So far, we have focused on how gendered constructions of masculinity are both relevant to and overlooked in common cultural reactions to three social problems: public harassment, school violence, and domestic abuse. In this section, though, we turn more specifically to how normalized masculinity(ies) are socially prescribed and become culpable in these problems' persistence. Following Foucault, again, "in fact power produces; it produces reality; it produces domains of objects and rituals of truth" (1990). Here, ontologically speaking, normalized masculinities are part and parcel of the rituals taken as "truth" embedded in "boys will be boys"—explanations that sometimes become "alibis" for otherwise imminent violence. Many gender theorists have extrapolated on the destructive expectations inherent in normalized masculinity, although, arguably, Robert W. Connell has been most important in detailing these pressures on different groups of men.

Connell (1995) explains that relations of domination operate between men and women, and among men themselves. To describe the complexity of masculinity(ies)—at once similar in some respects and different in others—Connell identifies four types: hegemonic, subordinate, marginalized, and complicit. Hegemonic refers to the form of masculinity most legitimate in a given society; in contemporary contexts, this has tended to include military heroes, successful businessmen, or powerful politicians. Men who appear to be hegemonic are thought to embody stereotypical masculine traits such as detachment (or lack of emotion), toughness, authoritativeness, and controlling qualities. Males who can most obviously differentiate themselves from women and homosexuals are classified in this category, apparently at the top of masculinities' hierarchy.

On the other hand, gays and men perceived as gay are relegated to the bottom of the hierarchy: their masculinity has become subordinated. Marginalized masculinity refers to men within stigmatized groups relating generally to race or economics in a culture where white, heterosexual, wealthy men are given the opportunities to be most powerful. Complicit masculinity refers to the majority of men who do not display omnipotent expectations of manhood, but who subsequently benefit from the subordination of women and gays. Even though they are not hegemonic, they receive a "patriarchal dividend" in that they reap status-power benefits just by virtue of being men (Connell, 1995, p. 79).

Connell argues that inequalities among masculinities often breed violence against females and/or against males perceived as gay or feminine. In Connell's words,

> Many members of the privileged group use violence to sustain their dominance. Intimidation of women ranges across the spectrum from wolf-

whistling in the street . . . to murder by a woman's patriarchal owner. Most men do not attack or harass women; but those who do are unlikely to think themselves deviant. On the contrary they usually feel they are entirely justified, that they are exercising a right. They are authorized by an ideology of supremacy. (1995, p. 83)

Thus, subordinating women is a ritual for asserting masculinity, and an opportunity for men to declare that they are "not women." In fact, dominating women becomes a central aspect of demonstrating masculinity. Men as well as younger adolescents (and even children) are taught to display their superiority and control over women. Thus hegemonic masculinity embodies the "boys will be boys" explanation that excuses so much violence perpetuated by men. Men are often taught, and indeed encouraged, to prove their affiliations through the exercise of hegemonic masculinity.

And consequently to be beaten by a girl, for instance, may still be a source of great humiliation in many social and professional cultural milieus, especially if the victory was displayed in front of other males who are taught that judging and being competitive are necessary to successfully attain masculinity. Women are made, not born, said de Beauvoir in 1951, but this is clearly the case for men as well. Normal masculinity expectations are set high, if not at levels impossible to attain, and many—indeed most—are encouraged to spend their lives trying to demonstrate hegemonic achievements.

Connell's second category of masculinity—subordinated masculinity—is particularly apt for understanding the school violence problem as described above. For subordinated masculinity often breeds reactive violence as males who believe they are perceived as feminine, and therefore lower on the masculinity hierarchy, try to reinstate a perception of themselves within a hegemonic formation, especially as a public performance for other men. Interestingly, though, this also suggests that in the other two social problems this chapter highlights—public harassment and domestic violence—aggressive and extreme "macho" behaviors may likewise be aimed at least as much at demonstrating status vis-à-vis other men as it is aimed at women. Subordinated masculinities are built on the many social and institutional practices by which men can be made to feel inferior in the face of impossible expectations; in such circumstances, normalized masculinity calls for visible demonstrations of an invulnerable, dominant, and invincible exterior. Again, one form

of this subordination is evident in the school violence cases where heterosexual boys, perceived as feminine, are subjugated in the same way
as hegemonic men are encouraged to dominate women and gays. Similarly the phenomenon of gay men being harassed in public, as Brooks
Gardner describes, also fits within Connell's description of subordinated
masculinity. As Connell himself describes, "Gay masculinity is the most
conspicuous, but it is not the only subordinated masculinity. Some heterosexual men as well as boys are expelled from the circle of legitimacy.
The process is marked by a rich vocabulary of abuse, including wimp,
nerd, sissy, mama's boy, dweeb, geek. . . . Here too, the symbolic blurring
with femininity is obvious" (1995, p. 79). In the school violence cases,
the boy perpetrators consistently said they acted violently because they
were tired of being teased, and each referenced perceived challenges to
their manhood. The discomfort that is socially attached to a subordinated
masculinity is often relieved when men demonstrate a greater power associated with hegemonic masculinity, clearly a motivating factor in these
crimes.

Relentless attacks on these adolescents' masculinity seemed to inspire
a fierce assertion of rebellion through violence. Lynne Segal explains
that homophobia is used as a means to keep all men in line by oppressing gay men and expressing contempt for men when they express emotional qualities associated with femininity (1990, p. 158). Consequently,
attacks by the hegemonic boys (popular preps and jocks) were motivated
by the same homophobic impulses as the defensive terror and rage these
assaults engendered in the victims-turned-killers. Segal says boys are
taught to despise the "feminine enemy within themselves" and to try
to destroy any person that draws attention to these rejected aspects of
their personality (ibid.).

In public harassment, a visible demonstration of manhood is reas-
serted through the uninvited remarks made towards women. In domestic
violence, a more private assertion is levied, demonstrating to a female
partner (though certainly some victims are male) the hierarchy in the
relationship and the superior position that the aggressor holds. Susan
Faludi (1999) conveys that contemporary men may be more motivated
to demonstrate a dominant form of masculinity in the face of economic
insecurities, that is, fears of losing one's job, extensive downsizing, and
other institutionalized experiences that breed feelings of inferiority. Such
domination in the face of pressures to demonstrate hegemonic masculin-

ity may contribute to ongoing patterns of violence and domination. As social mores persist, men who are subordinated in one way or another try to find ways to display their ultimate power and ability to dominate.

Connell calls a third kind of masculinity "marginalized." Again, this refers to some males feeling unable to reach the "standards" of other men, perceived as hegemonic, who are usually white, financially powerful, and heterosexual. One might expect, then, that both "subordinated" and "marginalized" men might feel motivated to incite some form of violent rebellion to transform perceptions of their "inferior" predicament. It is not difficult to comprehend the idea that marginalized masculinity, relating to institutionally enforced oppressions—like discrimination, or social/other exclusions—often relate to class or race. Thus men who are oppressed systemically in a particular society might look for other avenues to demonstrate their ability to be powerful or dominant, consistent with the hegemonic masculinity otherwise expected of them. Clearly, then, contradictions arise amid pressures to demonstrate hegemonic masculinity and experiences of widespread subordination in mainstream society, including but not limited to gender-based discrimination. However, marginalized masculinity is not limited to conditions relating to race and class.

Michele Fine et al. (1997) coined the phrase "white loss" to describe how white males, too, might make sense of a perceived lack of power. Men, more generally, can face realistic concerns relating to economic insecurity as well as common fears and pain unacceptable in traditional masculine identities; these "limitations" are constantly compared to omnipresent expectations for a highly visible dominating masculinity. These contradictions may motivate some men to go to extreme measures to prove their affiliations with a more powerful masculinity. Consequently, Fine et al. argue that, in the face of perceived dwindling power bases, many men faced with such contradictions look for someone to blame.

"While the workings of capital, the flight of jobs, and the devastation of the public sector escape largely unnoticed, black men, white women, and gays/lesbians are held accountable for their white misery" (Tonso, 2002, p. 393). Ferber (1999), too, has argued that this reaction is by no means limited to working-class men. Looking at the school shooting cases, white loss seems applicable. Shooters were generally less wealthy and less powerful/popular then the "preps and jocks" that seemed to rule the school. Many of the shooters identified with ideologies associated with Nietzsche, Satan, and Hitler, perspectives they might have used to try to fight the images of weakness with which they felt saddled. Persuading themselves of their own ability to wield power—whether through sheer will, demonic powers, or race-based fascism—may have been another disturbed effort to address a form of white loss. Even though they were white, they did not seem to get the "patriarchal dividend" (in Connell's words) that men receive by virtue of being male. They set out to reclaim that anticipated privilege.

Among the school shootings, boys seemed to have responded to pressures to demonstrate masculinity through exhibits of strength and power, especially in the face of emasculating remarks. All the surviving perpetrators said they felt more important after they committed their crimes. "Murder is gutsy and daring," announced Luke Woodham in Mississippi (Popyk, 1998). Michael Carneal, in Kentucky, said he brought the guns to school because he was "trying to get people to like him. . . . I just wanted the guys to think I was cool (Blank, 1998). After the incident, Carneal said, "I was feeling proud, strong, good, and more respected. I didn't think I would get in trouble, I thought it would make me popular" (ibid.). These boys conveyed that dominating and devastating their peers at school was, in their eyes, a way to unquestionably display their ability to wield power and control and thus be associated with a socially glamorized hegemonic masculinity. "One second I was some kind of heartbroken idiot," explains Woodham, "and the next second I had the power over many things" (Popyk, 1998).

While Connell's work depicts the workings in relation to one or another of multiple forms of masculinities, hegemonic masculinity is consistently most explicit and framed as the ideal to which men often feel they must adhere. Such a manifestation of normalized masculinity, implicated in the social problems described here, is held as the highest ideal for men to strive to achieve and measure themselves against. Social psychologists Robert Brannon and Deborah David summarize this dominant form of masculinity as a four-tiered composite:

1. "No Sissy Stuff"
2. "Be a Big Wheel"
3. "Be a Sturdy Oak"
4. "Give 'em Hell" (Kimmel, 1990, p. 8)

No Sissy Stuff   Masculinity exists on an extreme end of a masculine-feminine continuum. In other words, men are cautioned to distance themselves from anything remotely associated with femininity, including homosexuality or expressions of vulnerable (feminine) feelings such as crying. Relentless teasing, often in the form of negative references to gay sexuality, becomes a way to compel men to comply with this expectation; such baiting becomes a type of surveillance administered both individually and collectively in many a social sphere.

Be a Big Wheel Success, domination, status, victories, and other forms of "winning" are stressed in the aspect of masculinity. Men acquire a higher masculine standing with an association with some type of triumph or conquest. This facet of masculinity is visible in all three social problems discussed here, relating to males who try to dominate women in public harassment, display superior power towards spouses in intimate violence, and decimate their peers in school shootings.

Be a Sturdy Oak This is another invective to communicate invulnerability; men are expected to hide their emotions and appear confident, in control at all times, and unafraid. This chapter discusses in some depth the ramifications of this demand for emotional control in the face of human vulnerabilities. By acting "appropriately" tough and autonomous, men may disguise feelings of vulnerability and loss by creating what William Pollack, a social psychologist specializing in the study of young men, calls a "mask of masculinity." Instead of the range of emotions available to women, boys are permitted only anger and the means to control their other feelings with "calm and cool" fronts (Pollack, 1999). This expectation further complicates the ability for males to deal constructively with the contradictions inherent in expectations for hegemonic masculinity.

Give 'Em Hell This is a dictum to act aggressively, to dominate, to show them all "who's the boss." Men are expected to retaliate against perceived slights, intrusions on property, or to protect a sense of honor. This may manifest in the form of expectations to "fight back" when a bully teases a boy at school (exhibited tragically in the school shooting cases), or in demonstrations of superior power in the case of intimate violence, or in the aggression displayed in public harassment. The demand also invokes responses to moral dilemmas; men who believe they are slighted have one choice within hegemonic masculinity—some form of revenge.

Together these aspects of hegemonic masculinity enforce a strict code of behavior (while prohibiting others), a specific approach to life, narrow emotional parameters, and, some might argue, an antiquated view of morality. Masculinity expectations are coercive and unforgiving—and the social ramifications are tragic. Perhaps normalized masculinity should not be considered so "normal." Yet "boys will be boys," with all its implications, serves to perpetuate and sustain this construction.

Popular and scholarly books explaining and analyzing masculinity(ies) are still flooding the market as well as academe. In many different ways, writers grapple with the seemingly irresolvable conflicts between pressures for men to display hegemonic masculinity in the face of their all-too-human vulnerabilities. It is now apparent that many young boys and men—so afraid to admit, or sometimes even to perceive, their own human frailty—have been unable to admit to serious emotional challenges like depression; this significantly skews social perceptions of the extent of such suffering and prevents the kinds of intervention needed for relief.

To show something of this phenomenon statistically, Pollack contributes important insights to the National Institute of Mental Health (NIMH) research on depression. According to the NIMH, 12 percent of women and 7 percent of men experience a major depressive illness each year (NIMH, 1999). While this is disturbing in itself, Pollack's findings provide even more staggering information. He writes that because of the "boy code," boys feel compelled to appear tough and independent even when they are truly depressed. As a result of these socially imposed and finally internalized pressures, they are less likely to report their genuine pain on psychological studies or surveys. Pollack says advanced research conveys that boys are just as depressed as girls but don't necessarily "look" depressed to others. Pollack also notes a recent epidemic in suicides for young men (Pollack, 1999). The NIMH officially recognizes that while women report attempting suicide about twice as often as men, males are more likely than females to die by suicide (NIMH, 1999). Without socially acceptable vehicles for emotional expression, men may spend their whole lives building up difficult feelings. In fact, white elderly males have the highest rate of suicide in the United States—a rate three to four times higher than the general population. Gerontology researchers Sheikh and Yalom (1996) attribute this to the "social construction of gender in this society that teaches most men at a very early age to internalize their emotions." The "big boys don't cry" message is everywhere, and the end result is a rampant myth that men aren't depressed simply because they do not show it in ways that are easy for others to recognize (p. 9). Girls may talk about their feelings more, but if boys were allowed the same socially sanctioned vehicles of self-expression, we might hear more about their pain; instead boys are more likely to act on their despair. This, of course, may help explain externally directed violence in addition to the internally focused violence inherent in suicide.

Pollack writes that with the intention of "making men," destructive masculinity pressures begin when males are children; sometimes "as young as five or six, and then again in adolescence," boys "are often forced to separate prematurely from their parents, and expected to be independent" (Pollack, 1999, p. 11). This early separation understandably brings out emotional vulnerabilities in young boys, and then engenders extreme performances of hegemonic masculinity as a means to create distance from such "feminine" emotions, and to avoid socially proscribed feelings like shame that boys are taught to associate with most emotional expressions.

Another well-known theory of masculinity's problems was offered by Chodorow—when boys separate from their mothers (typically the primary caregiver), they tend to feel forced to differentiate themselves as "not female" or "not the qualities embodied by their mother." Masculinity pressures begin very young, and boys may work to establish a masculine identity from the onset. Since their mothers are often the people to whom they are most connected, they may feel compelled to repress needs for love and relationships during this separation process. This becomes a burgeoning conflict as males as well as females crave intimacy, and yet men feel they must demand "from women what men are at the same time afraid of receiving" (Chodorow, 1978, p. 199). Lack of intimate relationships and connection combined with pressure to suppress their emotions can boil into an uncontrollable and lethal rage ultimately erupting in violence. Pollack added more recently that the invariable "mask of masculinity" developed from such conflicts played a role in all the school shooting cases (p. 3).

This section has tried to address the potential origins, construction, enforcement, and ramifications of normalized masculinity and, as is most relevant here, the inextricable link between normalized masculinity and public harassment, school shootings, and domestic violence as well as their incipient everyday behavior enforced through a complex social surveillance—as described also through Connell's masculinities—that works to great detriment. The central role of normalized masculinity in these intrusive-to-assaultive-to-violent behaviors also raises issues about whether and how such highly gendered constructions continue to be maintained through so many interlocking social and institutional practices. What can be done, and where should we start?

Returning to Basics

Gender structures in everyday life, and masculinity norms in particular, need to be transformed. While ideas for how, where, and why such change should take place are increasingly forthcoming in academe, if not in popular literature, little has been done to significantly alter outside the academy the destructive gender constructions implicated in social problems that include the ones reviewed here. Change needs to occur throughout social institutions that include the criminal justice system, the media, education institutions, and traditionally oriented families.

We have shown that normalized expectations of masculinity are involved in public harassment, school shootings, and intimate violence. We have also discussed how the otherwise glaring culpability inherent in normalized masculinity is overlooked in responses to these behaviors. Normalized masculinity and its requisite expectations for victory at all costs, invulnerability, aggression, domination, and sometimes violence becomes hidden in everyday dynamics. The "boys will be boys" refrain has absolved many from civil offenses and sometimes crimes with a belief that boys cannot control their aggressive impulses. While much has been written about the specific ability of humans to advance pro-social ends, and our drive on some level to create civilized communities in spite of possible discontents, males have somehow been excused when such offenses clash with normalized masculine expectations. School bullies, public harassers, and perpetrators of domestic violence (statistically mostly male), have at one time or another been given carte blanche to behave as they do.

While those that commit domestic violence are perceived today as deviant, not too long ago the idea that men should control and tame their wives was socially acceptable. When Dora famously slams the door in *The Doll House*, and with the advent of the women's liberation movement in the 1970s, such issues became public discussions; previously acceptable systems of control were reexamined, rendered increasingly unacceptable, and sometimes criminalized. While this does represent some progress, the extent to which violence exists on a continuum of normalized masculinity—and of aggressive-to-violent behaviors—is still not acknowledged nor sufficiently addressed. Similarly, while schools certainly acknowledge the atrocities of violence that have occurred within them, the role of bullies as a significant antecedent is only beginning to be seen. Popular discourse still minimizes the impact of such everyday aggression, again with a "boys will be boys" refrain, and refuses to recognize the gay harassment and dating violence inherent in this aggression. In fact, when discussing these issues informally with educated and progressively identified parents, teachers, and university professors, one of the authors heard the same typical response: "bullying will always take place" and sometimes "they just have to fight back." So while the problem of bullies is ever so slowly entering public consciousness, the role of normalized masculinity is almost entirely absent in public discourse and ultimately in prevention and intervention strategies. The "boys will be boys" refrain helps normalized masculinity to stay entrenched and immune to efforts to dislodge it. Finally, public harassment is barely acknowledged as a social problem in the first place—much less the implicated role of normal masculinity expectations.

With such a lack of awareness, traditional gender structures are maintained and perpetuated rather than transformed. Consequently, as conversations change regarding domestic violence, as schools finally confront bullying as a social problem and even a criminal act, and as public harassment slowly seeps into public consciousness, the envelope needs to be pushed further still, much further. Because even if disciplinary tactics are increased, as is the current trend—such that there are more immediate and stringent consequences for battering, bullying, and harassing—the basic gender frameworks that manifest in these social problems will persist with "normal" "boys will be boys" exemptions. Lower-level everyday violence of this nature, that which manages to escape definitions of criminality, will continue with immunity.

We hope that across class, race, and ethnic differences, people will discuss, reflect on, and transform deeply embedded and destructive rules for gender. Such awareness needs to begin in early childhood curriculums, not just college, with the same force that has made progress by integrating the study of racial and ethnic diversity throughout U.S. education. Representations in popular culture can also be influential in initiating needed discussions and self-reflection.

Men's discussion groups or, more specifically, "batterer intervention programs," perhaps "discussions for those accused of bullying," and even groups for public harassers could go far in helping men resolve the contradictions with which they have been struggling; such intervention could provide meaningful avenues for individual change in the context of newly approving communities, thus influencing discussion and expectations in the larger society.

We see gender norms as destructive for the victims of these problems, but also for the individual perpetrator as well as for larger communities. Thus, change needs to take place within an individual who committed a crime or other aggressive act as well as in larger cultural contexts. Taken together, these kinds of interventions might help to break down the bravado that hegemonic masculinity encourages, which is revealed here as culpable in so many crimes. Groups can offer individuals the room to accept their own vulnerabilities, change their perceptions of a compulsory masculinity, and ultimately explore and confront their own individual paths and personal histories.

The ordinary definitions of masculinity need to be transformed—specifically "boys will be boys" discussed here—but also the institutional oppressive practices that incite so many men to try to demonstrate that they have a more dominant and powerful manhood. Racism, class discrimination, and bias of all kinds serve to diminish the self-esteem of all people but specifically aggravate the dictum within normalized masculinity to retaliate somewhere, somehow. As we create smaller forms of community and individual change, the interconnection among all prejudice needs to be held in the foreground. A transformed perception of what normal masculinity is might well engender a more cooperative and peaceful approach to changing other oppressive social practices. Ultimately, an approach and a gender identity for both men and women that is satisfactory will have to integrate masculinity and femininity; it will have to involve cooperation and not just victory, control but also vulnerability, negotiation and not just retaliation. Such a rich and more-encompassing gender identity could go far to ameliorate social ills, create more equality and good will, and grant both men and women much fuller possibilities for being human.

References

Ambert, A. (1994, February). A Qualitative Study of Peer Abuse and Its Effects: Theoretical and Empirical Implications. *Journal of Marriage and the Family*, 56(1), 119–130.

Angel, M. (1999, Spring). Symposium: Abusive Boys Kill Girls Just Like Abusive Men Kill Women: Explaining the Obvious. *Temple Political & Civil Rights Law Review*, 283.

Applebome, P. (1998, March 29). Round and Round in the Search for Meaning. *New York Times*, sec. 4, 1.

Blank, J. (1998, October 12). The Kid No One Noticed: Guns Would Get His Classmates' Attention. *U.S. News.* Retrieved July 11, 2001 from http://www.usnews.com.

Brooks Gardner, C. 1995. *Passing By: Gender and Public Harassment.* Berkeley: University of California Press.

Carlson, C. N. (2003, Spring). Focus Section: Violence against Women: Invisible Victims: Holding the Educational System Liable for Teen Dating Violence at School. *Harvard Women's Law Journal, 26,* 351.

Chancer, L. S. (1992). *Sadomasochism in Everyday Life.* New Brunswick, NJ: Rutgers University Press.

Chodorow, N. (1978). *The Reproduction of Mothering: Psychoanalysis and the Sociology of Gender.* Berkeley: University of California Press.

Cline, V. B. (Ed.). (1974). *Where Do You Draw the Line?* Provo, Utah: Brigham Young University Press.

Connell, R. W. (1995). *Masculinities.* Berkeley: University of California Press.

Faludi, S. (1999). *Stiffed: The Betrayal of the American Man.* New York: Perennial.

Ferber, A. (1999). *White Man Falling: Gender, Race, and White Supremacy.* Lanham, MD: Rowman and Littlefield.

Fine, M., Weis, L., Addelston, J., & Maruszxa, J. (1997). White Loss. In M. Seller & L. Fine (eds.), *Beyond Black and White: New Faces and Voices in U.S. Schools* (p. 283–301). Albany: State University of New York Press.

Foucault, M. (1990). *The History of Sexuality.* New York: Random House.

Foucault, M. (1991). *Discipline and Punish: The Birth of the Prison.* New York: Random House.

Friedman, T. L. (1999, May 4). Kosovo and Columbine. *New York Times*, Op-Ed, 31.

Hall, S. (1999, 22 August). The Bully in the Mirror. *New York Times Magazine*, 31.

Kimmel, M. (Ed.). (1990). *Men Confront Pornography.* New York: Penguin.

Klein, J., & Chancer, L. (2000). Masculinity matters: The role of gender in high-profile school violence cases. In S. Spina (ed.), *Smoke and Mirrors: The Hidden Context of Violence in Schools and Society* (pp. 129–162). New York: Rowman & Littlefield.

McGuffey, S. C., & Rich, L. (1999, October). Playing in the Gender Transgression Zone: Race, Class, and Hegemonic Masculinity in Middle Childhood. *Gender and Society, 13*(5), 608–627.

Moore, M. (Director). (2002). *Bowling for Columbine* [motion picture].

National Institute of Mental Health (1999, July 18). Women Hold Up Half the Sky. http://www.nimh.nih.gov/publicat/womensoms.cfm.

Pollack W. (1999). *Real Boys: Rescuing Our Sons from the Men They Will Become.* New York: Owl Books.

Popyk, L. (1998, November 9). I Knew It Wouldn't Be Right. *Cincinnati Post.* Retrieved June 12, 1999, from http://www.cincypost.com.

Savastana, M. A. (2003, Spring). Tattle-Telling on the United States: School Violence and the International Blame Game. *Dickinson School of Law, Carlisle, PA, Penn State International Law Review,* 649 (online). Available via LexisNexis.

Segal, L. (1990). *Slow Motion: Changing Masculinities, Changing Men.* New Brunswick, NJ: Rutgers University Press.

Sheikh, J., & Yalom, I. (1996). Depression. In *Treating the Elderly* (p. 3–43). San Francisco: Jossey-Bass.

Spina, S. (Ed.). (2000). *Smoke and Mirrors: The Hidden Context of Violence in Schools and Society.* New York: Rowman and Littlefield.

Spitzer, R. J. (1995). *The Politics of Gun Control.* Chatham, NJ: Chatham.

Talbot, M. (2002, February 24). Girls Just Want to Be Mean. *New York Times.* Retrieved December 18, 2002, from http://query.nytimes.com/gst/abstract.html?res=F30414F9355B0C778EDDAB0894 DA40.

Tomsho, R. (2003, February 20). Schools' Efforts to Protect Gays Face Opposition. *Wall Street Journal,* B1.

Tonso, K. L. (2002, Winter). Reflecting on Columbine High: Ideologies of Privilege in "Standardized" Schools. *Educational Studies, 33*(4), 389–403.

PART TWO

Epistemology and Crime

Epistemology is the study of what we know and how we come to make knowledge claims. Thus, a philosophy of crime that was sensitive to epistemological pursuits would examine the basis on which criminological knowledge assertions are made and legitimized. In this model of inquiry, various assumptions about truth telling and meaning figure prominently into the overall analysis.

Chapter 3 addresses the epistemological dimension of crime and criminology. The production of criminological knowledge is considered here as both the result and the source of a deeply social practice of tribal communality. Drawing inspiration from what is known as "actor-network theory," the chapter's main thesis states that the process of knowledge production, both in criminals and in criminal communities, appears to be a tribal process. Tribal dynamics in both generate particular "knowledges," and those in turn lead to further tribal dynamics, with the search for communality and tribal sociality being of paramount importance in this process.

"Knowledge," always particular to the tribal context in which it emerges, is conceived of here as a particular "assemblage" (of assemblages) that circulates between tribal members who negotiate with each other about its tribal appropriateness. Although this chapter has no encyclopedic ambitions, connections with the more familiar literature on epistemology and philosophy of science are made throughout. Evoking a variety of illustrations from the criminological literature, the chapter provides a sustained criticism of "linearity" and "rationality"—the province of the Cartesian subject—that dominated earlier, modernist epistemologies. Using actor-network theory, however, this chapter attempts to avoid the unnecessarily rigid modernity-postmodernity dichotomies.

Chapter 4 also explores the epistemology of crime. Like many fields of inquiry that attempt to explain "realities" of one kind or another, criminology lacks a clear, rational, and generally accepted epistemology to guide theory testing. This situation appears in part to be due to and maintained by two seemingly unsolved philosophical problems: the problem of induction and the problem of theory-laden observation. In this chapter, these two problems are examined, but no definitive solution is proposed. The examination is organized to support a healthy level of skepticism and openness to alternative methods of theory testing. It begins with an attempt to explain why the problem of induction makes the verification of nomothetic theories an unobtainable goal and the falsification of such theories problematic. This is followed by an account of how the problem of theory-laden observation affects all empirical tests, and how it results in a seemingly unavoidable paradox. Finally, it is suggested that these two problems can be used to rationalize the adoption of an "ironist" orientation toward theory testing, a perspective that rejects the correspondence theory of truth and embraces the goal of self-creation.

While chapter 3 offers a more allegorical appraisal of epistemology's role in fashioning knowledge claims about crime, criminals, and criminal communities, chapter 4 uses the logic of epistemology to challenge conventional wisdom about theory testing in criminology. Strikingly, both chapters draw attention to the taken-for-granted assumptions embedded within criminology proper and the manner in which these assumptions result in problematic assertions about what constitutes crime, which persons represent criminals, and how best to make truth claims about both. In short, these two chapters demonstrate where and how philosophical inquiry sheds additional and provocative light on the very foundations of criminological *verstehen*.

THREE

Crime, Criminology, and Epistemology: Tribal Considerations

RONNIE LIPPENS

In his essay "On Ethnographic Self-Fashioning: Conrad and Malinowski" (1988), James Clifford, one of the most distinguished voices in theoretical ethnography, developed an interesting thesis. Comparing writing styles and strategies in literature (Joseph Conrad's novels in particular) and ethnography (Bronislaw Malinowski's anthropological works), Clifford argues that, like literature, ethnographical writings are just that: writing (see also on this topic Geertz, 1988). Like literature, ethnographical works seem to be largely the result of authors who, more or less desperately, are trying to build, or, at least, to stabilize themselves through the use of particular writing strategies, styles, and forms. More often than not, the anthropologist or ethnographer finds him- or herself in a more or less uneasy position. Anxieties about the unfamiliar abound. The "others" are to some extent still "other." The own self starts to lose its footing in a sea of fluid uncertainties. This is the predicament whence the ethnographer or the author begins to develop or employ strategies and styles that (so it is hoped) will bring some stability. Much of ethnographical writing, claims Clifford, results from attempts to gain or, better, to regain stability of the self. In producing a more or less coherent story about a more or less coherent and therefore more understandable "other," the own self appears to stabilize again.

This is an important insight for both epistemology and criminology. Clifford's essay suggests that the tasks for epistemology (the theory of knowledge, or knowledge about knowledge) ought to include at least considerations about the *human, all-too-human* context of knowledge production (the phrase, by the way, is the title of one of Friedrich Nietzsche's books). That which ends up in texts as "knowledge" seems to be a matter of strategy, style, and form rather than substance. Criminologists very often rely on ethnography to produce criminological "knowledge." Like anthropologists, criminologists often aim to produce "knowledge" about "others," about "them," about those who allegedly are not like us. Clifford's message deserves to be heard by anyone who is involved in the production of criminological knowledge.

In this chapter, we will explore the human, all-too-human context of criminological knowledge, or, to put it in other words, knowledge about insiders and outsiders. For reasons that remain to be elaborated below, we will consider this human, all too human context not just as authors' writing strategies, styles, and forms aimed at the stabilization of individual selves but rather as the deeply social practice of tribal communality. Yes, our intention here is to stay with the tropes of anthropology, ethnography, tribalism, and otherness. The chapter includes two sections. The first section develops the thesis of *knowledge as the social practice of tribal communality.* In the second section, this thesis is applied to and illustrated with criminological themes and issues. We will end on a note that connects the themes and issues explored in this chapter to a text on knowledge that has arguably been one of the most defining in recent decades. This chapter has no encyclopedic ambitions. However, connections will be made throughout with the perhaps more familiar literature on epistemology and philosophy of science. Reference will also be made to the postmodernist debates that have figured in much of the literature of the 1980s and 1990s. Let us note in passing that the framework that provides the theoretical backdrop for much of this chapter, namely actor-network theory, was and still is, in my view at least, one of the more successful attempts at dealing with the unnecessarily rigid modernity-postmodernism dichotomies that have dominated so many of those end-of-the-century debates.

Knowledge about Insiders and Outsiders

Tribal Connections

Let us, by way of introduction, describe an everyday scene from the highland jungles in Papua New Guinea. Marilyn Strathern, an anthropologist, witnessed such scenes when she was doing fieldwork there and described them in her book *Partial Connections* (1991). Strathern has since become known as one of the representatives of actor-network theory. We will get back to actor-network theory later, as this strand of social theory is providing the thread of reasoning that underpins this chapter at hand. Let us for now just describe a scene in the Papuan jungle. Please bear with me. Picture a hut in a village. In front of the hut, a number of men are squatting. All of them have adorned themselves with a number of extensions such as bird feathers and other materials gathered from the forest. The men watch each other, they scrutinize each other's adornments, and they talk. Only the men, by the way, adorn themselves in such manner. The women carry nets on their backs that hold dear or useful objects that, in the course of their individual lives, they have been able to gather. Now this difference between genders is in itself very interesting. Women's lives appear as individual trajectories of past experience, while men's lives appear to be centered around what we will call expressed, as well as becoming, *tribal knowledge* about insiders and outsiders. For our purposes here and now, we will therefore focus on the tribesmen. The extensions worn by the men are typical of their particular tribe. Watching closely, we will indeed notice how the extensions on each of the men are more or less similar. However, they are not completely similar. There is some degree of variation to be noticed. The men look at each other, they talk, and again look at each other. In particular they look at each other's adornments. They assess them and evaluate to what extent they are similar or different, and to what extent they demonstrate tribal communality. We should be more precise here: watching and assessing each other's extensions, the men assess each other's *knowledge* of tribal community. This knowledge, if communally accepted, may *express* some level of tribal community that is already present, or it may help to produce some level of tribal community that is yet to *become*. Now, either the men themselves or we watching them will probably never be in a position to be able to distinguish *expressions* from *becomings*, but for our purposes, that does not matter much. What does need some emphasis is the idea that, in Papuan jungles, knowledge often seems to boil down to knowledge about who is *in* and who is *out* and that this knowledge, embodied as it is in visible extensions, is constantly assessed and negotiated while it is put to use to constitute or, eventually, reconstitute tribal communality. And in turn, tribal communality appears as that which is the result of (mostly visually) negotiated knowledge. Knowledge is both the result and the source of tribal communality, while the latter, tribal communality, is both the result and the source of knowledge. And this mutual constitution of knowledge and tribal communality proceeds in and through the visual arrangement and tribal negotiation and assessment of artifacts (the carriers of knowledge and tribal communality) that were gathered in some allegedly outside space, that is, the jungle, *out there*. The careful reader will already have noticed that this story is not just about Papua New Guinean jungles and that there is much more in all this than meets the eye. But before we make the issues more explicit or *visible* (see also Lippens, 2003), let us, for a while, continue with the exploration of the case of the tribal village in the jungle.

Sometimes tribal men will find some of their extensions to be defective or just missing. They will then have to fetch or find substitutes in the jungle. Depending on what they find in the forest, or depending on the emotional state of the tribesman, or on the state of his relationships with other members of the tribe, he will "find" this or that artifact (and no other) and fashion it into an extension. Upon his return in the village, the tribesman will again be watched and scrutinized, and in a series of talks and negotiations, the other men will, depending on the emotional and relational state of village life, decide whether the newly adorned tribesman's adjusted knowledge of tribal communality (visible as it is in his newly fashioned extensions) is acceptable as tribal, communal knowledge (they even may decide that their tribal, communal knowledge should be changed in order to bring it into line with the tribesman's) or whether his knowledge is unacceptable as tribal knowledge and the tribesman therefore qualifies as an outsider. The outcome of this bout of assessment and negotiation, however, is never certain. The outcome, as said, depends on a sheer inexhaustible number of (consciously known or unconsciously known) factors. Now the tribesman himself is likely to have been aware (whether consciously or not) of all this before he went into the forest. He will have been aware (consciously or not) of the deeply tribal nature of knowledge. He will have been aware (consciously or not) of "knowledge," that is, a combination of artifacts gathered in the world out there, being the source *and* outcome of tribal, communal life. He will have been aware (consciously or not) of the uncertain outcome of tribal knowledge and tribal communality. He will have been aware (consciously or not) that, despite all the seemingly indestructible traditions of tribal life, tribal knowledge and tribal communality is never completely stable. Change can, and sometimes will, occur. And it won't always be accepted. It can, and sometimes will, get rejected. It depends. . . . It depends, for example, on whether the tribesman chose to stick to the century-old forest paths or whether he chose to stray away from them. It depends on whether he stumbled upon some *new* kind of artifact, and, therefore, also upon an opportunity (or *risk*) to arrive at new knowledge. The tribesman, finally, will have been aware, whether consciously or not, that knowledge (combinations of objects stumbled upon, *out there*) and tribal communality (talks, assessments, in short: negotiations) are two sides of the same coin, that is, tribal life, as it *expresses* itself, or *becomes* (or both?), in negotiations and renegotiations about who's in and who's out.

The Boundary between Inside and Outside

But more is to be said about the hilly jungles in Papua New Guinea. Let us try and determine the boundaries of tribal life. Picture yourself hovering above the village. The village (a collection of huts, basically) is situated in a clearing in the forest. Now, where are the boundaries of the village? The tree line around the huts of course is clearly visible, but is that the boundary? If you watch carefully, you will notice that people regularly cross that boundary in order to go into the forest, for example, to forage or to find materials for making or adjusting extensions. Sometimes they do so using the age-old paths (which are clearly visible) but sometimes they do so sneakily, using or inventing nearly invisible tracks as they go. Thus, the boundary of the village, one could argue, also includes this multitude of sneaky little tracks and unexpected turns. The boundary of this village, and of tribal village life as such, may not be as clear-cut as it looked at first sight. Indeed, the forest (source of knowledge, source of extensions, source of village life) is as much part of the village as the village (source of hundreds of paths that snake into the greenery) is part of the jungle. When it comes to tribal communality and the knowledge it is made of, it seems to be difficult to strictly separate the world "out there" from the world "inside." The (visual) appearance of a tribesman, adorned with extensions, already tells us how this allegedly "outside" forest, as tribal knowledge, builds individual selves, tribal identities, and communal sensibilities.

A number of important issues need to be raised at this point. First, *how* the village impacts on the allegedly "outside" forest and *how* this forest impacts on the village, or, to put it in other words, how exactly the world "out there" on the one hand and tribal knowledge on the other (remember, both are sides of the same coin) mutually constitute each other—all this does not seem to be a matter of cut-and-dried obviousness, a priori connections, and stable patterns. Also in the jungle of Papua New Guinea, this ongoing process of mutual constitution appears to be a matter of both sneaky links as well as age-old tracks, of well-established, possibly rigid traditions as well as spontaneous change, of benign recognition and acceptance as well as suspicious distrust. That implies that tribal knowledge, which is produced in this encounter between villagers and the forest, and between each other (i.e., when they look at, discuss, and assess each other's extensions taken and fashioned from forest materials), will tend to be inherently unstable. However stable it may appear to be at a particular time or moment in tribal village life, knowledge is always open and prone to change. One never knows beforehand which track individual villagers are going to use when they venture into the forest. One never knows completely for sure what particular materials the tribesman is going to stumble upon in the jungle. One can never accurately predict what number and what kind of materials the tribesman is going to collect and fashion into which extensions. One never knows how the other members of the tribe, upon the tribesman's return, are going to react. Are they going to accept the tribesman's interpretation of the world "out there"? Are they going to accept his *body of knowledge* (literally!), or are those subtle and perhaps not so subtle negotiations going to end up with the tribesman being excluded or punished? Or is this process going to lead to adjustments, to possibly new tribal knowledge? And how will all this affect the next tribesman's venture into the forest? Is he going to anticipate and take account of tribal knowledge, or, should we say, tribal sensibilities? None of these questions is likely to be answered with a clear "yes" or a clear "no."

There is a second issue to be mentioned here. Tribal knowledge appears to be produced in and through a process whereby materials are connected with each other, a process, that is, where *assemblages* are made. First, the tribesman combines tracks in the forest. Then, he combines materials into a number of extensions. Then, he combines extensions. He goes on to combine those with his body into an assemblage that authors like Marilyn Strathern (1991) or Donna Haraway (1991) would call a *cyborg*. Upon his return in the village, he combines (t)his cyborg appearance with words, emotions, anticipation, and desire. With his fellow tribesmen, he will continue to add words and materials into an assemblage that we could call "tribal knowledge," and this assemblage, "knowledge," can and will be used in turn by others who will combine it, or splintery parts of it, with yet more words and materials, on their own travels in the jungle. This assemblage of assemblages then circulates amongst tribesmen; this "knowledge" finally connects men into tribal communality. Out of this assemblage of assemblages, knowledge (and, as the other side of the coin, tribal life) is produced. Stronger still, as the French philosopher Gilles Deleuze (e.g., 1995) would venture, this process of assembling assemblages, which to Deleuze is essentially a process of negotiation, *is* tribal life, or, at the other side of the coin, this process of assembling assemblages, *is* knowledge. Assemblages, however, are things and practices. That means that they take place at particular times. In other words, they are located in time and space. They are particular to particular times and particular places. Indeed, it seems impossible to assemble the totality (of assemblages) of the world into one, infinitely huge assemblage. Now this insight may sound like a truism (a banal one at that) but then one has to remember that Gilles Deleuze and his colleague, Felix Guattari, felt obliged to explicitly write a punned phrase like "we only believe in totalities [that are] at the side" (my translation from French) as late as 1972, in their classic but hugely complex book *Anti-Oedipe* (1972, p. 50). Note the words "believe" and the plural "totali*ties*." Assemblages therefore seem to be always partial, and inevitably so. Moreover, as assemblages of a variety of materials, they are also hybrids. Tribal knowledge (or tribal life) seems to be inevitably partial, limited, particular, hybrid, and, to make matters more complicated, imbued with emotions and desire (e.g., the desire to be part of a tribe or, alternatively, the desire to unsettle tribal knowledge).

This notion is going to be of crucial importance in the subsequent section of this chapter. Let us now point to just one consequence of what we have been developing so far. The world "out there," the jungle, will always be bigger than any assemblage (of assemblages) that is made out of its materials. That means that for any assemblage of tribal life that results from ventures into the jungle, a sheer limitless number of alternatives are possible. The latter may not yet have been realized, and tribesmen may not yet have "realized" this enormous reservoir of potential assemblages, but this mass of possibility nevertheless is there. As potential, as possibility, it is there. It may not have been explored yet by tribesmen. It may not emerge during village negotiations in front of huts. It may not enter the consciousness of individual tribesmen. But it is there, that is, a source of potential, possible change. In principle infinite, this "unrealized" potential for change is ever present (in all its absence) whenever assemblages of tribal life, or tribal knowledge, for that matter, take shape in time and space. Indeed, in a very direct sense it is precisely this absence, the unspoken and unrealized forest of possibility, that allows for assemblages to take shape. Assemblages can only be assemblages of particular materials. They cannot be assemblages of everything. It is the possibilities that are unrealized (or deliberately discarded) that *make it possible* for some particular assemblages to emerge, precisely *because* some others are unrealized. What emerges as tribal knowledge therefore rests upon unexplored, unspoken, silent, possibly discarded or forgotten possibilities. The latter are the *condition sine qua non* of the former. Ernesto Laclau and Chantal Mouffe (1985), for example, inspired by the Italian prewar political theorist Antonio Gramsci, by the French philosopher Michel Foucault, and by his fellow French philosopher Jacques Derrida (e.g., 1970) in particular, have used the phrase "constitutive exterior" to describe this alleged outside of unspoken possibility that, however absent, is nevertheless that on which *particular* discourses (including those with hegemonic or universalizing pretensions) ultimately depend. The importance of this cannot be overestimated. Although the "constitutive exterior" of a particular discourse (a particular tribal knowledge, for example, a particular view on the causes of crime) is unspoken, it nevertheless works inside the very core of the particular discourse it silently allows to be assembled. Within every discursive assemblage, in a way, this process of silencing of alternative assemblages has left a trace. There, at the heart of each particular discourse, even of those that have hegemonic pretensions, traces of this process of silencing are the location where the possibility for fragments of the "constitutive exterior" to slip inside is kept alive. Just like the tribesman who, having explored unknown tracks and passages, one day returns to the village adorned with slightly adjusted extensions (and who is probably unaware, like us, of the outcome of this experiment), splinters of this vast "constitutive exterior" of possibility can and very often *do* slip within. When that happens, trusted traditions and tribal knowledge once deemed so stable may start to crumble (or begin a process of renewal). Tribal knowledge is always open to change: the unexplored or unspoken outside on the one hand, in Laclau and Mouffe's words, offers the "conditions of possibility" for assemblages such as tribal knowledge to emerge at all, but on the other, and simultaneously so, it also holds their "conditions of impossibility."

Tribal Knowledge and Tribal Sociality

Let us now expand on a third and, for our purposes here, final attribute of tribal knowledge, that is, its deeply social character. Tribal knowledge, claims Rorty (1979), is not like the reflection in a mirror of what objects "out there" radiate, nor is it something that emerges from the inner depths of individual selves or souls. Tribal knowledge, as we have seen, appears to be the result of practices of assemblage. In order to arrive at tribal knowledge, a variety of things (e.g., desire, motivation, experience, words, objects and materials, negotiations, acceptance, rejection, inclusions, exclusions, and so on) need to be put together in an assemblage. Following philosophers such as Martin Heidegger, Michel Foucault, and Richard Rorty, one could indeed argue that the production of knowledge, first and foremost, involves a pragmatics. Knowledge is the result of a *practical* venture (Westphal, 1998). Knowledge assemblages come into the world, first and foremost, as technologies, that is, as machines that have some practical purpose or other. Martin Heidegger (1962), for example, claimed that underpinning all "knowledge" is a primordial, prereflexive understanding of the world as something that is "ready-to-hand." Michel Foucault introduced notions such as "technologies of the self" (see Martin, Gutman, & Hutton, 1988). According to Foucault, "knowledge" is produced in a field of power relations and often takes the form of particular "technologies" that can then be used by people, for example, to fashion their own (mostly subordinated) "self," a process that also allows for governance "at a distance" more easily. Note how such notions could describe events in Papuan jungles very well. And there is probably no great coincidence underlying Gilles Deleuze's and

Felix Guattari's decision (1972, 1980) to give their vitalist philosophy of desire a *machinic* twist (in their philosophy, the boundary between vital desire and machinic assemblage has collapsed, with the latter being the source as well as the result of the former, and vice versa). Now, this practice of assemblage appears to be a thoroughly *social* practice. The definition of "good" tribal knowledge is a social, indeed tribal event. Decisions to reject assemblages as "bad" knowledge, or indeed the decision to accept them and therefore to change tribal knowledge, are decisions that are made *socially*, in, through, and by tribal collectives. The tribesman who leaves the village to venture into the forest does so as a member of a tribal collective. He does so as a social being. The state of his relationship with the tribe, to a large extent, is likely to affect the choices he is going to make (whether consciously or not) on jungle paths. Returning to the village, the tribesman again will do so as a thoroughly social being. The presentation of his assemblage and the discussions and negotiations that will follow again are social, collective events. Tribal knowledge, it could be argued, is the social product of assemblages, or better, it is *social assemblage.* This phrase is important. It has at least two meanings. Tribal knowledge is produced socially (first meaning) and its pragmatics are also implied in the production or reproduction of the social, that is, social relations, community, or tribal collective (second meaning). Indeed, knowledge assemblages, like extensions, or—better still—*as* extensions, are what circulate between tribal members. These are what they carefully watch and study, negotiate around, and finally make decisions about. These are what glue members of the tribe together, or, as the case may be, these are what may drive them apart. Tribal community is constituted in and through this process of circulating assemblages that, in a way, simultaneously embody both the expression of already established tribal communality and the becoming of yet unrealized tribal potential. Knowledge assemblages, in the words of Strathern, do not only *partially connect* the world "out there" with the tribal world "within." They also partially connect tribal members with each other. In other words, as assemblages, or machines, they are also technologies of connection; they are pragmatically used to express and/or to produce tribal communality. Such connections, however, as we have seen above, are never complete. They can only be partial. The boundary between tribal knowledge assemblages and their alleged "outside," like the boundary between the village and the forest "out there," tends to be extremely jagged and highly porous. Furthermore, the alleged "inside" of tribal knowledge assemblages is not evenly solid. Like any other assemblage, its hybrid "inside" is full of holes, gaps, hiatuses, and contradictions (but see Lippens, 2004, for more detail). New assemblages can and often do emerge in the spaces of open possibility that are inherent in, indeed that are the *sine qua non* of any assemblage. Tribal knowledge, just like tribal life itself, is a matter of *partial connections,* and is therefore prone to instability and change. One can never know for certain what the tribesman, a partially connected "body of knowledge" (in one sense), bearer of partially connected "bodies of knowledge" (in another sense), is going to be looking for in the forest, and how he is going to interpret the materials he finds, or how he is going to assemble them.

Before we move on to a discussion of epistemological and criminological issues in the next section, let us deal with one more aspect of the Papuan jungle. So far we have considered tribal knowledge and tribal communality (tribal life, in short) to be quite distinct from the forest "out there." We have, admittedly, argued that the boundary in between tends to be extremely jagged and porous, but we may have given the impression that, ontologically, both sides of the boundary are distinct, just as "culture" would be distinct from "nature." In the next section, we will explore in more detail how actor-network theory would deny any such ontological distinction (actor-network theorists consider actors *in* networks, but also actors *as* networks, or networks *of* actors, but also networks *as* actors). Here is the place to redress the false impression we may have been giving and to draw some preliminary epistemological conclusions. The forest, of course, does not contain only rocks and trees. It also includes tracks and passages; it includes villages (note the plural here) and all sorts of human artifacts. It contains "bodies of knowledge," chatter and negotiations. Its tracks and villages are strewn with assemblages of all sorts. Some are similar, but many do differ quite substantially from each other. And its villages, its "bodies of knowledge," its people in turn are full of forest materials. In Papuan jungles, tribesmen venturing in forests stand a good chance of stumbling upon artifacts, "bodies of knowledge" or assemblages of some sort, particularly in the vicinity of other villages. Those often are used to make other assemblages, which then in turn will be part of the forest. Now, if this is already the case in hilly jungles, then it should not really come as a surprise that authors such as the French philosopher Jean Baudrillard (e.g., 1983), who wrote about highly mediatized, "hyperspatialized" societies (the United States in particular), claim something similar. These ultramodern societies, as

Baudrillard has it, seem to have turned into "hyperreal" worlds where everything is a "simulacrum," that is, an image, or a simulation of images that in turn are nothing but simulations of simulations of simulations and so on. In those hypermodern, hyperreal worlds, Baudrillard claims, every speck of rock-solid soil has disappeared and, with it, any difference between reality and illusion. In hyperreal worlds, where everything is just a mediatized image of mediatized images, says Baudrillard, it is impossible to know what the "real" world looks like. In Papuan language: there is just an endless stream of assemblages, or bodies of tribal knowledge, the one partially simulating the other. However, we need not go so far as to follow Baudrillard into "hyperspace." Assemblages are what people use to build bodies of knowledge. This is what they use to simply build their lives and their worlds. And those—that is, their lives, their worlds, their bodies of knowledge—are what others in turn are going to use (at least splinters of them) to make theirs. And so on. As one of the main founders of actor-network theory has argued (Latour, 1993) modern societies, even ultramodern societies, in at least one respect do not differ substantially from premodern ones: the production of knowledge has always been a matter of producing assemblages. In such a world, it is indeed impossible to find out what the world "really" looks like. The world comes to us *as* an assemblage of assemblages.

Epistemology, Criminology, and Academic Tribalism

Epistemological Considerations

Let us now take leave of the tribal villages in the Papuan jungle and focus on the epistemology of crime and criminology. As it happens, like the bodies of knowledge in jungles, both epistemology and criminology seem to be about boundaries, about negotiations and about decisions about who or what counts as in and who or what counts as out.

Epistemology, it is said, is the theory of knowledge. Epistemology, broadly, deals with five questions (see Williams, 2001, pp. 1–2). Epistemology asks questions about the nature of knowledge. What is knowledge, and how does it differ from other ways of seeing and talking about the world? What is good knowledge? A second question is the one about the boundaries of knowledge. What can be known, and what can't? These questions have been drawing epistemologists' attention for a long time. Traditional epistemologists like Robert Audi (1998), for example, have made a huge effort to meticulously list and categorize problems and pit-falls (e.g., sensory, cognitive, biographical, social factors) one is destined to encounter on the road to "good," reliable, valid, in short, stable knowl-edge. The third question is also a familiar one. It is the question about method: how can knowledge be obtained? What is the best method to arrive at knowledge? Fourth, epistemology tries to deal with the "prob-lem of skepticism," a "problem" that, according to most epistemolo-gists, lies at the heart of epistemology. Indeed, early modern philosophers such as René Descartes, for example, who wrote in the seventeenth cen-tury, literally placed "doubt" at the very methodological center of scien-tific endeavor. Cartesian philosophy could therefore be called a strand of skepticism. Despite being partial to skepticism, though, Descartes did assume that stable, certain knowledge was possible, but only if it was arrived at by a rational subject who, starting from a position of "doubt," had applied "reason" to the world "out there." Other skepticisms later rejected this methodology. Some postwar philosophies, particularly the strands that have become known as poststructuralism and postmodern-ism, have severely undermined (or "deconstructed") this Cartesian trust in "rationality" and "reason," words that, according to deconstructionists, like "truth"—or any other sign for that matter—have no fixed meaning at all. But poststructuralism or postmodernism are by no means the only strands of philosophical and cultural analysis that have pushed skepti-cism beyond Cartesian modernism. Bruce DiCristina, for example, in his primer on criminological methodology (1995), has aptly shown how Paul Feyerabend's (1975) anarchic philosophy of science not only offers a skep-tical and therefore *more democratic* antidote to the law-and-order politics of dogmatic scientific communities, but it also provides us with at least the hope that, if we can move beyond the "thought police" of dogmatics, we will end up with more diverse, and therefore better knowledge (please note the paradox involved). Epistemology finally asks questions about the purpose of knowledge. What do we use "knowledge" for? Answers to questions like these have over the years been varied, and some will be rehearsed below.

Bodies of Criminological Knowledge

An underlying current of all these questions seems to involve a quest to determine a particular boundary, that is, the boundary between "good" knowledge and "bad" knowledge (or non-knowledge), or between "good" methods and "bad" methods, or, simply, between *in* and *out*. But this appears to be very similar to what is going on in and through the production of tribal knowledge. When it comes to criminal knowledge (i.e., knowledge that is generated or reproduced in and through crime) or criminological knowledge (i.e., knowledge that is generated or reproduced in and through academic communities), the same principles and dynamics as those in Papuan jungles seem to be at work. Someone like Bruno Latour, who himself started off as an anthropologist of science in the 1970s (he produced ethnographies of physics and biology labs in particular), would not be surprised to find that this indeed is the case.

Let us note how this boundary between "in" and "out" is a recurring theme of gang life, for example, where so much of gang members' energy goes towards defining and maintaining correct or stable knowledge of signs, practices, methods, threats, defenses, and, more generally, behaviors. Or consider the example of a *community* (please note the use of this word here) of crack dealers in El Barrio (Bourgois, 1995). How much of Primo's, Candy's, and Caesar's (Philippe Bourgois's protagonists) efforts go into establishing correct or stable knowledge of life in East Harlem, into acquiring stable and reliable knowledge about social codes (dress codes not in the least) for them to be able to venture into the world of regular employment, or into attempts to produce correct knowledge about the dynamics of retail crack trade? Or let us take the example of a board of directors (why not Enron's?) where good knowledge about what constitutes "good" (i.e., acceptable or, in a sense, internally legitimate) accounts is paramount in any decision that the board may take. In a situation like this one (the board meeting), one has to be either very foolish or very brave (depending on your viewpoint) to produce alternative "good" accounts. Or imagine a professional group of mediators who spend a lot of time acquiring stable knowledge about criminal etiology, about "restorative justice," and about interpersonal dynamics and standards of professional practice. Imagine how they will tend to demonstrate their "good" knowledge of these issues, circulating it among their colleagues through talk and visual display, hoping perhaps (whether consciously or not) to be accepted by their fellow mediators as "one of us" or, as the case may be, hoping to be recognized as an "innovator," a "risk taker," or, why not, simply as an "outsider."

Now picture yourself a criminology department where faculty as well as students will tend to be eager to acquire good and stable knowledge about gangs and gang members, about crack dealers in El Barrio, about

Enron's boardroom dynamics, about "restorative justice," about media-tors and their professional standards, about who or what counts as "in" and who or what counts as "out," and so on. Like the gang member, the crack dealer, the board member, the mediator, or the tribesman, the crimi-nology faculty member will venture into the forest of knowledge assem-blages that are already available in libraries, in scholarly publications, in the biographies of gang members and board members, in the thoughts of mediators who have tried to express them during interviews (it will be noted in passing that it is an impossible task to find out whether there is a "real" match between thought and expression), in what can be observed in neighborhoods or read in the press. The faculty member will then select a number of splinters from these assemblages in order to produce his or her assemblage. This assemblage in turn will end up circulating among the criminologist's fellow faculty members or among criminologists more generally, where, in various places, processes of assessment and negotia-tion of some sort may then begin in order to ascertain whether, and to what extent, the criminologist is "one of us." Ultimately this particu-lar assemblage will join the flood of knowledge assemblages (those are assemblages of assemblages in their own right) that the world "out there" is made of. This criminologist's assemblage will be particular; it will be partial. Its articulation will depend not just on the few connections he or she has managed to make between a limited number of materials, but also on the vast and limitless number of possible alternative connections that he or she, for a number of reasons, has been unable to make. One can never be certain what materials the criminologist is going to stumble upon by coincidence, leave unnoticed, or consciously and purposefully select. Sensory, cognitive, biographical, and social factors will all influ-ence this scholar's ventures as well as the choices he or she makes.

Just to illustrate: the presence and strength of some form of "thought police" or "political correctness" may lead him or her to avoid particu-lar explorations of alternative assemblages (e.g., alternative interpreta-tions of data). As with the whistle-blower's alternative "accounts" at Enron's board meeting, it takes a certain amount of foolishness or brav-ery (depending on your viewpoint) in some corners of today's academia to question particular dogmatic "truths." In many cases this issue is one of the reasons why researchers or scholars are reluctant to explore particular topics or to make alternative connections between particular data sets and/or theoretical approaches (see, for example, the work of recent whistle-blowers such as Fekete, 1994; Hoff-Sommers, 1995; Patai

& Koertge, 1995). We will later see how factors that we have touched upon above (i.e., tribal desire and tribal fashion, notably) may push researchers and academics to focus their attention on particular, desirable topics and on particular, fashionable interpretations of them. Ultimately, however, the ventures and choices of the criminologist, researcher or scholar, are not predictable. Their trajectories and choices cannot be stabilized in stable knowledge of stable patterns. The hybridity as well as the holes that are characteristic of knowledge assemblages (e.g., the assemblages that are in the scholar's "body of knowledge" as he or she sets out to conduct research) allow for too much leeway, particularly in times, such as ours (say, the early 21st century), when the forest of scholarly life has been churned into an astonishing multitude of knowledge assemblages, each one a multiplicity in its own right that, at least potentially, is *partially connected* to all others. This has been the case particularly within the assemblage that we have come to know as criminology, the field of knowledge about boundaries par excellence, if you wish, where border crossing, reassemblages and thus *change* are rife. "The image that I prefer," Stanley Cohen once wrote, "is that of a friendly parasite that grows by turning on itself, constantly reproducing internally but also trying to adapt to changes in its host organism" (1988, p. 16).

Let us illustrate this. A few years ago (in 1999), the renowned British criminologist Jock Young published *The Exclusive Society*. We will get back to this book in a moment. Young, it will be remembered, was one of a small group of critical criminologists who, in the early seventies, were at the forefront of a movement that broke with what then used to be called "mainstream criminology." For a number of reasons (it would take us too far to explore them here), these critical criminologists *desired* to relinquish membership in this mainstream criminological community. Critical criminologists quickly started to make new knowledge assemblages and built, as it were, their own tribal villages, that is, organized their own conferences and research groups (e.g., the European Group for the Study of Deviance and Social Control) and founded their own journals (e.g., the U.S.-based journals *Crime and Social Justice* and *Contemporary Crises*). It shall be noted in passing that this chimes with Foucault's (1975) claim that knowledge—for example, criminological knowledge—emerges in and from institutional provisions or, in other words, from institutional assemblages, such as prisons. The presentations at those conferences and the contributions in those journals, most of which were broadly inspired by an assemblage of interactionist, Marxist, and abolitionist knowledge assemblages, and which were mostly assembled with materials obtained through the application of "qualitative" ethnographic research methods, quickly circulated as extensions between the newly emerging and steadily growing membership. Critical criminologists' extensions, like any other, were *hybrid* assemblages. They were full of contradictions and gaps—contradictions and gaps that kept them together but that, at the same time, also provided a space whence rupture or reassemblage could suddenly, unpredictably, spring.

In the early 1980s, Young again made another rupturing move. At the forefront of yet another criminological breakup, Young defined much of critical criminology's assemblages as "idealist" and started working on what he proposed to be a "left realist" criminology, that is, a left-wing criminology that would take crime "seriously" (much crime was *found* to be "intraclass") in order to keep the "working class" from being lured into the trap of neoconservative politics. In the 1990s, Young again seems to have made a number of explorations outside his tribal village. On his ventures, he stumbled upon previously unnoticed assemblages, *bodies of literature* that made him desire to move on yet again. It all "started off," the tribesman-criminologist tells us, "as [a book on] criminology and ended up as one on cultural studies and political philosophy" (Young, 1999, p. v). Having stumbled upon knowledge assemblages that dealt with notions such as "blurring boundaries," "border crossing," and "hybridity," and having decided to adjust his extensions during his meanderings in a previously unexplored part of the academic forest, Young produced a new assemblage of assemblages. In *The Exclusive Society* as well as in subsequent works, the most conspicuous extensions are images of *bulimic* tribesmen on the one hand and *cannibals* on the other. Both refer to issues and problems of inclusion and exclusion, or, to put it in other words, to boundaries and boundary crossing. In his recent work, Young seems to be preoccupied with the idea (well accepted in the tribe of "postmodern" theorists and *cyborgologists* such as Latour, Strathern, and Haraway) that, in today's cyborg age, boundaries between selves, communities, and cultures tend to be highly porous, and that there is now a constant and often almost frenzied transfer of materials (e.g., motivations, desires, practices, styles, interpretations, and so on) that assemble and reassemble across those boundaries. In a cyborg age, boundaries are losing much of their bounding qualities anyway. Gilles Deleuze and Felix Guattari, whom we have already met, wrote it like this, back in 1972: "me and non-me, inside and outside, that doesn't mean a thing anymore" (Deleuze

& Guattari, 1972, p. 7; my translation). And here is how Kathleen Kirby, a cultural geographer, expressed it a few years ago: "things begin to circulate, and no longer know their places. Foundations and frameworks crumble and things loop and circle and shift and spin: the inside flies to pieces and explodes outward, the outside melts and fragments, and elements of both sides drift freely across an indifferent boundary" (1996, p. 102). At a time when boundaries seem to be blurring almost anywhere, in and across neighborhoods, in and across academic communities, in and across cultures, Young ventured beyond his *left realist* village to find that, indeed, many had left their own village before. He seems to have noticed how the assemblages that he found during his boundary-crossing ventures were themselves the result of boundary-crossing ventures of others. What some inner-city youngsters seem to be doing and saying, what some institutions seem to be doing and saying, what some academics seem to be doing and saying, all this points to a boundary-crossing age. The space of contemporary tribal life, the space in and between villages, academic or other, is strewn with assemblages and "bodies of knowledge" that have reached high levels of boundary-crossing hybridity. These high levels of hybridity have provided those assemblages (as well as those who carry them as extensions) with a propensity for yet higher levels of boundary crossing. Young stumbled upon, as he calls it, "late modern" life. The *left realist* village has meanwhile been largely dismantled. Too many explorations have now started from the very gaps, incoherencies, and contradictions that kept it apart/together. So many wanderings, so many explorations, into such a vast forest, with so many villages, and with so many cyborgs that, having turned into extremely complex and hybrid assemblages themselves, now have the capabilities and makeup to venture much farther afield, way into the vastness of assemblages that stretch beyond particular tribal knowledges. This is important. Accepted as a member of the tribal village of boundary-crossing theorists ("cultural studies and political philosophy," he claims), Young is now likely to use this newly acquired assemblage of knowledge assemblages as his base for further ventures into the forest of late modernity. He is likely to make use of the assemblages he has made or acquired as guides in order to find, or to stumble upon yet more boundary-crossing assemblages. This of course is in line with what epistemologists have been saying for a long time: facts are not just "out there," they are found, or stumbled upon, because one's explicit or implicit theoretical framework allows for it. However, as we have seen, theoretical frameworks are assemblages, and as assemblages, they are full of holes and contradictions. Things just might happen on one of Young's next explorations that might urge him to desire to leave or, possibly, negotiations and tribal indulgence permitting, to change the boundary-crossing tribe.

One more thing needs to be said here. Although Young's tribal desire to be "in" or "out" has led him to assemble bodies of knowledge that are quite varied and different from each other, none of them is *completely* different from the others. A recurrent theme that runs as a common thread in all of Young's assemblages is the search for social justice. Indeed, assemblages, particularly late modern assemblages, are never completely different nor completely the same. Assemblages also tend to carry both change and continuity. But this should not surprise us. Already in Papuan jungles, assemblages are both *expression* of something that is already there (e.g., a desire to count as "in" or a desire to go "out") and *becoming* of something that is yet to come (again, a desire to count as "in" or a desire to go "out"). The space, or tension, between expression and becoming is what we have called "negotiation," and it is precisely that space where assemblages of the old and the new are pondered.

"We Have Never Been Modern"

Here is the place to get back to Bruno Latour (1993), who denies that modern science or modernity more generally have ever seen a real divide between something called "nature" and something called "culture," or between something called "object" and something called "subject." Moderns like to think they have succeeded in establishing such divides. Such a belief is the *condition sine qua non* for a scientific culture that assumes that nature can be truthfully reflected (as in a mirror, Rorty would say) in knowledge about it. Knowledge is then the province of knowing subjects (themselves the province of culture if you like) who possess the faculty of turning experience (i.e., contact with an outside world) into a sound and eternally valid and reliable reflection or image of this world. Epistemology, then, according to this belief, is the search for ways to purge any trace of "culture" or "subjectivity" from this process of reflection in order to reach the pure, natural object, or "objectivity." This particularly modern process of purging the subject from scientific "truth" could be read from a psychoanalytic point of view. The process then demonstrates an inevitably subjective desire to exclude the subject from the production of knowledge while, simultaneously and paradoxically (although the paradox is rarely noticed or acknowledged), a particular "subject of science" (i.e., the Cartesian subject) is presupposed, but "forgotten," in this very act of purging (see on this, e.g., Caudill, 2003). But this belief in "objectivity," Latour says, is just that: a belief. It is just an assemblage, like so many others. If anything, the world is turning ever more rapidly into a world of "quasi-objects," i.e., assemblages of thought, motivation, desire, and matter that circulate through networks of actors (or actors *as* networks) that, as technologies, they help to produce. In a world of quasi-objects, it is impossible to distinguish nature from culture, object from subject, world from word, or desire from knowledge. Quasi-objects are both. In a now-classic article, Latour goes on to claim that scientific practice is a question of "drawing things together" (Latour, 1990). Quite literally: various materials (in biology: microbes, strategies, ambition, enzymes, strings of words, images, resources, and so on) are *drawn* together (in the sense of being expressed or represented) into what Latour calls "immutable mobiles." The latter are often two-dimensional hybrids such as textbooks, articles, images, graphs, and so on. These hybrids are immutable, in the sense that they seem to express a certain stability, but they are highly mobile in the sense that they tend to be circulated (a "center of calculation" may make sure that this happens) through the network of actors (the actor-network) as an extension, Strathern might say, for other actors to pick up and, possibly, to join in the production of the tribe/knowledge. However, immutable mobiles, being hybrid assemblages, are never completely immutable. Once assembled, once "drawn together," they will, as an encircled consistency, continue to circulate across the network, but simultaneously, its inherent gaps and contradictions will start cutting across the immutable mobile and scatter its fragments through the network. Both the encircled consistency as well as the fragments will become part of the network and will thus end up as parts of yet other hybrid assemblages or as yet other extensions in or through which actors produce knowledge as well as themselves. Latour's immutable mobiles, in a way, are what appears when actors draw together, or assemble, things from the network. Their hybridity is what gives hybrid collectives (e.g., British left realists during the eighties) a certain coherence and consistency; but it is also what ultimately makes hybrid collectives splinter and scatter across the network. We are basically talking about technology here. The "body of knowledge" called "symbolic interactionism," or Marxist theory, or the book *The New Criminology* (1973), or the "European Group for the Study of Deviance and Social Control," or strings of words that were uttered by drug takers during unstructured interview sessions, or ethnographic impressions noted down by prison research-ers, or interpretations of "established facts," and so on . . . all are made of disparate materials from the network that have been drawn together. All can be and were used as extensions. All can and indeed did end up as part of an attempt to draw together collectives. All can and did end up being fragmented, the fragments scattering across the network to be used in ever so many other bouts of drawing things together. Force and power are in them. Indeed, they have been *drawn* together, and this requires force. Force and power give them a certain coherence and con-sistency. Force and power will tear them apart.

Modernity, claims Latour, is no different from what went before. The only thing that does seem to have happened at the end of the fif-teenth century, or at the onset of modernity, is the sudden emergence of new technologies such as the printing press that allowed for the almost instant assemblage and circulation of often very disparate and often very contradictory materials at the same time and in the same place. It is this disparity and contradiction, assembled at the same time and in the same place, says Latour, that have triggered modern inquisitiveness and there-fore modernity. But nothing fundamentally new happened. This brings us to another point. A world of "quasi-objects" and "immutable mobiles" that are "drawn together" is a world where knowledge and community emerge or disappear in and through force (i.e., the force to draw things together), mobility (i.e., the mobility of circulating quasi-objects and actor-networks), openness (i.e., the gaps that make possible the hybridity of assemblages), and desire. This is not likely to be a world where stasis or linearity is dominant. Although force, mobility, and openness are nec-essary conditions for any quasi-object (e.g., a knowledge assemblage) to emerge and, possibly, for it to be able to temporarily stabilize the flow of desire, they are also, and simultaneously so, the very conditions that eventually will break up this stability from the "inside" as well as from the "outside." This process of stabilization and destabilization tends to be unpredictable. Indeed, the current and significant appeal of complexity theory and chaos theory, also in criminology (e.g., Milovanovic, 1997), illustrates how notions such as unpredictability and instability have themselves become attractive assemblages ("attractors," chaos theorists would say) that somehow have managed to stabilize attempts to understand the restlessness of the world as well as the restlessness of attempts to understand this restlessness (the attentive reader will have grasped that both forms of restlessness are not distinct).

Knowledge of Tribal Community

Let us now focus on this temporary stability that emerges (better: that is *expressed* while it *becomes*) when assemblages, knowledge assemblages for example, assemble. We have already touched upon the place of tribal desire in processes of knowledge assemblage. Tribal desire sends tribesmen into the world "out there." Tribal desire arms them with the provisions with which they will decide what particular assemblage they will make and which particular tribal knowledge they will adopt, join, or, as the case may be, leave, discard, or generate. When restless desire temporarily crystallizes into assemblages (into "bodies of knowledge") that in turn will produce or reproduce tribal assemblages of actor-networks, stability expresses itself and becomes. In Deleuze's and Guattari's language (1972, 1980): flows of desire assemble into "abstract machines" that circulate and are put to use, enigmatically and largely unpredictably (i.e., "rhizomatically"), in and through "desiring machines," that is, in and by actor-networks of tribal communality. This notion of communality and its corollary, community, are important. That which keeps quasi-objects, immutable mobiles, and actor-networks apart/together, in other words, that which provides stability, however temporarily, is communality, the promise and possibility of community. Now, many philosophers of science have recognized this before. Let us just mention two. Thomas Kuhn, for example, in his classic *The Structure of Scientific Revolutions* (1970) hinted at this. Kuhn's main thesis, it will be remembered, stated that scientific knowledge does not steadily and progressively accumulate until, one final day, universal and eternal truth will be reached. Instead, Kuhn argued, scientific progress is not really progress; it is a succession of paradigmatic revolutions. A *paradigm* is a collection of beliefs, assumptions, methods, interpretations, and so on that predetermine and structure the observation and the production of "facts" and knowledge. Now, each paradigm that has succeeded in acquiring predominance is destined to be overthrown at some point by another. It is, for our purposes here, interesting to note that Kuhn situates the production of knowledge in "scientific communities," where knowledge is often produced in and through the unreflective application of often unspoken yet paradigmatic practical scripts and guidelines. Kuhn's use of the word "community" is important. Knowledge appears to be a matter *of* as well as *for* community. It appears to be a matter of *communal practice.* So thinks the philosopher and literary critic Stanley Fish, who introduced the phrase "interpretive communities" (see, e.g., Fish, 1980, 1989). Knowledge, says Fish, is interpretation. Nothing else. As Fish claims, "like it or not, interpretation is the only game in town" (1980, p. 355). Now this is consistent with what more traditional epistemologists have been claiming for a long time, namely, that justifications for particular beliefs (i.e., "knowledge") always refer to other justifications (e.g., Williams, 2001, pp. 61–68). Any particular justification rests upon other justifications that are linked in a network that is, in principle, limitless. This network is rarely explored in its entirety. It is too vast. At best, believers of "knowledge," stuck in time and space, only have at their disposal a limited number of justifications that they regularly evoke and employ in bouts of "circular" reasoning. Interpretive communities, according to Fish, interpret the world in *particular* ways. At least this is so according to Fish and his fellow members of this *particular* interpretive community of scholars who believe that the world is how it is interpreted in interpretive communities. "Knowledge," they claim, is always interpretation. Better still, it is interpretation of interpretations: the criminologist-ethnographer, for example, who decides to produce or assemble observational "knowledge" about a police department, or about a community of crack dealers, or about a group of female gang members does not just produce interpretations of those worlds. He or she produces interpretations of police officers' interpretations of their world. He or she interprets crack dealers' or female gang members' interpretations. He or she interprets interpretations. Moreover, "knowledge" is always particular: it is that which is produced in interpretive communities, and interpretative communities are particular, that is, they evoke, use, mobilize, and circulate *particular* interpretations of *particular* interpretations. Sometimes this "knowledge" is then presented as universal knowledge. Indeed, most of the history of modernity could be read as a succession of historical attempts to produce and present universal knowledge. But, says Fish, all knowledge is the result of what goes on in particular interpretive communities, and that goes for allegedly universal knowledge too. Western, Cartesian, "reasoned" knowledge, produced by "rational" subjects and therefore "universally" valid, for example, cannot escape its *particularity:* it is Western, it is Cartesian, it claims it is "reasoned" and "rational," it believes it is "universal," while it depends on all and everything other that it discards or excludes from its interpretive community (please remember the passages on this above).

According to Deleuze and Guattari, for whom, as I mentioned above, the boundary between the machinic (culture, technology, the subject) and the vital (nature, desire, the object) has collapsed, the world is a world of *multiplicities;* each of those multiplicities allows for a multitude of interpretations that, each, are partial and particular. What we have been at pains to elaborate here is the idea that this particularity can be interpreted as *tribal* particularity. Tony Becher (1989) once used the trope of tribalism to describe what goes on in academic or scholarly communities. What academics consider to be "good" knowledge or "valid" knowledge, says Becher, is largely a matter of tribal desire and tribal fashion. I tend to agree. In our tribe, we believe that "knowledge" is inherently social, communal, and tribal. Maybe it took someone like the French sociologist Michel Maffesoli to make us aware of this. In his *The Time of the Tribes* (1996), Maffesoli describes our age as the age of the "neo-tribes"—tribal assemblages where pure and often Dionysian, sensual sociality (what Maffesoli calls tribal *puissance,* or force) reigns. But these sensual assemblages of tribal desire tend to very short-lived. They come and go dazzlingly chaotically. Contemporary cyborgs are well prepared to latch onto some of them, but only to leave them whenever the *affects* of Dionysius have sizzled out. However, it is not just our age that sees tribal life assembling, fragmenting, and reassembling everywhere. Having explored the above, I feel slightly compelled to repeat Latour's tribal knowledge: we have never been modern.

White-Collar Tribe

Before concluding this chapter, let me illustrate what went before. Let us use the notion of "white-collar crime" to that end, a notion that is fraught with "ambiguities" (Nelken, 2003). Due to space restrictions, I will only be able to briefly sketch the tribulations (or should I say, *tribalations?*) of this concept, but even this brief sketch will, hopefully, illustrate a number of positions. As is well known, Edwin Sutherland developed the notion of white-collar crime in a number of articles that appeared in the early 1940s (see also Sutherland, 1949). According to Sutherland, it did not make sense to limit criminology to the study of ordinary crime (e.g., burglary) when so many more kinds of harmful acts were committed by "respectable" people in the course of their business. In many cases, those harmful acts were not criminalized and penal sanctions were therefore not provided by the criminal law. But, claimed Sutherland, there is no reason why criminologists should not be interested in studying or analyzing them, even if the only sanctions provided by the law are in civil or administrative law. Sutherland's notion was not a revolutionary one. Indeed, he remained firmly within the bounds of state definitions of harm, or "crime," and Sutherland himself often explicitly stated that his critique of white-collar "crime" was ultimately based on quite unspectacular concerns with citizenship. Sutherland's concern was not to destabilize criminology, much less so American business culture, or capitalism for that matter. His concern was merely to stress the need for businesses too to act responsibly. Sutherland merely wanted to contribute to the *civilization* of American capitalism that, as such, he thoroughly endorsed. The lens through which Sutherland looked at white-collar crime could hardly be called revolutionary. Like ordinary crime, such as burglary or simple theft, said Sutherland, white-collar crime occurs in and through processes of "differential association." Sutherland just transposed his theory of "differential association," which he developed in the 1930s, to a topic that he stumbled upon on one of his forays in the world of crime and criminology, and that he claimed should be of interest to criminologists, that is, harmful acts committed by respectable but "differentially associating" individuals: businessmen and functionaries. Most criminologists would now agree that Sutherland's notion and theory of "white-collar crime" is one of the most important "assemblages" in the history of criminology. Indeed, Sutherland's assemblage, however unspectacular it may now seem to have been, did prefigure quite a few fundamental developments in criminology. Labeling perspectives, for example, which would emerge fully fledged by the early 1960s, were foreshadowed in Sutherland's work. At the time of Sutherland's first publications on white-collar crime, however, his work was unable to have a serious impact on the criminological community of the time. There were some critical reactions—some conservative and hostile—but, on the whole, Sutherland's work was largely ignored and very little at the time seemed to indicate that the criminological community would later enthusiastically pick up on his ideas. To continue our Papuan analogy here, we could say that Sutherland, during his travels into the forest of life and criminology (in both cases, we are talking about the very same forest), produced an extension that he brought back to the village of the 1940s criminological community only to find, after some negotiation (i.e., the few reactions in a number of journals), that his fellow tribesmen decided that at best it was irrelevant to the tribe's needs and desires and, at worst, inappropriate. There was no tribal community ready to recognize, accept, or build on Sutherland's notion and theory, and he himself did not make a substantial effort to start a tribal community that would. In other words, Sutherland himself did not begin to institutionalize his knowledge, for example, in a new *White-Collar Crime* journal or a Business Crime Institute. Only from the 1960s onwards would the criminological community see the gradual emergence of a body of literature on white-collar crime. In the forest of life and criminology, the conditions then seemed to have grown sufficiently ripe for a significant number of criminologists to get interested in the issue. Strangely enough, this interest was not widespread among labeling criminologists and interactionists. In a now-classic article, Alex Liazos, for example, complained as late as 1972 that so many among the latter were only interested in writing about "nuts, sluts, and perverts" (Liazos, 1972), apparently unaware of the huge importance of power differentials and power structures. Only when, around the time of the publication of *The New Criminology* (Walton, Taylor, & Young, 1973), the analysis of political economy (largely Marxist-inspired) got combined with interactionism and when a distinct and very vocal community, or "tribe," of radical criminologists began to institutionalize their "knowledge" (see discussion of this issue above), did the topic of white-collar crime again appear on criminology's agenda. This was due not just to developments *within* criminology or *within* radical or critical criminology in particular. Throughout the social sciences and the humanities, indeed throughout society as a whole, a severely antistatist and at times even a sheer anti-institutionalist vogue had institutionalized itself (please note the paradoxical contradiction). This anti-institutionalism in many cases provided a common ground for otherwise often very contradictory movements, schools, and, indeed, institutions. It would take us too far to expand on this here and now. Let it suffice to mention that this development did allow for an ever-growing number of radical and critical criminologists, thriving on shared sociality, and bent on criticizing all manner of institutionalized oppression or domination (see on this the highly influential paper by the Schwendingers, 1970), to gather and to produce fitting assemblages or, in other words, to show and circulate "extensions" and to negotiate over them. It is against this backdrop that Sutherland's work was rediscovered. His book, originally published in 1949, was eventually republished in 1983 in an uncut version (Sutherland had to omit names of companies in the first version). Sutherland's original notion and theory however were quickly adjusted to the exigencies of radical criminology's newly emerging anti-institutional, Marxist-inspired critical framework. During the 1970s, this occurred in a number of separate studies, but from the early 1980s onwards the critical and often highly radicalized analysis of what was now called "corporate crime"—which clearly transcended Sutherland's narrowly defined "white-collar crime"—developed ample momentum. Corporate crime tended to be studied and analyzed in connection to problems of national (first) or international (later) political economy. Works like those by the British radical criminologist Steven Box (1983) and empirical work by mainstream criminologists who had meanwhile joined in this momentous development (e.g., U.S.-based researchers Clinard & Yeager, 1980) gave a clear impetus to this process. Journals such as *Corruption and Reform* (later to be incorporated in *Crime, Law, and Social Change*) provided institutional anchoring. With hindsight, one might note how this gathering, sometime during the early 1980s, of former radical or critical criminologists and mainstream criminologists around the issue of "corporate crime" (now focusing predominantly on "corporate structure" and "corporate culture") happened at a time when the old antistatist and anti-institutionalist common ground that previously, during the 1970s, held the motley "tribe" of critical criminology together, was beginning to crumble away. Again it would take us too far to elaborate this point. Suffice to say here that the emergence of British left realism was one of the factors that formed the backdrop of this process. But the theme of "corporate crime" survived, and has since, in and through its many institutionalized communities, spawned innumerable studies that, as "immutable mobiles," are not just circulating in the forest of criminology but in the forest of corporate life as well. Some of these "immutable mobiles," by the way, still have some of the early radicalism about them (e.g., Pearce & Tombs, 1990; Slapper & Tombs, 1999). Others have found it worthwhile to produce their own peculiar assemblages of assemblages. James Messerschmidt's influential paper (1997) on the Challenger disaster is a case in point. In connecting feminist inspiration, theories of masculinity, and Giddens's structuration theory (1984), and in applying this assemblage to conflicting managerial styles that, according to Messerschmidt, were at work before and during the shuttle launch, he brought a novel approach to the study and analysis of corporate crime. Yet others have tried to venture beyond the everyday scope of criminology's communal knowledges (e.g., Ruggiero, 1996, 2000) and are now arguing for a thorough rethinking of the issues involved in "organizational crime," particularly in an age of "blurring boundaries," that is, in an age when the boundary in between the (alleged) inside and the (alleged) outside of organizations and organizational experience is slowly evaporating (see, e.g., Lippens, 2001). Two comments may be added here. Each new move in the criminological knowledge about white-collar crime or corporate crime, or, to put it in other words, each new adjustment of extensions and tribal adornments (e.g., Sutherland's, Box's, or Ruggiero's) was or is at the same time already an expression of what already had emerged, and a foreshadowing of what was or is yet to become. This, as we have seen previously, is what makes assemblages both stable and unstable. Further change, or further adjustments, can and will set in. And the more adjustments that ultimately end up both in the forest of criminological literature and in the forest of corporate life (but once again, we are talking about the same forest), the greater the potential for yet more connections and assemblages, and the greater the chance of yet more change occurring. And it is not just criminological tribesmen who then are going to put to use all these emerging assemblages in yet other assemblages. All those who take part in organizational life or corporate life will equally do so when assembling *their* corporate or organizational assemblages.

By Way of Conclusion

One of the most defining texts of the latter half of the twentieth century is *The Postmodern Condition* (1984) by the French philosopher Jean-François Lyotard. The book was written as a "report on knowledge" for the Quebec government. Since its publication, the humanities and the social sciences have never been quite the same again. Modern Western "knowledge," claims Lyotard, was and still is the result of a *particular* "language game." It boils down to what "experts" define as "knowledge." It is "knowledge" that, *because* it is "expert" knowledge, ignores basic questions such as "how do you prove the proof" or "who decides the conditions of proof" (1984, p. 30). It is knowledge that takes the form of "homology." That means that the stories "experts" produce tend to present themselves as the only stories ("metanarratives") that really matter. They tend to present their particular stories as universal truth. In view of what we have developed above, we may, like Lyotard, have some serious doubt about the universality and ultimate truthfulness of modern "knowledge." Lyotard himself celebrates a "postmodern" moment that he defines as "incredulity toward metanarratives." It is a moment that appreciates difference, and that tries to substitute "paralogy" for "homology." When it comes to "knowledge," Lyotard goes on, we ought to learn to "tolerate the incommensurable," and to respect "heterogeneity," diversity, and the deviance of "invention" (1984, pp. xxiii–xxv). It will probably come as no surprise that, after a little *negotiation* of some sort, I largely agree with Lyotard. However, rather than consider knowledge as a matter of mere "language games" and narration, I have tried to look at knowledge as *the social practice of tribal communality*. Splinters of Lyotard's knowledge assemblage, his "body of knowledge," have ended up here, in this assemblage of ours, in our "body of knowledge." We are *partially connected* with Lyotard and with others who, like us, desire to express and simultaneously (and paradoxically so) become tribal communality with those who try to re-think knowledge about insiders and outsiders.

References

Audi, R. (1998). *Epistemology: A Contemporary Introduction to the Theory of Knowledge*. London: Routledge.

Baudrillard, J. (1983). *Simulations*. New York: Semiotext(e).

Becher, T. (1989). *Academic Tribes and Territories: Intellectual Inquiry and the Cultures of Disciplines*. Buckingham: Open University Press.

Bourgois, P. (1995). *In Search of Respect*. Cambridge: Cambridge University Press.

Box, S. (1983). *Power, Crime, and Mystification*. London: Tavistock.

Caudill, D. (2003). Lacan, Science, and Law: Is the Ethnography of Scientism Psychoanalytic? *Law and Critique, 14*, 123–146.

Clifford, J. (1988). On Ethnographic Self-Fashioning. In *The Predicament of Culture*. Cambridge, MA: Harvard University Press.

Clinard, M., & Yeager, P. (1980). *Corporate Crime*. New York: Free Press.

Cohen, S. (1988). *Against Criminology*. New York: Transaction Books.

Deleuze, G. (1995). *Negotiations*. New York: Columbia University Press.

Deleuze, G., & Guattari, F. (1972). *Anti-Oedipe*. Paris: Editions de Minuit.

———. (1980). *Mille Plateaux*. Paris: Editions de Minuit.

Derrida, J. (1970). Structure, Sign, and Play in the Discourse of the Human Sciences. In R. Macksey and E. Donato (eds.), *The Languages of Criticism and the Sciences of Man: The Structuralist Controversy*. Baltimore: Johns Hopkins University Press.

DiCristina, B. (1995). *Method in Criminology: A Philosophical Primer*. New York: Harrow and Heston.

Fekete, J. (1994). *Moral Panic: Biopolitics Rising*. Montreal: Robert Davies Publishing.

Feyerabend, P. (1975). *Against Method.* London: New Left Books.

Fish, S. (1980). *Is There a Text in This Class?* Cambridge, MA: Harvard University Press.

———. (1989). *Doing What Comes Naturally.* Durham, NC: Duke University Press.

Foucault, M. (1975). *Discipline and Punish.* New York: Vintage.

Geertz, C. (1988). *Works and Lives: The Anthropologist as Author.* Cambridge: Polity Press.

Giddens, A. (1984). *The Constitution of Society.* Cambridge: Polity Press.

Haraway, D. (1991). *Simians, Cyborgs, and Women.* New York: Routledge.

Heidegger, M. (1962). *Being and Time.* New York: Harper and Row.

Hoff-Sommers, C. (1995). *Who Stole Feminism?* Carmichael, CA: Touchstone Books.

Kirby, K. (1996). *Indifferent Boundaries.* New York: Guilford Press.

Kuhn, T. (1970). *The Structure of Scientific Revolutions.* Chicago: University of Chicago Press.

Laclau, E., & C. Mouffe (1985). *Hegemony and Socialist Strategy.* London: Verso.

Latour, B. (1990). Drawing Things Together. In M. Lynch & S. Woolgar (eds.), *Representation in Scientific Practice.* Cambridge, MA: MIT Press.

———. (1993). *We Have Never Been Modern.* Cambridge, MA: Harvard University Press.

Liazos, A. (1972). The Poverty of the Sociology of Deviance: Nuts, Sluts, and Preverts. *Social Problems, 20,* 103–120.

Lippens, R. (2001). Rethinking Organizational Crime and Organizational Criminology. *Crime, Law, and Social Change, 35*(4), 319–331.

———. (2003). Imagining Lines, Assembling Criminologies, Towards Negotiation. In K. L. Kunz & C. Besozzi (eds.), *Social Reflexivity and Qualitative Methods: Toward a Criminological Self-Understanding in Postmodern Society.* Bern: Haupt Verlag.

———. (2004). Imaginary. Boundary. Justice. In R. Lippens (ed.), *Imaginary Boundaries of Justice.* Oxford: Hart Publishing.

Lyotard, J.-F. (1984). *The Postmodern Condition: A Report on Knowledge.* Minneapolis: University of Minnesota Press.

Maffesoli, M. (1996). *The Time of the Tribes.* London: Sage.

Martin, L., Gutman, P., & Hutton, P. (Eds.). (1988). *Technologies of the Self: A Seminar with Michel Foucault.* Amherst: University of Massachusetts Press.

Messerschmidt, J. (1997). Murderous Managers. In *Crime as Structured Action.* London: Sage.

Milovanovic, D. (Ed.). (1997). *Chaos, Criminology, and Social Justice: The New Orderly (Dis)order.* Westport: Praeger.

Nelken, D. (2003). White-Collar Crime. In M. Maguire, R. Morgan, & R. Reiner (eds.), *The Oxford Handbook of Criminology.* Oxford: Oxford University Press.

Patai, D., & Koertge, N. (1995). *Professing Feminism.* Basic Books.

Pearce, F., & Tombs, S. (1990). Ideology, Hegemony, and Empiricism: Compliance Theories of Regulation. *British Journal of Criminology, 30,* 423–443.

Rorty, R. (1979). *Philosophy and the Mirror of Nature.* Princeton: Princeton University Press.

Ruggiero, V. (1996). *Organised Crime and Corporate Crime in Europe.* Aldershot: Dartmouth.

———. (2000). *Crime and Markets: Essays in Anti-Criminology.* Oxford: Oxford University Press.

Schwendinger, H., & Schwendinger, J. (1970). Defenders of Order or Guardians of Human Rights? *Issues in Criminology, 5,* 123–157.

Slapper, G., & Tombs, S. (1999). *Corporate Crime.* Harlow: Longman.

Strathern, M. (1991). *Partial Connections.* Lanham, MD: Alta Mira Press.

Sutherland, E. (1949). *White-Collar Crime.* New York: Holt, Rinehart and Winston.

Taylor, I., Walton, P., & Young, J. (1973). *The New Criminology.* London: Routledge and Kegan Paul.

Westphal, M. (1998). Hermeneutics as Epistemology. In J. Greco & E. Sosa (eds.), *Epistemology.* Oxford: Blackwell.

Williams, M. (2001). *Problems of Knowledge: A Critical Introduction to Epistemology.* Oxford: Oxford University Press.

Young, J. (1999). *The Exclusive Society.* London: Sage.

FOUR

The Epistemology of Theory Testing in Criminology

BRUCE DICRISTINA

Since the Enlightenment, scholars have constructed and evaluated many different theories of law, crime, and punishment. Unfortunately, there is relatively little agreement among criminologists regarding the quality of these theories and little reason to believe that a consensus will be reached any time soon. Criminology is a multidisciplinary field comprised of conflicting theological, philosophical, biological, psychological, and sociological perspectives, not to mention other relevant disciplines that do not fall neatly into these categories. It endures persistent disagreements over the political and economic interests supported by various criminological theories, a situation that seems unlikely to change in the foreseeable future. Moreover, like many (if not all) other fields that attempt to explain "realities" of one kind or another, criminology lacks a clear and rational epistemology to guide theory testing. The primary purpose of this chapter is to examine two dimensions of this latter issue—two seemingly unsolved philosophical problems that plague the testing of criminological theories and, for that matter, empirical evaluations of perhaps all nomothetic theories. The first is the problem of induction; the second is the problem of theory-laden observation.

This chapter consists of four parts. The first part attempts to clarify the idea of "theory testing" and the scope of the present inquiry. The second part outlines the problem of induction as it relates to the verification and falsification of nomothetic theories. The third part examines the problem of theory-laden observation as it relates to the verification and falsification of any theory (nomothetic or idiographic); here, special attention is given to the paradox of observational theories, a problem that encourages a fundamental reinterpretation of many empirical studies in criminology. The final part explores the nature and use of theory testing in the context of a postmodern orientation that rejects the correspondence theory of truth and embraces the goal of self-creation—namely, the "ironist" perspective described by Richard Rorty.

Theory Testing

In general, to "test" a theory, one must compare it to one or more conceptually distinct criteria, standards that are not part of the theory itself, though they certainly may be another part of the "disciplinary matrix" upon which the theory has been constructed.[1] Conceived broadly, the criteria may include empirical "facts," rules of formal logic, intersubjective agreements, political and economic ideals, and other "significant" standards that can be used for purposes of evaluation. Preferably, the selected criteria will be better established and more plausible than the theory itself at the time of the test, yet this is not always the case. As explained below, it is here that subjectivism and relativism enter the testing process in a problematic way, at least if one's goal is to identify the theory that best corresponds to reality.

In criminology (and, of course, the natural and social sciences in general), when reference is made to a "test" of a theory, the term typically means an "empirical test," an effort to compare the theory with observations of the segment of reality it is designed to represent (i.e., empirical "facts"). In such a test, the credibility of the theory depends on its fit with the "facts." If the "facts" are largely consistent with the theory, the theory is said to have empirical support; if there is a marked inconsistency, the theory is said to lack support. If several such tests indicate a lack of empirical support, the theory may be declared inadequate and in need of significant revision. At the extreme, it will be rejected entirely, an outcome that is more likely when there is an alternative theory that better fits the "facts."

The emphasis on empirical tests in the sciences is reflected in the common contention that a theory must be empirically testable to be scientific. This certainly is evident in the literature of criminology. For example, according to Ronald Akers, "A scientific theory must be testable by objective, repeatable evidence. If a theory cannot be tested against empirical findings, it has no scientific value" (2000, p. 7). Likewise, Daniel Curran and Claire Renzetti contend, "Whatever the source of the theory, to qualify as scientific it must satisfy at least the two criteria of logical integrity and empirical verifiability" (2001, p. 2). The priority accorded systematic empirical inquiry may be a useful reference point when demarcating science from theology and philosophy, but some caution ought to be taken to avoid overstating its significance, which can be and has been questioned in some fundamental ways.

Although theories can be compared against other criteria, the primary focus of this chapter is on empirical tests. In assessing the nature and value of the conclusions generated by such tests, many different issues warrant attention; indeed, there are too many to be reviewed here. Consequently, only two of the most important are examined, the problem of induction and the problem of theory-laden observation.

The Problem of Induction

To appreciate the problem of induction as it relates to theory testing, it is necessary to have a basic understanding of the distinction between two kinds of theory (nomothetic and idiographic) and two general research orientations (verification and falsification). The problem of induction pertains primarily to the testing of nomothetic theories rather than idiographic theories, and the failure of verification advocates to solve the problem of induction has contributed to the popularity and development of falsificationism.

The primary distinction between nomothetic and idiographic theories is a distinction between the general and particular. A nomothetic theory is comprised of a set of general propositions ("law-like statements") designed to explain a general phenomenon, a phenomenon that may occur again and again in different places and at different times. It can be thought of as a "universal theory," at least in the conditional sense. It does not necessarily apply in all places and at all times, but rather is held to apply beyond a particular place and particular time. Most of the theories presented in criminology texts are of this kind. They attempt to explain laws, crime, punishment, or some other relevant variable in general—that is, among different people, in different places, and at different times, even at future times.

On the other hand, an idiographic theory is comprised of a set of particular propositions designed to explain a particular phenomenon and nothing more; it is designed to explain a phenomenon that occurred in a particular place at a particular time. This is the kind of theory historians typically construct to explain a single historical event; it also is the kind of theory prosecutors and defense attorneys construct to explain a single alleged criminal act. In criminology, a theory designed to answer any one of the following questions, and nothing more, would be an example of an idiographic theory: Why did California enact a habitual offender ("three strikes") law during the 1990s? Why did the official rates of violent crime in the United States increase between 1960 and 1990? Why have incarceration rates increased in the United States since the 1960s?

Nomothetic theories could be used to explain these particular phenomena, but by definition such theories would be presented as explanations of other phenomena as well. For example, a nomothetic theory could be constructed to explain variations in violent crime rates in developed capitalist societies. Given its general nature, such a theory may explain the increase in official violent crime rates in the United States between 1960 and 1990, but it also would explain violent crime rate variations in other places and at other times. On the other hand, the explanatory scope of an idiographic theory would be limited to just the one phenomenon.

The distinction between verification and falsification can be somewhat elusive. Verification, an orientation associated with logical positivism, involves an effort to accumulate "facts" that are consistent with a theory. As such "facts" grow in number, especially as they grow relative to contradictory observations, the theory is said to be more credible. On the other hand, falsification, an orientation associated with the "anti-positivist" philosophy of Karl Popper (1959, 1963, 1972),[2] involves an effort to accumulate "facts" that challenge a theory.[3] At first glance, the distinction between verification and falsification may appear superficial, more of a semantic game than anything else. However, this initial impression is misleading, since the former can be completed only by comparing a theory against all (or almost all) the "facts" it is designed to explain, while the latter can be completed by comparing the theory against a small proportion of those "facts," perhaps even a single "fact."

The Verification of Nomothetic Theories: A Seductive Delusion?

Because a nomothetic theory is designed to explain a general phenomenon that occurs in different places and at different times (past, present, and future), it cannot be compared directly to all instances of that phenomenon, to all relevant "facts." The phenomenon it attempts to explain may occur an infinite number of times, since it is not limited to a particular place and time.[4] Accordingly, a nomothetic theory cannot be verified through direct observation alone. Moreover, an appeal to "probabilistic verification" does not solve this problem, for it cannot be demonstrated directly that a given nomothetic theory fits the "facts" in most cases. The phenomenon at issue is general, and thus there will always be an unknown and possibly infinite number of unobserved occurrences of the phenomenon across space and time. In other words, the verification of nomothetic theories, if it is at all possible, must occur indirectly through an inductive reasoning process and, thus, depends on the validity of the "inductive principle."[5]

Induction, to borrow the words of John Stuart Mill, is a process through which we infer "from what we have perceived, or been directly conscious of, to what has not come within our experience" (1846, p. 184). Thus when we systematically generalize our observations to the future or to unobserved portions of the past or present, we are engaging in an inductive reasoning process. This process often is characterized as a useful approach to theory construction; but as just noted, it also is necessary for the indirect verification of nomothetic theories. Such verification can be no more rational than the inductive principle upon which it is based. If we can establish the truth of this principle, if we can demonstrate that "the course of nature is uniform," it may be possible to make the observations necessary for the verification of nomothetic theories.

Unfortunately, the rationality of inductive reasoning has been contested for centuries and remains unsettled (Salmon, 1995). David Hume usually is credited with being the first philosopher to articulate "the problem of induction."[6] Hume asked whether we are logically justified in having any confidence in our inductive inferences and came to the skeptical conclusion that we are not. In his words, "even after the observation of the frequent or constant conjunction of objects, we have no reason to draw any inference concerning any object beyond those of which we have had experience" (Hume, 1739/1967, p. 139). The inductive principle may provide the rationale for such inferences, but it is an assumption that cannot be verified, even in its more moderate (probabilistic) forms.[7] As Bertrand Russell noted, "We can never use experience to prove the inductive principle without begging the question" (1912/1999, p. 47).[8] After all, the inductive principle is a general (nomothetic) proposition, yet it is precisely that kind of proposition that it is used to verify. The following comment by Russell captures nicely the basic problem:

> It has been argued that we have reason to know that the future will resemble the past, because what was the future has constantly become the past, and has always been found to resemble the past, so that we really have experience of the future, namely of times which were formerly future, which we may call past futures. But such an argument begs the very question at issue. We have experience of past futures, but not of future futures, and the question is: Will future futures resemble past futures? (Russell, 1912/1999, p. 44)[9]

The disconcerting nature of the problem of induction is clearly expressed in one of Hume's best-known statements: "That the sun will not rise tomorrow is no less intelligible a proposition and implies no more contradiction than the affirmation that it will rise" (1748/1969, p. 197). If our expectations rely on the inductive principle, but its use cannot be logically justified, then all expectations become conjectures of essentially the same logical quality. If one asserts that the strongest and most stable association identified by the empirical literature of criminology will not hold tomorrow, the assertion is no more erroneous than the claim that the association will remain the same.[10] As a result, there is good reason to regard all nomothetic theories as conjectural, as guesses; and while this conclusion may be obvious as far as criminological theories are concerned, it also extends to the best "established" theories, a point that is supported by the implications of Einstein's theory of gravity. As Popper comments, "There never was a theory as well 'established' as Newton's, and it is unlikely that there ever will be one; but whatever one may think about the status of Einstein's theory, it certainly taught us to look at Newton's as a 'mere' hypothesis or conjecture" (1972, p. 9).

In short, because the inductive principle cannot be proved, inductive inferences, even if stated as probabilities (see Popper, 1972), remain indemonstrable conjectures. As such, they cannot empirically verify nomothetic theories; they cannot demonstrate that such theories are in close correspondence with reality. Moreover, there appears to be no other way to verify such theories, since their scope extends to unobserved phenomena of the past, present, and future. Thus, to the extent that criminologists accept the inductive principle and pursue the verification of nomothetic theories, they may be accused of following an "irrationalist epistemology." Yet, in view of what has been argued to this point, it still *may* be possible to avoid irrationalism.

The Falsification of Nomothetic Theories: A Rational Alternative?

The foregoing analysis suggests that the verification of nomothetic theories lies beyond the realm of rational empirical inquiry, since such verification depends on the verification of the inductive principle, which, itself, is nomothetic in character. If this line of reasoning is compelling and we still wish to create theories and rationally judge them by their empirical fit, we may continue to be hopeful (at least for the moment) since two obvious possibilities remain: (1) We can pursue falsification rather than verification; or (2) we can create and test idiographic theories rather than nomothetic theories. The rest of this section considers the rationality of the first possibility; the next section examines a philosophical problem that can lead one to question both possibilities.

Thus far, nothing has been said that would rule out the possibility that nomothetic theories can be directly falsified through a process of deductive reasoning, at least if the idea of falsification is not extended to "probabilistic falsification." Popper, perhaps more than any other philosopher of science, developed and defended falsification as a "rational" alternative to verification. He maintained that falsification could be rational because it does not depend on inductive reasoning; it does not depend on the indemonstrable inductive principle. Indeed, he concluded, "there is no such thing as induction by repetition," in either a logical or psychological sense (Popper, 1972, pp. 6–7). As noted earlier, falsification involves an effort to accumulate "facts" that challenge a theory but seemingly does not require the theory to be compared against all or most of the "facts" it is designed to explain. Through a deductive process, the theory may be "refuted" following a comparison with a relatively small proportion of those "facts." For Popper, "the assumption of the truth of test statements sometimes allows us to justify the claim that an explanatory universal theory is false" (1972, p. 7).[11]

Unfortunately, falsification has been plagued by at least two general problems: (1) the question of how many contradictory "facts" are necessary to reject a theory, and (2) that of how to create and evaluate different statements of fact. The remainder of this section examines the first problem; the second is the subject matter of the next section. Thomas Kuhn provided a concise summary of the first problem:

> If any and every failure to fit were ground for theory rejection, all theories ought to be rejected at all times. On the other hand, if only severe failure to fit justifies theory rejection, then the Popperians will require some criterion of "improbability" or of "degree of falsification." In developing one, they will almost certainly encounter the same network of difficulties that has haunted the advocates of the various probabilistic verification theories. (Kuhn, 1996, pp. 146–147)

The first part of this argument should be very easy for criminologists to understand. Clearly if we rejected every general criminological theory that failed on one occasion or another to fit the empirical world it was intended to explain, we would be left with untestable, untested, and undertested theories only. Of course, even with this considerable limitation, it still may be argued that falsification is more rational than verification; if our tests are restricted to "facts" that represent directly observed phenomena and those "facts" are true, we can rationally falsify testable nomothetic theories, but we cannot verify such theories. However, this does not mean that falsification necessarily is more useful than verification.

To establish falsification as a rational *and* useful principle for the testing of nomothetic theories (if it is at all possible), its critical edge must be tempered. At first glance, it may appear as though this can be accomplished through the development of some criterion of improbability (i.e., some form of probabilistic falsification), but this, as Kuhn (1996) implied, leads us back to the problem of induction. To establish the improbability of a nomothetic theory, it is necessary to make inferences about the future, as well as the unobserved portions of the past and present; yet as noted above, such inferences depend on the inductive principle, which cannot be proved. In effect, this probabilistic solution reduces falsification to a form of verification, with the primary difference being one of vocabulary.[12]

Popper (1972, pp. 17–21) attempts to avoid this problem by rejecting probabilistic theories of preference and replacing them with the idea of "corroboration," a criterion that involves an evaluation of the empirical testability of a theory, the extent to which it has been tested, and how well it survived these tests. If a theory is testable and consistent with the "facts," if it has survived the "crucial experiments" it has faced, it receives some degree of corroboration. However, corroboration "says nothing whatever about future performance" and is neither a probability nor improbability criterion. According to Popper, when compared to "competing theories" (other theories designed to explain the same phenomenon), the "best" corroborated theories often are the more "improbable" ones, because they are the most testable and have the greatest "informative content." Yet ideally, at a given point in time, they will explain all that their competitors explain as well as some things their competitors fail to explain.

Prelude to the Next Problem

There have been many efforts to solve the problem of induction, but not one of the proposed solutions, as Wesley Salmon (1995) notes, is generally accepted as correct. Nonetheless, I will assume that Popper's reasoning successfully evades this problem, and that falsification (as low corroboration relative to one or more competing theories) still warrants examination as a potentially rational approach to the empirical testing of nomothetic theories. In view of what has been argued to this point, it would be difficult to draw the conclusion that criminologists who reject the inductive principle and pursue falsification in this sense are following an irrationalist epistemology. However, this conclusion may be easier to reach upon consideration of the next problem, the problem of theory-laden observation.

Before proceeding to this problem, it should be acknowledged that we can avoid the problem of induction without resorting to falsification; that is, we can avoid it if we are willing to set nomothetic theories aside and settle for the testing of idiographic theories. Such a reorientation, however, involves a considerable sacrifice. Idiographic theories certainly can be useful (e.g., when judging guilt or innocence in particular criminal cases), but their range of practical application is not nearly as great as that of nomothetic theories. Because they are designed to explain phenomena that have occurred in particular places at particular times (and nothing more), idiographic theories cannot be used *directly* to make predictions or guide efforts to control oneself or one's environment. They do not provide information that can be used directly to guide the prediction of crime trends, the reduction of crime and suffering, or improvements in the efficiency of the criminal justice system. To use an idiographic theory in any of these ways, it first must be generalized beyond the particular situation it was designed to explain, but this act of generalization would involve transforming it into a kind of nomothetic theory. Thus nomothetic theories have a greater range of practical application, and a shift in subject matter to the testing of idiographic theories would represent a significant sacrifice.

For this reason, I will continue to focus on the possibility that nomothetic theories can be falsified through rational-empirical means. Nevertheless, the problem of theory-laden observation plagues empirical tests of all theories, nomothetic and idiographic. To this point, it has been assumed that statements of fact are not problematic as long as they are based on careful observations made in particular places at particular times—that is, as long as they are not generalized. But of course, statements of fact pertaining to specific perceptions can be very problematic in that they appear to be unavoidably theory-laden. This is a problem for both verification and falsification, regardless of whether one is testing a nomothetic theory or an idiographic theory.

The Problem of Theory-Laden Observation

Perhaps the most important issue to examine when assessing the nature and value of the conclusions generated by empirical tests in criminology is the problem of theory-laden observation. To appreciate this problem as it relates to theory testing, it once again is necessary to draw a distinction between two kinds of theory—in this case, "explanatory theories" and "observational theories." I begin with an outline of this distinction and then proceed to a description of the paradox of observational theories. My examination of this problem has been shaped largely by the language and arguments of Lakatos (1969) and Kuhn (1996).

Explanatory and Observational Theories

If the process of theory testing involved only one theory, if the only conjectures involved were those of the theory being tested, the inaccuracy of a testable theory could be readily established in many cases. Unfortunately, the idea that researchers can create mono-theoretical testing situations seems untenable. When conducting an empirical test of a theory, at least two theories always appear to be involved: (1) the theory one wishes to test (the explanatory theory) and (2) a more-or-less distinct theory that is used to "collect" the "facts" (the observational theory). Thus, while an empirical test requires a comparison between an explanatory theory and a set of "facts," it in effect entails a comparison between an explanatory theory and an observational theory, since the "facts" depend on the latter (see Lakatos, 1969).

In the field of criminology, different observational theories are used to construct official crime data, victimization data, self-report data, and other "facts" on crime, such as the data set used by Jeffrey Reiman (2001). Likewise, different explanatory theories—such as the various explanations developed in the feminist, Marxist, learning, anomie, and control traditions—are designed to explain (and are compared against) some of these "facts." In other words, the test situation is not simply a matter of comparing an explanatory criminological theory (e.g., social learning theory) against the reality it attempts to explain and measuring its success relative to other competing explanatory theories (e.g., general strain theory and social bond theory). Implicitly or explicitly, an empirical test in criminology, as in other fields, involves a comparison between one or more explanatory theories and an observational theory. The paradox that results from this situation will be examined later. At this time, the scope and general content of explanatory and observational theories will be outlined.

Explanatory theories can be either nomothetic or idiographic, and can vary markedly in terms of their complexity and scope. However, to maintain conceptual clarity (to keep them distinct from observational theories), the term "explanatory theory" will be limited to single explanations. In other words, as used here, the term refers to a single set of interrelated propositions arranged in an effort to explain a general or particular phenomenon. Thus Emile Durkheim's (1900/1969) explanation of penal evolution would represent an explanatory theory, but his overall "social theory" would not, for it includes explanations of punishment, law, crime, suicide, the division of labor, the common consciousness, social solidarity, and many other phenomena. In the same way, Friedrich Engels's (1845/1993) explanation of working-class criminality and Sigmund Freud's (1915/1959) explanation of "criminality from a sense of guilt" represent explanatory theories, but "Marxist social theory" and "Freudian psychoanalytic theory" are too broad for this label, since they both entail a large collection of explanations.

Two additional points regarding explanatory theories and empirical tests need to be mentioned at this time. First, while explanatory theories must be empirically testable (if one wishes to empirically test them), the idea of testability, as suggested below, becomes somewhat obscure in view of the problem of theory-laden observation. Second, as noted above, more than one explanatory theory can be involved in a particular test. If you are attempting to find the best theory from a pool of competing theories, your research may involve an effort to find one theory that explains everything the other theories explain and more. However, to avoid getting lost in lengthy digressions, I will focus on test situations that involve one explanatory theory only.

Regarding observational theories, they are constructed primarily to guide and "justify" the research procedures used to describe (measure) key variables and variable relations. They are comprised of conjectures that shape and rationalize the decisions made during the "data collection" and data analysis processes. However, observational theories are rarely presented in a complete and explicit manner.[13] In fact, it is somewhat misleading to refer to them as theories, since they often amount to rather loose sets of conjectures and conditioned perceptions. They represent a kind of "background knowledge" (Popper, 1963), both explicit and "tacit" (Kuhn, 1996; Polanyi, 1958). Nevertheless, I will continue to use the term observational theory since it effectively communicates the speculative nature of this kind of "knowledge."

To better understand the content and scope of observational theories, it is useful to take a closer look at some of the ways they shape both "data collection" and data analysis. Regarding the process of data collection, observational theories influence *where we look* for relevant facts, *how we look*, and *what we perceive*.

To begin, data collection requires that we make a choice as to whom or what we are going to question or observe. The explanatory theory will suggest one or more relevant populations, but direct observation of all cases of even a single population frequently is impossible. For example, we may not have the resources to question all members of a relevant population, so we may select a simple random sample. The belief that observations of a simple random sample are a useful substitute for observations of an entire population, as well as our choice of a simple random sample over a nonprobability sample (e.g., a purposive sample), can be rationalized in terms of probability theory. In this case, probability theory would be part of our overall observational theory; it would be a distinct theory that is used to guide the construction of "facts" against which our explanatory theory can be compared.

Next, we must "choose" how we are going to question or observe those people or things. The explanatory theory will specify the variables that need to be measured and should provide at least nominal definitions. However, an observational theory is necessary to answer the following questions: should "facts" be "gathered" through survey research, field research, or some other method? If a survey methodology is used, precisely what questions should be asked? How should they be worded? In what order should they be asked? And how should they be administered (e.g., self-administered questionnaires, telephone interviews, or face-to-face interviews)? When visual observations are part of the plan, when, where, and from what angle should they be made? Answers to all these questions require a distinct set of conjectures (i.e., an observational theory), and different answers (i.e., different observational theories) can result in significantly different "facts."

In addition, we must organize the stimuli we experience into perceptions (sensations), which represent another part of the "data collection" process that is shaped by observational theories. When exposed to the same stimuli, when carefully and systematically looking in the same place with the same observational instruments, it is possible for different observers to see different things. Kuhn (1996, pp. 111–135, 174–210) provided one of the more persuasive descriptions of this problem. He argued that in the natural sciences perceptions are shaped by past exposures to "exemplars," "concrete problem-solutions" that are employed as "examples." Exemplars are "paradigms" in the more limited and, for Kuhn, "appropriate" sense (pp. 186–187). They are used to teach students to literally see things in a certain way; they are used to shape perceptions. Thus a paradigm-shift is comparable to a switch in visual gestalt.[14] To paraphrase Kuhn, what are seen as ducks in the context of one paradigm can be seen as rabbits in the context of another (p. 111).[15]

Overall, and in general terms, Kuhn's reasoning suggests that our past experiences shape what we see, and that we can be trained to see things in one way and not another (to some degree at least). This suggestion pushes relativism beyond the comfort threshold of many criminologists, and even Kuhn (1996, pp. 186, 191, 205–207) attempted to distance himself from the relativist (and subjectivist) implications of his argument. Nonetheless, it is a persuasive and interesting line of reasoning that warrants attention when examining the epistemology of theory testing in criminology.

The extent to which personal and group experiences result in contradictory perceptions among criminologists is difficult to assess. Yet it seems reasonable to assume that people with different life experiences, with different educational backgrounds, may see something fundamentally different when observing the same behavior or conditions. For instance, when examining a highly competitive business practice, the exemplars of critical criminology may train some scholars to *see* an act of cruelty or deception, whereas the exemplars of conservative criminology may train other scholars to *see* hard work and perseverance. This is an important point, and the key to understanding its significance is to recognize that the issue is one of perceptual differences and not merely interpretive differences.[16] The observers in this case do not see the same thing and then choose to interpret it in different ways; rather they see very different things (some see ducks and others see rabbits, so to speak). Moreover, following Kuhn, the observers probably cannot see it any other way at the time; typically, an observer cannot choose to step back from his or her perception and see things in a different way.

Before proceeding, two additional points need to be made regarding these three general ways in which observational theories shape "data collection." The first concerns the choices available to a researcher, while the second concerns the degree of separation between explanatory theories and observational theories. When choosing *where to look* and *how to look* for relevant facts, we may have a meaningful choice, and that choice may be guided by a more-or-less explicit and distinct observational theory, one that is clearly separable from the explanatory theory. But the situation changes with the issue of *what we perceive*. Perception is largely an involuntary response shaped by one's past experiences (e.g., the exemplars one has been exposed to during one's education) and, thus, involves a "tacit" dimension of observational theories. Moreover, the experiences that shape perceptions may include repeated exposures to concrete applications of an explanatory theory, in which case the distinction between observational and explanatory theories becomes blurred.

Moving beyond data collection, observational theories also guide and rationalize at least two aspects of data analysis—namely, the interpretation of perceptions ("raw facts") and the identification of concept relations. In each of these areas, we once again can have a meaningful choice, and that choice may be guided by a more-or-less explicit observational theory.

On the one hand, while the explanatory theory tells us what we should expect from our data, the interpretation of perceptions is shaped by much more than just this theory. For example, interpretations frequently are influenced by the meanings and rules of ordinary language (e.g., the English language) that we choose to apply. If the perceptions in question consist of respondent statements, alternative interpretations are always possible,[17] and we must select the "best" interpretation to establish "the facts." Accordingly, if a respondent provides information in English, we typically will select certain meanings and rules from this language, ideally giving due consideration to relevant local or individual variations (e.g., the unique vocabulary of deviant subcultures). These selected meanings and rules will guide our interpretation and, thus, comprise part of our observational theory.

On the other hand, observational theories guide and rationalize the selection and application of one or more techniques for identifying patterns among "the facts." After "the facts" have been established, it generally is necessary to choose a technique for testing proposed concept relations, a choice that typically requires conjectures of one kind or another. For instance, the statistical techniques commonly used to examine variable relations and test hypotheses in criminology are based on different assumptions and arguments that rationalize their application. These assumptions and arguments often concern the nature of the samples, the shape of a relevant sampling distribution or population distribution, and the level of measurement. When a particular technique is chosen, the line of reasoning that "justifies" its use (or simply the assumption that its use is justified) becomes part of the observational theory of the study.

In short, in the ways just described (and other ways as well), observational theories shape data collection, data analysis, and ultimately the "empirical facts" used to test explanatory theories. But of course, because they are theories, because they are comprised of conjectures and conditioned perceptions, they are not necessarily accurate reflections of reality and can lead to very distorted data sets and conclusions. Clearly, criminological research methods often are based on highly questionable conjectures. Consider some of the assumptions that frequently shape survey research data in criminology: the members of the sample who respond are adequately representative of the population of interest; the respondents pay close attention to the questions being asked and understand them; the respondents have the knowledge necessary to answer all questions accurately; the respondents answer all questions truthfully, even when asked about their own criminal behavior; coding and data entry is completed without significant mistakes; and so forth. Each conjecture represents a point at which reality may be distorted, and the overall result, in the context of theory testing, is a very problematic paradox.

The Paradox of Observational Theories

Lakatos (1969), in his examination of "nafalsificationism" (an analysis built around Kuhn's interpretation of Popper's philosophy of science),[18] provided a useful description of the paradox of observational theories:

> One can easily see that when we devise an experiment in order to test, to criticize a theory, we always use some "observational theories" or "touchstone theories" (or "interpretive theories") uncritically if we want to make its "falsification" possible. *Nafalsificationism demands, therefore, that at least in a given critical situation, the body of science be divided into two, the problematic and the unproblematic* (the unproblematic is usually understood to be the well-corroborated). But this demand is irrational and dogmatic. Often "unproblematic background knowledge" is not even well-corroborated, and the clue to progress may lie in its overthrow. And even if it is well-corroborated, nothing prevents us from inferring from a negative result to its falsehood. (Lakatos, 1969, pp. 156–157; emphasis in the original)

In this sense, a paradox infects efforts to empirically evaluate theories. If the knowledge claims of the explanatory theory conflict with the "facts" generated through the application of a particular observational theory, we still must confront the question of which theory is wrong. Is it the explanatory theory, the observational theory, or both? *The central problem is that the knowledge claims of the explanatory theory can be reinterpreted as a set of "facts" that can be used to evaluate the observational theory.*[19] This aspect of theory-laden observation appears to be commonly overlooked by criminologists during the process of theory testing. Most criminologists do comment on the limitations of their methods, but they rarely weigh the plausibility of their observational theories against that of their explanatory theories. The routine is to acknowledge the existence of methodological limitations and proceed as if the observational theories involved are less problematic than the explanatory theories.[20] But of course, this is not necessarily the case, because some of the observational theories used by criminologists have a relatively low level of plausibility.

The important thing to keep in mind is that the conclusions of a given study can be reversed (literally) if it can be successfully argued that the explanatory theory as a whole is more plausible than one or more conjectures of the study's observational theory. If such an argument can be made and the explanatory theory is consistent with the data, the study may do little or nothing to support the explanatory theory, although it may provide some support for the observational theory. Conversely, if there is an inconsistency, if the data do not support the explanatory theory, one may conclude that the observational theory is problematic and not the explanatory theory. As the following example suggests, a greater awareness of this paradox may prompt a fundamental reinterpretation of many studies that claim to verify, corroborate, or falsify criminological theories.

To illustrate the paradox of observational theories, consider a recent study that involved the use of self-report data to test a nomothetic life-course theory of adult criminal behavior (Simons et al., 2002). Consistent with current research norms, the authors acknowledge several limitations of their study (p. 429–430) but overlook the paradox just described.

Among other things, the life-course theory examined proposes that involvement with an antisocial romantic partner has a direct positive effect on criminal behavior and an indirect positive effect through the development/preservation of deviant friendships. It is reasoned that antisocial romantic partners are more likely to tolerate and reinforce criminal behavior and deviant friendships, whereas conventional partners are more likely to discourage such behavior and friendships. Although the theory includes several additional variables and propositions, for purposes of illustration, I will treat this learning component as the explanatory theory. The inclusion of all variables and propositions would not resolve the paradox but only make it more complex and more problematic.

The observational theory that is applied in this study includes a variety of conjectures regarding the adequacy of the sample of young adults who were questioned (236 couples), the validity of the self-report data, and the accuracy of the statistical techniques used to analyze this data (e.g., structural equation modeling and OLS regression). Once again, in an effort to keep this example clear, my focus will be on just one part of the theory at issue—in this case, a conjecture that underlies the self-report data that was used. Specifically, the observational theory of this study assumes that young adult offenders, when questioned by researchers (who are probably strangers), will generally provide accurate information about their own criminal behavior.

If we assume that all other conjectures of the observational theory are true (which seems unlikely), we can reduce our problem to a single question. Which idea is more plausible: the idea that close friendships with antisocial individuals increase the likelihood of criminal behavior, *or* the idea that young adult offenders generally will provide researchers with accurate information about their own criminal behavior? If you conclude that the latter idea is the most plausible, the study and its conclusions may appear reasonable. If you conclude that the former idea is the most plausible, the study and its conclusions probably will appear unreasonable or inverted, at least with regards to the learning component of the life-course theory that was tested.

Unfortunately, in this particular study, this problem was overlooked, and, arguably, the former idea is more credible than the latter. Not only does the idea of a positive relationship between friendships with antisocial individuals and criminal behavior seem more reasonable in terms of "common sense," it is quite possible that more empirical studies support this proposition, since it is at least indirectly supported by studies that have corroborated learning theories in general. On the other hand, the idea that people generally will provide researchers with accurate information about their own criminal behavior seems directly contrary to "common sense"; and while several studies offer some support for self-report measures of unlawful behavior (see Thornberry & Krohn, 2000), the support is hardly overwhelming.[21]

The groundwork is now in place for a fundamental reinterpretation of the results of the Simons et al. study. Most of the analyses conducted by the authors suggest a significant relationship between close friendships with antisocial individuals and criminal behavior. However, in view of the observational theory paradox, this finding may tell us more about the observational theory than the explanatory theory. If the explanatory theory is more plausible than the observational theory, it seemingly makes more sense to view this study as a test of the observational theory. In this connection, the explanatory theory can be reinterpreted as a set of "facts" that can be used to evaluate the observational theory. Upon doing this, it can be argued that the study does more to corroborate the observational theory than the explanatory theory; that is, it appears to provide some support for the use of self-report data but has little or nothing to say about the quality of the learning component of the life-course theory that was examined.

To complete this illustration of the observational theory paradox, assume that the authors of this study found no evidence of a relationship between close friendships with antisocial individuals and criminal behavior. In other words, assume that they "discovered" contradictory "facts" and concluded that the explanatory theory appears to be false. Their conclusion, in this case, could be criticized in the same manner. If it can be successfully argued that the explanatory theory is more plausible than the observational theory, it makes more sense to view the study as a test of the observational theory. Therefore, the more "reasonable" conclusion would be that the study does more to falsify the observational theory than the explanatory theory; that is, it would represent a challenge to the rationality of self-report data but would say little or nothing about the quality of the learning component of the life-course theory.

In sum, efforts to verify or falsify theories often take the form of a game, one in which the speculative nature of an observational theory is downplayed relative to that of the explanatory theory being tested. Regrettably, a rational alternative to this game, a solution to the problem of theory-laden observation, may not exist. When judging the explanatory and observational theories of a study to determine which is the most plausible, it appears as though we have recourse only to other theories and, thus, cannot escape the paradox. How does one avoid circularity among, or an infinite regress of, observational theories? Without a solution to this problem, all empirical tests—all attempts to verify or falsify theories, whether nomothetic or idiographic—must include some degree of relativism.[22]

Ironism, Self-Creation, and Theory Testing

To this point, it has been argued that both verification and falsification are problematic whether one wishes to test a nomothetic theory or an idiographic theory. Indeed, some readers may believe the skepticism of the argument has been taken too far, since it can be used to challenge seemingly all empirical tests in criminology. Yet, because the problems of induction and theory-laden observation appear to be unresolved, I will follow through with this skeptical line of argument and conclude this chapter with a brief overview of a postmodern orientation that attempts to reduce the relevance of these problems—namely, the "ironist" perspective described by Richard Rorty.

The Ironist Perspective

Since the publication of *Philosophy and the Mirror of Nature* (1979),[23] Rorty has established himself as one of the more interesting contemporary philosophers, and one of the more intriguing parts of his work is his description of the ironist perspective. Ironists reject the correspondence theory of truth, appreciate the contention that "truth is made rather than found," are deeply concerned with "self-creation," and are inclined to see their work as "poetic" rather than theological or "metaphysical" (Rorty, 1989).[24]

According to the correspondence theory of truth, language is a medium of expression and representation; it is a means by which we can express "the essential nature of the human self" and represent the essences of the world outside ourselves.[25] Vocabularies, given this theory, are comparable to pieces of a jigsaw puzzle—that is, with the right words arranged in the right way, we can accurately express or represent what is real. Words are held to designate facts ("chunks" of an intrinsically divided reality), and these designations supposedly become more exact as a language becomes more developed. More importantly, from this viewpoint, "facts," which are believed to transcend language, provide us with the criterion for choosing between alternative vocabularies, including alternative theories. A sentence, on this account, is true if it corresponds to the essences of the human self or the world, and false (or at best approximate) if it does not.[26]

Rorty (1989) contends that the correspondence theory of truth is no longer useful and should be set aside. He asserts that we should abandon the notion that the human self and the world outside us have an "intrinsic nature," that the world provides us with a language to speak, and that our language is a medium of expression or representation. Instead, Rorty, following Donald Davidson and Ludwig Wittgenstein, believes we should treat different languages more like alternative tools that we have created. From this viewpoint, when a group asserts that a theory is a step toward the truth, it simply means that they have come to perceive it as "useful" for one purpose or another, not that it expresses or represents the true nature of reality better than competing theories.

Upon abandoning the correspondence theory of truth, it becomes easier to appreciate the idea that "truth is made rather than found." If we discard the notion that languages are mediums of expression and representation, we are prompted to see truth and falsity as creations resulting from the construction and comparison of sentences, for they can no longer be seen as discoveries based on comparisons with facts. Rorty summarizes this idea in the following way: "since truth is a property of sentences, since sentences are dependent for their existence upon vocabularies, and since vocabularies are made by human beings, so are truths" (1989, p. 21). In other words, a sentence can be true or false only in the context of a given vocabulary, all of which are human constructs. If a sentence is constructed that does not have a place in a vocabulary (if it is a "metaphor"), it can be neither true nor false.

Rorty (1989) describes ironists as being inclined toward both of these positions—toward abandoning the correspondence theory of truth and toward appreciating the idea that truth is created rather than discovered. Ironists do not believe in efforts to discover the intrinsic nature of the human self and the external world. They have "radical and continuing doubts" about the vocabularies they use to justify their beliefs and actions, their "final vocabularies." They do not believe that the vocabularies they use are any closer to reality than the vocabularies of others, and they remind themselves of this by frequently using terms such as "perspective," "conceptual framework," and "language game." Moreover, they do not believe that the unique vocabularies of different people are "destined to converge," but instead they are oriented more toward expanding the number of alternative vocabularies.[27] Thus they prefer to speak more in terms of making and diversification rather than finding and convergence.

In addition, ironists are concerned with the goal of "self-creation"—which, for Rorty, involves efforts to modify the language one has been taught. Through a process of continual redescription, ironists hope to make the best possible selves for themselves.[28] To this end, they try to become familiar with the vocabularies of "strange" people, groups, and communities because they do not want to be trapped by the vocabulary of their initial socialization. Rorty goes on to add that self-creation, nonetheless, is a project that can never be completed, because we can never escape entirely the language we have been taught (and even if we could, this may not be desirable in that no useful language can be entirely private).[29] Further, ironists are "never quite able to take themselves seriously," for they believe "anything can be made to look good or bad by being redescribed" and are "always aware that the terms in which they describe themselves are subject to change" (Rorty, 1989, pp. 73–74).

Not surprisingly, Rorty suggests that ironists are comparable to "poets," people who make "things new," people who try to "achieve self-creation" and dread the thought of finding themselves to be "only a copy or a replica." What is more, ironists prefer dialectical argument over logical argument, pitting a wide variety of vocabularies against each other. "Ironists take the writings of all the people with poetic gifts, all the original minds who had a talent for redescription . . . as grist to be put through the same dialectical mill" (1989, p. 76). In contrast, most "intellectuals" start by putting these writings into categories, by drawing rigid distinctions between theology, philosophy, science, literature, and other such categories.

While the ironist perspective, like all perspectives, can be criticized in several different ways, two criticisms deserve special attention. On the one hand, ironists have been censured for embracing relativism. For some scholars, this may represent a fundamental shortcoming, yet it is difficult to evaluate its importance and relevance. As noted above, without a solution to the problem of theory-laden observation, some degree of relativism is inevitable in the construction of empirical data and the testing of theories. Moreover, this criticism loses much of its meaning when viewed from an ironist perspective. On this matter, Rorty simply contends that the charge of relativism "should not be answered, but rather evaded" (1989, p. 54). He asserts that it is no longer useful to draw distinctions between absolutism and relativism, nor between rationality and irrationality, morality and expediency, or logic and rhetoric. These terms are part of a vocabulary we should replace.[30]

On the other hand, ironists may be reproached for encouraging cruelty, since redescription can have some disconcerting and painful consequences. In Rorty's words, "The best way to cause people long-lasting pain is to humiliate them by making the things that seemed most important to them look futile, obsolete, and powerless. . . . The redescribing ironist . . . suggests that one's self and one's world are futile, obsolete, and powerless. Redescription often humiliates" (1989, pp. 89–90). However, redescription and its potential negative consequences also are a part of theology, traditional philosophy, and science. What makes ironist redescriptions potentially more painful, according to Rorty, is that ironists redescribe "in the name of the imagination" and these other orientations redescribe "in the name of reason," claiming that they are educating, empowering, and freeing their audience. An ironist cannot make such claims. For this reason, Rorty considers the possibility of "liberal ironism."

Liberal ironism is an orientation that tries to strike a compromise between the liberal's interest in reducing cruelty[31] and the ironist's emphasis on contingency and self-creation.[32] However, liberal ironists do not attempt to integrate or synthesize liberalism and ironism; rather they attempt to accommodate the two by dividing their vocabularies into two spheres: public and private. In the public realm, redescriptions are to be shaped with the actual or potential suffering of others in mind and, accordingly, opportunities for self-creation are limited. In the private realm, one's redescriptions are no one else's business; they are not necessarily constrained by concerns about the suffering of others, allowing more room for self-creation. In this connection, liberal ironists have two reasons to pursue an awareness of as many different vocabularies as they can: (1) it allows them to better avoid being cruel to other people through their redescriptions, and (2) it facilitates self-creation, as noted earlier.

While Rorty's description of liberal ironism is interesting and may even be used to develop a new variety of criminology, it is the element of ironism and its relation to theory testing in criminology that is the primary concern of this section.

Ironism and Theory Testing in Criminology

The ironist perspective can guide an alternative way of thinking about theory testing in criminology. Because this viewpoint rejects the correspondence theory of truth and embraces the idea that "truth" is made, it does not consider empirical tests to be means through which we come closer to understanding the essential nature of law, crime, or punishment. From this viewpoint, empirical tests are tools through which the "truth" or "falsity" of a theory is created; they are not means through which truth and falsity are discovered. The different modes of theory testing are ways of creating support for or opposition to different pictures of criminological phenomena and not techniques for discovering truly superior or inferior knowledge. While a given theory may come to be accepted as more "useful" for one purpose or another, an ironist would not view it as more accurate, not in the sense that it expresses or represents reality better than competing theories. In this connection, an ironist would acknowledge that the quality of criminological theories, along with the concepts of crime and justice, are subject to continuous redescription and that "anything can be made to look good or bad by being redescribed."

Moreover, from this perspective, the modes of theory testing become tools that may be used for purposes of self-creation. Criminologists who adopt an ironist orientation would be interested in different ways to create "knowledge" that could further their own self-creation, and they may be inclined to see other criminologists as creating, defending, and criticizing "knowledge" for this purpose. In general, the construction and evaluation of criminological theories can be part of a process of self-creation. By creating and testing theories, consciously or unconsciously, we may be redescribing ourselves and, in this sense, creating ourselves to a degree. Some attempts at theory construction and evaluation may be better described as unconscious efforts at self-redescription; that is, they may say more about the author than the phenomena they are designed to explain. By describing certain conditions or people in a particular way, it is possible to describe oneself indirectly. For instance, conservative criminologists who employ quantitative quasi-experimental methods may frame themselves (implicitly) as people of science who represent the antithesis of the "street criminal," while critical criminologists who are involved in participatory action research may frame themselves (implicitly) as humanitarian researchers who represent the antithesis of the white-collar, corporate, or political criminal.

Likewise, similar to researchers of the symbolic interactionist tradition, criminologists who adopt an ironist orientation would be inclined to contemplate ways in which some "rule creators," "rule enforcers," and "deviants" may be creating themselves through their words and actions.[33] "Moral crusaders," "experts," and other rule creators can redescribe both themselves and particular behaviors through the rules they shape and advocate. Police officers, prosecutors, judges, correctional officers, and other criminal justice personnel can redescribe both themselves and others by developing a unique language and taking particular actions against alleged offenders. Deviants, too, can redescribe themselves and others by developing a distinctive language and violating rules in particular ways. In short, from an ironist perspective, the creation, enforcement, and violation of law can involve individual efforts at self-creation; they can involve the struggle of particular individuals to create unique selves for themselves, consciously or unconsciously.

Overall, criminologists who adopt an ironist orientation would be more inclined to describe themselves as poetic, rather than scientific. They would see themselves as being involved in an ongoing process of creation, including self-creation, rather than an effort to discover the truth (the most accurate theory). In addition, they would not draw rigid distinctions between different styles of description and would not object to narratives of theology, philosophy, science, literature, the criminal justice profession, criminals, and perhaps any other kind being "put through the same dialectical mill" when evaluating a theory.

Conclusion

The foregoing examination of theory testing in criminology focused on empirical tests and was organized to support a healthy degree of skepticism. This chapter began with an effort to explain why the problem of induction makes the verification of nomothetic theories an unobtainable goal and the falsification of such theories problematic. This was followed by an account of how the problem of theory-laden observation—in particular, the paradox of observational theories—appears to infect all empirical tests, contaminating them with some degree of relativism. This problem plagues efforts to verify nomothetic and idiographic theories and, likewise, afflicts efforts to falsify such theories. Moreover, it was suggested that these two problems seem to be unsolved, may never be solved, and can be used to rationalize the adoption of a postmodern perspective, such as that of "the ironist."

Despite the disconcerting implications of this line of argument, its skepticism is liberating in at least two ways. First, it helps create and maintain room for the application of diverse research tools. By challenging the rationality of established methods and truth-claims, the problems of induction and theory-laden observation open a door to other methods of theory testing and the construction of alternative "realities." One still may appreciate and systematically apply the inductive principle and, more generally, the most fashionable observational theory as guides for research, but one also should have the opportunity to work "counter-inductively" and apply a variety of fundamentally different observational theories. Second, as suggested by the overview of the ironist perspective, this skeptical line of reasoning may help maintain or increase opportunity to create a unique self for oneself, something that would be valued by people who desire such an end.

Notes

1. Thomas Kuhn (1996, pp. 175, 181–187) defines "disciplinary matrix" as "the entire constellation of beliefs, values, techniques, and so on shared by the members of a given community." It is a "paradigm" in the more comprehensive and, for Kuhn, "inappropriate" sense.

2. Although the neo-positivists of criminology may embrace Popper's philosophy of science (or at least a distorted version of his work, namely, "dogmatic falsificationism"), there is a sense in which Popper was very much an anti-positivist, a point that was stressed by Bryan McGee: "The truth is that Popper was never a positivist of any kind; quite the reverse, he was the decisive anti-positivist, the man who put forward from the beginning the arguments that led (after an excessively long time) to logical positivism's dissolution" (1985, p. 47).

3. Imre Lakatos (1969) has identified three different interpretations of Popper's philosophy of science: "dogmatic falsification," "nafalsification," and his "growth" ("progressive problem-shift") orientation. In this section, my focus is on dogmatic falsification, an orientation that assumes theories can be disproved with complete certainty. While this form of falsification represents a distortion of Popper's perspective, it seems to be the form that is most commonly accepted by criminologists. In the next section, the orientation of nafalsification is addressed in connection with the problem of theory-laden observation.

4. If Popper is correct, this seemingly extreme statement may underestimate the nature of the problem. In his words, "An explanatory theory goes essentially beyond even an infinity of universal test statements; even a law of low universality does so" (Popper, 1972, p. 7).

5. To keep the problem of induction in focus, the problem of theory-laden observation will be ignored until the end of this section.

6. To avoid lengthy digressions, I have examined this problem as if it were a single problem. See Popper (1972) for a useful examination of several different problems of induction, including "the traditional philosophical problem," "the commonsense problem," "Hume's logical problem," and "Hume's psychological problem."

7. A probabilistic form of the inductive principle is represented by the following belief: the greater the number and consistency of associations observed between two or more phenomena, the more probable it is that the phenomena were, are, and will be associated in the unobserved cases of the past, present, and future.

8. Russell (1912/1999, pp. 41–48) provided a useful overview of the problem of induction and a four-part description of the inductive principle.

9. A similar problem is evident in Mill's examination of induction: "Whatever be the most proper mode of expressing it, the proposition that the course of nature is uniform, is the fundamental principle, or general axiom, of Induction. . . . I hold it to be itself an instance of induction. . . . Yet this principle, though so far from being our earliest induction, must be considered as our warrant for all the others, in this sense, that unless it were true, all other inductions would be fallacious" (1846, p. 184).

10. Russell concluded, "we must either accept the inductive principle on the ground of its intrinsic evidence, or forgo all justification of our expectations about the future" (1912/1999, p. 47).

11. Popper refers to "observation statements" or "test statements" rather than "facts." He defines such statements as "singular statements describing observable events" (1972, p. 7).

12. Russell noted an interesting twist to this problem: "The fact . . . that things often fail to fulfil our expectations is no evidence that our expectations will not *probably* be fulfilled in a given case or a given class of cases. Thus our inductive principle (if stated in probabilistic terms) is at any rate not capable of being *disproved* by an appeal to experience" (1912/1999, p. 47; emphasis in the original).

13. As Lakatos notes, "calling the reports of our human eye 'observational' only indicates that we 'rely' on some vague physiological theory of human vision" (1970, p. 107).

14. Kuhn (1996, pp. 113–115) emphasized that the gestalt switch experiments of psychology are "suggestive" of the kind of perceptual change that accompanies a paradigm shift in the developed natural sciences, but he also stressed that the two are not identical. For instance, in the experiments of psychology, the subjects usually are aware of the switch in their perceptions and can shift back and forth between alternative perceptions; in contrast, after a paradigm shift in a natural science, the shift in perception is rarely acknowledged and scientists typically cannot shift back and forth.

15. For some readers, it may seem odd that I have decided to use the term "observational theory" rather than "paradigm." The two terms do have much in common, but Kuhn uses "paradigm" in several different ways (see Kuhn, 1996; Masterman, 1970) and, thus, creates too much surplus meaning. In his "Postscript—1969," which he added to the second edition of *The Structure of Scientific Revolutions,* Kuhn explains that he used "paradigm" primarily in two different senses. The term was sometimes used to refer to a "disciplinary matrix" (see note 1 of this chapter), and as just mentioned, it was sometimes used to refer to an "exemplar." An observational theory, as I use the term, falls somewhere in between these two epistemic entities; it includes more than an exemplar, but it does not include "the entire constellation of beliefs, values, techniques, and so on shared by the members of a given community."

16. Kuhn (1996, pp. 121–123, 191–198) drew a distinction between perception

and interpretation, emphasizing that the former is an involuntary process, while the latter involves making a conscious choice between alternatives.

17. Most, if not all, languages allow considerable room for alternative interpretations, since their terms commonly have more than one acknowledged nominal meaning and their rules usually have some flexibility. Beyond this, a "standard language," such as the English language, can vary in important ways across locations and individuals.

18. Nafalsificationism is an intellectual orientation that rejects the idea that theories can be disproved with complete certainty (unlike "dogmatic falsificationism"), yet it accepts the idea that an explanatory theory must be rejected if it conflicts with the "facts" generated by a widely accepted observational theory (Lakatos, 1969).

19. Regarding the paradox of observational theories, Lakatos concludes, "The problem is not whether a refutation is real or not. The problem is how to repair an inconsistency between the 'explanatory theory' under test and the—explicit or hidden—'interpretive' theories; or, if you wish, *the problem is which theory to consider as the interpretive one which provides the 'hard' facts and which the explanatory one which 'tentatively' explains them*" (1969, p. 161; emphasis in original). Popper and Lakatos were optimistic that this problem could be solved rationally and, accordingly, that researchers (at least in the natural sciences) could avoid irrationalism.

20. In other words, the problems with particular research methods do receive much attention, but the manner in which they are framed often draws attention away from how serious they can be. When conceptualized as an observational theory paradox, their significance is not readily discounted. Likewise, although criminologists occasionally touch on this paradox in discussions of "construct validity," the issue tends to be framed in a way that draws attention away from its significance.

21. This issue is complicated by the fact that some of the studies that support learning theories of crime involve analyses of self-report data.

22. Although my viewpoint is skeptical, I have not ruled out the possibility that someone has created a rational solution to the problems of induction and theory-laden observation. Perhaps it exists as a variation of Popper's "growth" ("progressive problem-shift") orientation (see Lakatos, 1969, 1970). In any event, the solution, if it does exist, is not well established and may apply only to the most detailed natural sciences.

23. Other notable works by Rorty include *Consequences of Pragmatism* (1982), *Contingency, Irony, and Solidarity* (1989), *Objectivity, Relativism, and Truth* (1991), *Essays on Heidegger and Others* (1991), and *Truth and Progress* (1998).

24. Metaphysical thought, for Rorty (1989), includes scientific thought as it is usually conceived.

25. Rorty (1989) uses the terms "language," "vocabulary," and "language game" in a loose sense. They seem to subsume everything from the unique "final vocabulary" of a given individual to the shared vocabulary of Western civilization.

26. In other words, "beliefs are criticizable because they fail to correspond to reality. Desires are criticizable because they fail to correspond to the essential nature of the human self" (Rorty, 1989, p. 10).

27. "There is no way to step outside the various vocabularies we have employed and find a metavocabulary which somehow takes account of *all possible* vocabularies, all possible ways of judging and feeling" (Rorty, 1989, p. xvi).

28. Rorty describes a genius as someone who "has found a way to describe (a part of the) past which the past never knew, and thereby found a self to be which her precursors never knew was possible" (1989, p. 29).

29. "Metaphors are unfamiliar uses of old words, but such uses are possible only against the background of other older words being used in old familiar ways" (Rorty, 1989, p. 41).

30. For readers who are tempted to conclude that Rorty's viewpoint is contradictory, he notes that his work should not be read as if he were suggesting that his "sort of philosophy corresponds to the way things really are" (1989, p. 8), and he openly acknowledges that his perspective is not neutral: "When I say 'we should' do this or that 'we cannot' do that, I am not . . . speaking from a neutral standpoint" (1989, p. 54).

31. Following Judith Shklar (1984), Rorty suggests that liberals are characterized foremost by a "desire to avoid cruelty and pain"; they are "people who think that cruelty is the worst thing we do" (Rorty, 1989, pp. xv, 65, 74).

32. Rorty (1989) viewed Jurgen Habermas as "a liberal who is unwilling to be an ironist" and Michel Foucault as "an ironist who is unwilling to be a liberal" (p. 61).

33. Of course, in this paragraph, I have borrowed a few terms from Howard Becker (1973).

References

Akers, R. L. (2000). *Criminological theories: Introduction, evaluation, and application* (3rd ed.). Los Angeles: Roxbury.

Becker, H. (1973). *Outsiders: Studies in the sociology of deviance.* New York: Free Press.

Curran, D. J., & Renzetti, C. M. (2001). *Theories of crime* (2nd ed.). Boston: Allyn and Bacon.

Durkheim, E. ([1900] 1969). Two laws of penal evolution. *University of Cincinnati Law Review, 38,* 32–60.

Engels, F. ([1845] 1993). The demoralization of the English working class. In D. F. Greenberg (ed.), *Crime and capitalism: Readings in Marxist criminology* (pp. 48–50). Philadelphia: Temple University Press.

Freud, S. ([1915] 1959). Some character-types met with in psychoanalytic work. In E. Jones (ed.), *Sigmund Freud: Collected papers* (vol. 4, pp. 318–344). New York: Basic Books.

Hume, D. ([1739] 1967). *A treatise of human nature.* London: Oxford University Press.

———. ([1748] 1969). An inquiry concerning human understanding. In R. P. Wolff (ed.), *Ten great works of philosophy* (pp. 176–295). New York: Mentor.

Kuhn, T. S. (1996). *The structure of scientific revolutions* (3rd ed.). Chicago: University of Chicago Press.

Lakatos, I. (1969). Criticism and the methodology of scientific research programmes. *Proceedings of the Aristotelian Society, 69,* 149–186.

———. (1970). Falsification and the methodology of scientific research programmes. In I. Lakatos & A. Musgrave (eds.), *Criticism and the growth of knowledge* (pp. 91–196). Cambridge: Cambridge University Press.

Masterman, M. (1970). The nature of a paradigm. In I. Lakatos & A. Musgrave (eds.), *Criticism and the growth of knowledge* (pp. 59–89). Cambridge: Cambridge University Press.

McGee, B. (1985). *Philosophy and the real world: An introduction to Karl Popper.* La Salle, IL: Open Court.

Mill, J. S. (1846). *System of logic, ratiocinative and inductive.* New York: Harper & Brothers.

Polanyi, M. (1958). *Personal knowledge: Towards a post-critical philosophy.* Chicago: University of Chicago Press.

Popper, K. (1959). *The logic of scientific discovery.* New York: Basic Books.

———. (1963). *Conjectures and refutations: The growth of scientific knowledge.* New York: Basic Books.

———. (1972). *Objective knowledge: An evolutionary approach.* Oxford: Clarendon Press.

Reiman, J. (2001). *The rich get richer and the poor get prison: Ideology, class, and criminal justice* (6th ed.). Boston: Allyn and Bacon.

Rorty, R. (1979). *Philosophy and the mirror of nature.* Princeton: Princeton University Press.

———. (1982). *Consequences of pragmatism: Essays 1972–1980.* Minneapolis: University of Minnesota Press.

———. (1989). *Contingency, irony, and solidarity.* Cambridge: Cambridge University Press.

———. (1991). *Objectivity, relativism, and truth: Philosophical papers* (vol. 1). Cambridge: Cambridge University Press.

———. (1991). *Essays on Heidegger and others: Philosophical papers* (vol. 2). Cambridge: Cambridge University Press.

———. (1998). *Truth and progress: Philosophical papers* (vol. 3). Cambridge: Cambridge University Press.

Russell, B. ([1912] 1999). *The problems of philosophy.* Mineola, NY: Dover Publications.

Salmon, W. C. (1995). Problem of induction. In R. Audi (ed.), *The Cambridge dictionary of philosophy* (pp. 651–652). Cambridge: Cambridge University Press.

Shklar, J. (1984). *Ordinary vices.* Cambridge, MA: Harvard University Press.

Simons, R. L., Stewart, E., Gordon, L. C., Conger, R. D., & Elder, G. H. (2002). A test of life-course explanations for stability and change in antisocial behavior from adolescence to young adulthood. *Criminology, 40,* 401–434.

Thornberry, T. P., & Krohn, M. D. (2000). The self-report method for measuring delinquency and crime. In D. Duffee (ed.), *Measurement and analysis of crime and justice: Criminal justice 2000* (vol. 4, pp. 33–83). Washington, DC: National Institute of Justice.

PART THREE

Ethics and Crime

Discussions of ethics entail a deliberate engagement with the thorny, contentious, and timeless debates surrounding the nature of freedom and responsibility, being and becoming, personhood and citizenship. Accordingly, ethical inquiry pursues the meaning of living virtuously and acting morally in an organic, complex society. In relation to the philosophical foundations of crime, ethical inquiry investigates how nonnormative expressions of reason, desire, choice, and conduct are fundamental, rather than peripheral, to being fully human.

Chapter 5 examines the possibility of an ethics of crime or, more generally, an ethics that gives rise to criminal or nonnormative conduct understood as an ethics of freedom. Freedom is conceptualized as a core value, motivation, and commitment for individuals who pursue nonnormative behavior in light of their lived experiences. The relationship between ethics and human existence is examined, the possibility that freedom itself can be an ethic is addressed, and a framework from within which to understand kinds of freedom, kinds of human motivations linked to freedom, and kinds of human behaviors motivated by freedom are described. The proposed framework offers freedom a threefold role in human motivation, valuation, and behavior, namely (1) freedom experienced in the form on nonnormative choice, (2) freedom experienced in acts of nonnormativity, and (3) freedom experienced as a (potential) consequence of nonnormativity. This threefold framework yields three corresponding types of ethics: the ethics of the underground, the ethics of play, and the ethics of transformation.

Building upon this notion of crime or nonnormative conduct as a manifestation of "types" of freedom, chapter 6 first develops Deleuze's ethics integrated from Nietzsche and Spinoza. The notions of will to power and forces as well as deterritorialization are summarized. The chapter then applies these concepts to justice studies and the emerging interests in the "edgeworker." In studying Deleuze's notion of evaluation, chapter 6 incorporates a constitutive approach in defining harm. The final section engages in a dialogue with Williams's three ethics of freedom. It indicates some points of convergence as well as divergence.

Perhaps what is most provocative about the chapters in this section is how the authors endeavor to humanize the so-called offender by de-realizing the person's otherwise criminal motivations, choices, and actions. In other words, philosophical inquiry permits one to speculate on how the need for self-expression (e.g., experiencing increasing degrees of freedom through thrill seeking, nonnormative conduct, or choice making) represents a core constituent of human becoming. Thus, the ethical dimensions of our existence—and by extension the philosophical foundations of crime—cannot be understood absent a careful and systematic assessment of this underexamined phenomenon.

FIVE

Engaging Freedom: Toward an Ethics of Crime and Deviance

CHRISTOPHER R. WILLIAMS

In recent years, ethics has increasingly become a mainstay of criminological discourse. More and more, courses entitled "ethics and criminal justice" or "ethics of crime and justice" are entering university catalogs and program curricula. Textbooks and scholarly analyses of ethics and criminology are increasingly being published, entertaining variations on traditional ethical arguments and applying them to a host of controversial issues in crime, law, and justice. Continuing debates on discretion, use of force, and corruption in police behavior, on "zealous advocacy," plea bargaining, and discrimination in the courts, and on humane treatment, prisoners' rights, and capital punishment in corrections have benefited substantially from the infusion of ethical concepts and principles into more traditional criminological contentions. Most, if not all, of what criminologists study is inherently ethical in nature, and most, if not all, of what criminal justice practitioners do is inherently ethical in nature. For this reason alone, criminology cannot progress in any meaningful fashion without appropriating the materials that philosophical ethics has to offer.

At the same time that criminology has become increasingly concerned with ethical issues, its conception of what constitutes an ethically relevant issue has strayed little from conventional and somewhat obvious understandings of what ethics is and where it is applicable. The aforementioned concerns are each interested in establishing the ethical foundations of policies, practices, decisions, and behaviors issuing from *within* the system of justice. That is to say, "ethics and criminology" has become synonymous with the "ethics of police, courts, and corrections" (perhaps inclusive of law and punishment). Demonstrably absent from the emerging relationship between ethics and criminology are examinations of crime and criminal behavior with an eye toward the ethical. Put another way, the convergence of ethics and criminology has been almost exclusively understood as an opportunity to entertain what should or ought to be done *about* law, crime, and justice, rather than as a tool for furthering our understanding of what people are *doing* when they engage in criminal and deviant behaviors.

The remainder of this chapter represents an attempt to fuse ethics not with concerns of criminal justice but with those of crime and criminal behavior. Crucially, attending to the crossways of ethics and criminal behavior can enhance our understanding of crime and, in doing so, contribute to future research, policy, and practice in this area. Each of the following sections is an attempt to chart some location within this crossway. The first section sets the foundation of an ethics of crime by briefly examining conventional understandings of what ethics is and offering an alternative conception that allows for nonnormative commitments, valuations, preferences, and motivations to be understood in ethical terms. The next two sections establish the basis for the particular variation of ethics that the remainder of the chapter explores, namely, the relationship between ethics and freedom and that between freedom and value. The next section further examines the relationship between ethics and freedom by proposing a threefold root for a nonnormative ethic of freedom. In doing so, I explore three perspectives from which to understand human behavior, with three corresponding characterizations of nonnormative ethics. The final three substantive sections more thoroughly explore each of the three ethics issuing from this framework. I conclude by commenting upon the potential value of this framework for understanding crime as well as its implications for future research, policy, and practice.

(Re)Conceptualizing Ethics

At its inception, ethics was the philosophy of human character. From Socrates, through Plato and Aristotle, and into the meditations of Roman philosophers such as Thomas Aquinas, St. Augustine, and the Stoics, ethics was a mode of thinking about how human beings should *be*. The ancient virtue ethicists were not primarily interested in practical ethical concerns about what we should *do*; rather, they intended to establish certain characterological traits as beneficial to individual and social well-being. It is not surprising, then, that we should find criminal behaviors generally discussed under the broader category of vice or vicious character. Plato (see the introduction of this volume), for example, understood crime in moral psychological terms as ignorance, dis-order of the soul, and/or a dis-ease of the soul. The criminal disposition was a vicious disposition, characterized by lack of knowledge concerning what is good, and lacking the capacity to assert control over base impulses such as anger, passion, and pleasure. Quite clearly, the criminal was understood as she or he who *lacked* ethics, in the sense that to be "ethical" entailed the cultivation of understood virtues and rational control over the human inclinations toward vice.

The intellectual climate of modernity produced two competing and, perhaps more familiar, conceptions of ethics. Namely, Kant's deontological ethics promoted an ethics of rule/duty following, wherein "good will" or intention and acts themselves were "ethical" if and when they conformed to understood principles. Bentham and Mill, in turn, offered a teleological or consequentialist regard for ethics as the advancement of "good" consequences. While philosophers have since debated what is and how we determine what constitutes a worthy ethical principle, as well as what are to be classified as "good" consequences, the field of ethics has strayed little from orchestrations of ethics and morality that are organized around conceptions of the "good," "right," and "just." By all accounts, criminal behavior fails to be "ethical" in any popularly understood sense of the word. By all accounts, criminal actors or persons engaging in criminal activity fail to *be* ethical, *act* ethically, or produce ethically "good" consequences: as virtuous character and good will, criminal agents are lacking; as "right" conduct or rule following, criminal behavior demonstrably fails; and as the advancement of "good" consequences, criminal behavior often produces precisely the opposite.

Yet each of these conceptions—from virtue ethics to its deontological and teleological counterparts—resolves questions of ethics and morality by appealing to normative concerns of what is good, right, and/or just. "Normative," in this respect, refers to traditionally understood virtues, agreed-upon rules and principles, and popular delineations of good consequences. Arguably, however, regarding crime and criminal behavior merely as failing to approach normative conceptions of what *should* be or be done neglects crucial possibilities for understanding crime and criminal behavior on different ethical grounds. Critically, criminal behavior—or what might be better referred to in ethical terms as *nonnormative* behavior—may be just as "ethical" as its normative variants. The key to such an argument rests upon an alternative conception of what ethics, fundamentally, is. Rather than narrowly focusing on what should or ought to be done by referencing normative principles and guidelines (e.g., virtue, duty, the common good), ethics might be better regarded as encompassing *all* varieties of human behavior. In other words, we might regard all forms of human behavior—normative and nonnormative, virtuous and vicious, rule following and rule breaking, "good" and "bad"—as "ethical" in the broadest sense of the term. This, of course, requires redefining what we mean by "ethics" and "ethical," straying from if not challenging traditional, inherited understandings.

Fundamentally, ethics is a way of knowing, seeing, living, and experiencing human existence and the relationships that human beings maintain with themselves, others, and their world. Having an "ethic"—being "ethical"—reflects a commitment to certain ways of being and ways of relating, a valuing of certain forms of experience, a preference for certain things over and above others, and an underlying motivation to pursue these commitments, values, and preferences. Yet commitments, values, and preferences are rarely as simple as absorbing, assuming, and adhering to dominant, normative conceptions of what should be or be done. Instead, they are often dynamic products of experience: of the ongoing interplay between self and other, self and world; of our unique histories, understandings, feelings; of our personal and social struggles; of our past, present, and potential future social locations; and the like. In short, our commitments, values, and preferences are coterminous with who, where, and what we were, are, and want to be.

In this regard, one's "ethic" may be demonstrably nonnormative (cf., Matza, 1964, on neutralization theory). It may equally be consistent with, in variation from, or antithetical to dominant, normative conceptions of ethics and morality. The production and consumption of pornography, the choice and act of abortion, and the practice of social activism are each violations of or departures from normativity. They are each, in various circles, regarded as inherently unethical, immoral, and even illegal. They are each ways that we should not be, things that we should not do, or bring about consequences that we should not desire. Yet in each case the human realities at issue are not inherently unethical or immoral; rather, they represent alternative conceptions of morality and alternative ethical formations. Pornography, abortion, and social activism *can* represent commitments, valuations, and preferences as much as any other form of being or doing. The profanity of pornography, for example, represents a symbolic departure from the sacred space of intimacy, traditionally reserved for spiritually unioned, heterosexual couples. Yet such departures are not departures from the ethical; rather, they represent ethical creations of alternative spaces for human sexuality. They are, in some sense, commitments to, valuations of, and preferences for alternative ethical understandings.

Reconceptualizing ethics in this manner should not necessarily be read as a *defense* of nonnormative ethical formulations. It is, more so, a plea for attention to the complexities, ambiguities, and contextualities that characterize the notion of "ethics" and the "ethic" of any particular individual or group of individuals. In the context of crime and deviance, it becomes necessary to entertain such alternative commitments, valuations, preferences, and motivations on a conceptual level. As choice is the cornerstone of ethics, embodying our commitments, valuations, preferences, and motivations, we might ask why, for instance, one might "choose" nonnormativity. What experiences—histories, struggles, understandings, feelings, social locations—make nonnormative commitments, valuations, and preferences seductive alternatives to normativity? Granted that nonnormativity is valued over and above normativity, how is the experience itself of nonnormativity an affirmative experience? In what ways are the consequences of nonnormativity understood as valuable and desirable? These are the sorts of questions that an "ethics of crime" can and should entertain. In this sense, ethics becomes not a tool for judgment or formulation of principles but a conceptual medium for illustrating the meanings, values, commitments, and so on of criminal and deviant behavior.

Ethics, Crime, and Freedom: A Prospectus

The questions outlined above and the more general project of an "ethics of crime" could rely on a variety of philosophical, psychological, and sociological images. Hedonism, individualism, egoism, greed, and other images have been positioned in various ethical theories and criticisms. Indeed, images such as these have been and continue to be employed to describe motivations for and/or causes of criminal and deviant behavior. For the purposes of this chapter, however, I have chosen a somewhat different image with which to conceptualize criminal and otherwise deviant commitments, valuations, preferences, and motivations. Namely, I argue that an ethics of crime should account for the experience (or lack thereof) of human *freedom*.

The notion of freedom has played a crucial role in the history of metaphysical discourse and, by implication, in the metaphysics of ethics. In its most common form, by "freedom" is meant something closer to "free will." Freedom in this respect is commonly contrasted with determinism, becoming critically present in metaethical controversies over the very possibility of ethics. In simplest terms, the controversy hinges on the argument that if human beings are not free from the determining influences of divine, biological, psychological, and/or sociological forces, we are not "free" to choose and, therefore, cannot rightfully be said to be ethical, unethical, moral, or immoral. If our thoughts, feelings, and/or behaviors are determined by forces beyond our control, then the pursuit of ethics becomes a futile endeavor. We will, instead, think, feel, and behave precisely as we are determined to rather than as we choose to.

"Freedom," in what follows, should not be confused with this metaethical concern for "free will" and the possibility of ethical choice. Rather, my concern will be with the possibility that freedom itself can be a commitment, value, preference, and underlying motivation. In other words, freedom can be an ethic. Recast in this light, ethics may have something, perhaps quite radical, to say about crime and deviance. The notion of freedom can shed conceptual light on questions such as why one might choose nonnormativity; what experiences make nonnormative commitments, valuations, and preferences seductive alternatives to normativity; how the experience of crime and deviance can be affirmative; and how the consequences of crime and deviance can seem desirable as ends. In this respect, the ethics of crime as an ethic of freedom transcends strictly virtue-based, deontological, and consequentialist conceptions of ethics. Instead, it draws attention to how freedom can be a crucial component of intentions, actions, *and* consequences.

The following sections explore the possibility of an ethics of crime as an ethic of freedom. The "ethics of crime" is better understood as an ethic that gives rise to criminal and deviant behaviors. In particular, I reflect (though tentatively and provisionally) on how freedom might be understood as a commitment, value, preference, and motivation giving rise to a variety of behaviors that are regarded as nonnormative. I begin by briefly examining the relationship between ethics and human existence, particularly as they intersect at the notion of value. Next, I attempt to clarify what is meant by "freedom as an ethic," suggesting that various forms of freedom might be valued, thereby representing an ethic and providing incentive for nonnormative behaviors. In doing so, I offer a general framework (see the overview in the table below) from within which to understand several types of freedom, kinds of motivations linked to freedom, and forms of behavior motivated by the ethic of freedom. More specifically, the proposed framework offers freedom a threefold role in human commitment, valuation, preference, and subsequent behavior; namely, freedom is presented as (1) experienced in nonnormative *choice*; (2) experienced in *acts* of nonnormativity; and (3) experienced as a *consequence* or potential consequence of nonnormativity. This threefold role gives rise to three different but related ethics, discussed respectively as an "underground ethic," an "ethic of play," and an "ethic of transformation." While these three "ethics" are presented independently, they should not necessarily be regarded as mutually exclusive. Though different in important ways, each ethic might be understood as interrelated or simultaneously operative in given valuations of, commitments to, preferences for, or instances of crime and deviance.

Ethics and Values

The concept of "ethics" I have thus far described regards ethics as involving ways of knowing, seeing, living, and experiencing human existence. Having an "ethic," I have proposed, involves, among other things, a com-

Table 5.1

	Underground ethic	Ethic of play	Ethic of transformation
Type of freedom	existential/ontological	phenomenological	teleological
Perspectival basis	acting subject (choice)	act itself	results of act
Motivational basis	affirmation of choice	end in itself	means to an end
Type of affirmation (freedom to/for)	self-determination; self-constitution; self-creation	temporary dissolution of boundaries; free play of emotions, feelings, etc.	liberation; praxis; overcoming

mitment to certain ways of being and ways of relating, a valuing of certain forms of experience, a preference for certain things over and above others, and an underlying motivation to pursue these commitments, values, and preferences. Crucially, both traditional conceptions of ethics (e.g., virtue-based, deontological, teleological) and that developed in the present chapter are organized around the concept of value. Value is the fundamental of ethics: we commit ourselves to certain values; we display preference for understandings, experiences, relations, and behaviors that promote or provide opportunities to exercise certain values; and we are generally motivated to advance those values over and above others. Whether knowingly or unknowingly, consciously or unconsciously, values are reflected in the choices we make, the virtues we cultivate, the actions we undertake, and the ends we pursue.

"Value" can be understood as "desirability, worth, or importance" (Pollock, 1994, p. 8) or, applied, as "any object of desire, any 'inclination,' motivation, drive, attraction, whether instinctual or acquired, latent or aroused, whether 'end-in-itself' or means to another end" (Solomon, 1987, p. 93). One can, for example, value certain thoughts, feelings, experiences, objects, behaviors, or principles. Depending on what we value, our relation to it can be one of production or reproduction, nurturance, maintenance or preservation, personal possession, elimination, and so on (Lacey & Schwartz, 1996, p. 319). We may value sensual pleasure and be motivated to pursue experiences that produce or reproduce sensual pleasures. We may value physical health, thereby committing ourselves to activities that maintain or nurture physical health. Or if, as Bentham (1970) suggested, we are principally motivated to avoid pain, we may value experiences—or activities that produce experiences—in which some subjective sense of pain is eliminated or reduced.

Values, of course, can be beneficial or harmful to oneself, others, and society on the whole. We can value the "high" we get from inhaling THC in the same sense that we can value compassion and forgiveness; we can value danger and excitement as much as peace and serenity (many such valuations, of course, might be better regarded as subsumed within more basic, intrinsic values such as pleasure or happiness). Importantly, while the personal and/or social *desirability* of that which we value may be subject to unfavorable judgment, we are nevertheless deeply involved with value, and value, in turn, forms the basis around which an ethics can be orchestrated. It is in this respect that the underpinnings of criminal and deviant behavior are ethical; that is, criminal and deviant behaviors—as much as normative behaviors—reflect underlying valuations.

Because values are dynamic products of experience—products of the ongoing interplay between self and other, self and world; of our unique histories, understandings, feelings; of our personal and social struggles; of our past, present, and potential future social locations—criminal and deviant behaviors should be understood as embodying values that are created, developed, and modified within the context of lived human experience. Motivations, values, and objects of value are largely subjective. Valuations entail personal reflections (or interpretations) of worth, desirability, or importance that, in turn, are determined by way of reference to the experience of the valuing subject. One can value, for example, a "quality (or a practice) that gives worth, goodness, meaning, or a fulfilling character to the life a person is leading or aspiring to lead" (Lacey & Schwartz, 1996, p. 319). In other words, our values are often related to a life or lifestyle that we judge as personally and/or socially meaningful and fulfilling. Relatedly, what we value can be a "quality (or a practice) that is partially constitutive of a person's identity as a self-evaluating, a self-interpreting, a self-making being" (ibid.). In this respect, values become elements of identity, essential to the process of self-creation, development, and/or maintenance. Self-creation, in turn, can itself be a value or motivation, inclusive of related values such as freedom, autonomy, independence, and self-determination. In any case, what we value will often be a direct reflection of the ongoing struggles of our personal and social existence. These struggles, in turn, find embodiment in our valuations; our valuations are constitutive of our ethics; and our ethics ultimately manifest in our actions (or non-actions).

Values, then, can be regarded as "action-guiding principles" (Solomon, 1987, p. 93), informing and consequently reflected in our behaviors. "To choose a value is to act, in appropriate circumstances, on that choice; similarly, to act is to make value choices" (Bell, 1989, p. 114). Crucially, human behavior—including nonnormative behavior—provides us with some indication of the feelings, experiences, objects, and so forth that are valued by the acting subject, with some insight into what is valuable, worthy, and important to the acting subject. Human beings often value and thereby seek to attain what is experienced as absent, nurture what is in need of nurturance, maintain what is in need of maintenance, and eliminate what needs to be eliminated. In this respect, attending to the "ethics of crime" can potentially further our understanding of nonnormative behavior by offering insight into the struggles and experiences of criminal and deviant actors and groups. Likewise, understanding the struggles and experiences of criminal and deviant actors and groups can provide insight into how, why, and what values give rise to what ethics.

The portrait of nonnormative ethics explored in this chapter suggestively attends to one struggle in particular: that of *freedom*. We might understand all values to, ultimately, be grounded in freedom. On the one hand, values are products of (structured) choice, thereby partaking of freedom. More importantly, perhaps, freedom can be understood as "both the defining feature of human existence and its ethical ideal" (Arp, 2001, p. 7). Paralleling existentialist understandings, not only are human beings free to choose values and act in light of those values, but freedom becomes or can become *itself* an ideal to be attained, maintained, produced, and so on in experience. Consequently, freedom can itself be a commitment and motivation for human behavior, including behavior of a nonnormative nature. It is in this sense that freedom is itself simultaneously a value and the source of all (other) values (Sartre, 1956; see also Anderson, 1979; Detmer, 1988). As a source of values, we should be considerate of the ways in which other values (e.g., pleasure, friendship, material goods) are ultimately derived from the more generalized value of freedom. As a value itself, both normative and nonnormative behaviors become, in many instances, reflections of "the quest of freedom itself as such" (Sartre, 1973, p. 51).

Freedom as Experience; Freedom as Ethic

Both normative and nonnormative variations of human behavior can be understood from three perspectives: that of the acting *subject*; that of the *act itself*; and that of the *results* of the act (Balaban & Erev, 1995). Each perspective, though not necessarily exclusive, provides a different understanding of freedom as a value and, subsequently, of the embodiment of freedom in human motivation and behavior. Acting subjects, acts themselves, and results of acts each embody a different *idea* of freedom and *enable* a certain kind of freedom (ibid.). In other words, the meaning of freedom and the experience of freedom will be different, depending on whether importance is placed on the actor, act, or results of the act.

Each of these three perspectives can be thought of as valuing freedom in a slightly different sense, giving rise to behaviors in which freedom is experienced in different ways. If the freedom of the acting subject is of highest regard, significance lies in the experience of choice, independence, self-determination and self-constitution as affirmed through the acting subject herself or himself. If, on the other hand, the meaning and experience of freedom are embodied in the act itself, freedom *is* the act and the act *is* freedom. The ethics implied is an ethic of the act itself, wherein the act holds the possibility of the experience of freedom. Finally, if the meaning and experience of freedom are embodied in the consequences of human behavior, that behavior can be understood as a *means* to freedom or the experience of freedom. In the first two cases, human choice and human behavior are intrinsically valuable—they are ends in themselves. In the final case, human behavior is valuable only instrumentally—as a means to the end of freedom.

These three perspectives give rise to three different "ethics," each with freedom as its foundation and each giving rise to motivations that are linked to the experience of freedom. The meaning and experience of freedom, however, occur somewhat differently in each instance. From the first perspective (that of the human subject), the motivation for non-normative behavior is the experience of freedom in the form of moral self-determination or moral self-constitution (Balaban & Erev, 1995). While freedom remains the core value, its commitment and motivations are linked to freedom as experienced in choice. The ethic that emerges is one of *self-creation*, independent of (i.e., free from) structuring forces. Its sense of freedom is that experienced in the act of configuring oneself as an independent and self-chosen moral subject. Importantly, the resultant ethic stands largely independent of types and consequences of human behavior. In the more traditional language of ethics, it is neither an act-based nor a results-based ethics. It is, instead, closer to a Stoic ethic of self-government, with parallels to Kant's regard for autonomy and Nietzsche's concern for self-creation. The behaviors themselves and the consequences of those behaviors may be deemed immoral by conventional, normative standards. Yet conventional, normative standards are themselves forces that impede the self-creation of the subject. Important to this variation of the ethics of freedom is the experience and affirmation of one's freedom *from* forces that act to structure or impede the process of self-creation and self-determination. This form of freedom is best regarded as existential, approximating that alluded to by Sartre (1956). In relation to criminal and deviant behavior, the ethic in question might best be understood as an "underground ethic," committed to and motivated by freedom as experienced in the choice *not* to be ethical (by conventional standards, anyway).

The second perspective and its corresponding ethic bear on the meaning and experience of the act itself. Its commitment and motivations are to freedom as experienced in the active moment—the here and now. Motivated by physical or "spiritual" impulses, including curiosity, emotions, feelings, and the like (Balaban & Erev, 1995), its freedom lies in the experience of the act itself as an outlet for such impulses. Importantly, the behaviors in question carry their own merit—that is, they are irrespective of intentions, inclinations, and consequences. The acts are not a means to an end, but rather are ends in themselves. They represent activities undertaken for their own sake. The acts themselves are intrinsically valuable, deriving their value from the momentary experience of freedom accompanying the acts. Behaviors as seemingly disparate as burglaries, sexual deviations, BASE jumping, and auto theft are subsumed herein. To be sure, it is not uncommon to misrepresent such behaviors as motivated purely by pleasure; they are, in the ethical tradition of Aristippus and the Cyreniac School, understood as hedonistic—extracting their value from the sensual enjoyment produced by the act. While the acts themselves are indeed "pleasurable" in the common sense of the word, we might benefit from understanding their pleasure as a *derivative of the experience of freedom.* In other words, such activities are pleasurable *because* they are "freeing." In the context of deviant and criminal behaviors, this form of freedom is most closely related to the notion of deviance as "fun" (Riemer, 1981) and more generally that elaborated by Jack Katz (1988) in his *Seductions of Crime.* We can perhaps regard the ethic involved with this form of freedom as a "phenomenological ethic" or an "ethics of play."

Finally, human behavior can be understood from the perspective of its results; that is, it can be committed to certain ends, motivated by certain results. This perspective is perhaps most common in contemporary Western culture, often manifesting in various forms in sociological and criminological scholarship. The meaning and experience of freedom from this perspective is that which is brought about or *realized* as an end, the behaviors of which are merely means to the attainment of that end. In other words, criminal and deviant behaviors are *means to an end*, wherein the end is the experience of freedom (or some perceived increase in freedom). From this perspective, criminal and deviant behaviors might be understood as "transforming life into a means to life" (Balaban & Erev, 1995, p. 2). They are teleological in the traditional sense of being goal- or future-directed, where the end is an increase in positive freedom in the face of (subjectively) experienced constraints. Commitment is to the goal, and motivation is linked to the attainment of that goal. As such, the ethic that emerges from this perspective is less considerate of the means by which the goal is attained and the "morality" of the act or acts by any normative standards. Normative standards, in fact, may themselves be forces contributing to the experienced oppression and repression of the acting subject. In some such cases, it could be argued that nonnormative means are justified or even obligatory if the impeding or constraining forces are themselves immoral. Here, we might recall Dr. Martin Luther King Jr.'s (1963) appeal to the inherent morality of nonnormativity and the moral obligation to criminal action when normativity itself is immoral or unjust. For King, and within the lived experience of many others, the end is regarded as justifying the means, whether normative or defiantly nonnormative. The underlying ethic is one orchestrated around the *attainment* of freedom. In some ways, this ethic parallels popular explanations of criminal and deviant behavior as instrumental; that is, as motivated by the attainment of some desired consequence. Crucially, many such mainstream explanations focus on the attainment of material ends more than the attainment of freedom as an end. The latter, of course, may be attained *through* material ends but is conceptually independent of them. We might regard this ethic as an "ethic of transformation" or the "praxis of liberation" in the face of the lack of freedom. In the next three sections, I explore each of these three "ethics" in more detail.

The Underground Ethic: Freedom and the Choice *Not* to Be Ethical

The notion of the "underground ethic" reflects the embodiment and enablement of freedom in relation to the perspective of the acting subject. Less concerned with specific forms and consequences of behaviors, the freedom embodied in and enabled by the "underground ethic" is the freedom for self-constitution and self-determination. It is, in other words, a freedom organized around and experienced in the freedom of choice. Though most closely resembling the existential/ontological freedom espoused by Sartre, the relationship between freedom, ethics, and self-constitution was a central concern both for the Stoics and, much later, for Kant: "[o]n all sides I hear: 'Do not argue!' The officer says, 'Do not argue, drill!' The taxman says, 'do not argue, pay!' The pastor says, 'Do not argue, believe!' . . . in this we have examples of pervasive restrictions on freedom" (Kant, 1784/1983, p. 42).

For both Kant and the Stoics, much in the way of limitations on freedom are self-imposed; that is, we willfully submit to guidance from others and lack the courage to affirm our own freedom of choice (ibid.). For the Stoics, ethics was an exercise in self-examination—a critical, searching examination of one's culture and received values, beliefs, and so on. Ethics involves the development of the power of choice, the shaping and constructing of one's own soul, and the development of independence from the tyranny of convention (Nussbaum, 1994, pp. 316–358). Of course, both the Stoics and Kant emphasized the importance of reason in the exercise of choice and, to be sure, did not defend behaviors in violation of the law. Nonetheless, each recognized the interplay between ethics and freedom, between self-constitution and choice.

Somewhat closer to the notion of freedom in its "underground" form is Sartre's (1943, 1956) treatment of existential or ontological freedom. Sartre draws from Kantian concerns for the relationship between autonomy, self-legislation, and freedom while downplaying the Kantian emphasis on reason (e.g., Crowell, 2003). For Sartre, existential or ontological freedom is shared by and, consequently, available to experience for everyone, irrespective of situation. Sartre was concerned with human existence "as such"—independent of material considerations. In this regard, he argued, human beings are unconditionally free. Of course human existence—particularly *social* existence—imposes constraints on certain forms of freedom. Within these constraints, however, lies a human subject that is ultimately free in another sense; namely, in her or his capacity to choose and, thus, experience freedom through and within that choice. In noting that "freedom is the being of man" (Sartre, 1943, p. 516), Sartre is offering that human existence is *in itself* characterized by an unlimited, unrestricted, always present freedom that exists independently from and irrespective of the constraints of material reality.

In other words, regardless of what are usually perceived as limitations on freedom, human beings always retain the freedom to choose. No one and no thing can *force* choices upon them. While choices may be limited—sometimes substantially—human beings always enjoy a certain unbounded freedom that is contained within choice.

Notwithstanding the fondness of human beings for authority—"it is always easier to follow than to stand on one's own" (Nussbaum, 1994, p. 345)—choice can be an affirmative experience. Irrespective of actions that follow from choices, or the consequences that follow from those actions, the experience of freedom of choice is itself an affirmative experience. It is in this sense that the freedom of choice, or the experience of freedom in the act of choice, can reflect a commitment, valuation, motivation and, thus, an ethic. In the context of the "underground ethic" developed in the remainder of this section, the freedom at issue might be understood as the very choice to be ethical or, better stated, the *choice not to be ethical*. This idea of freedom implicates the experience of purposively deviating from convention, of choosing one's own values, of refusing to succumb to expectations, laws, rules, structures, and the like. In this deviation and refusal, one becomes a self-constituted, self-determined being. Free from the bounds of normativity, one becomes free to fashion oneself.

Much as being "ethical" by normative standards requires that one choose and commit oneself to normative principles (or selected virtues, consequences), one might equally choose or commit oneself to nonnormativity. One can choose *not* to be ethical or, perhaps, choose the unethical. One can choose amorality, immorality, or a "higher morality" that stands contrary to normative conceptions. If ethics is, in some sense, the practice of freedom (Foucault, 1997, p. 282), the choice to be ethical or unethical, moral, amoral, or immoral, is itself a practice of or exercise in freedom. The unethical, amoral, or immoral becomes itself an ethic or, better stated, an affirmation of freedom through ethical choice.

The unethical, we might say, is an ethic of affirmation in the sense that it affirms one's existential/ontological freedom through the exercise of choice—the choice *not* to submit to conventional moral structures. Normative ethical frameworks, inclusive of traditional virtues, categorical imperatives, and expectations of utility, can be experienced as diminishing one's freedom to choose to be otherwise. Consequently, it is to "choose to be unethical by celebrating one's ontological freedom by self-consciously rejecting all standards whatsoever" (Arp, 2001, pp.

93–94). The choice to be unethical is a choice inspired by the demand for freedom from *imposed* values. It is, in some ways, a nihilistic ethic where, following Turgenev's Arkady in *Fathers and Sons*, nihilism describes she or he "who does not bow down before any authority, who does not take any principle on faith, whatever reverence that principle is enshrined in" (quoted in Solomon, 1987, p. 90). For Nietzsche, such an attitude or, we could say, ethic is essential to a genuine, authentic human life. "Becoming who you are" is an ethical imperative for human beings; an imperative to pursue one's *own* virtue (Solomon, 1987). It is an ethic constituting "a reaction against the *'tyranny'* of reason and the authority of the church, morality, and 'the herd' in their disdain for 'the individual'" (ibid., 91).

For Barnes (1968), the choice of the unethical represents one of several possible ethical stances. While it may well be an ethical stance that is harmful to self and/or others and unethical or immoral by prevailing standards, it is nonetheless a stance that can be authentic. Authenticity in this sense does not imply any judgment or attachment of ethical value to the content of the choice that is made. It recognizes, rather, that the act of choice itself is an authentic exercise in the realization of one's freedom—it is to accept one's freedom and one's capacity for ethical choice rather than fleeing one's freedom by allowing others (e.g., religion, law) to choose *for* one. While not necessarily supportive of ethical subjectivism, the "ethic" at issue is certainly tied to it. Rejecting all authority, all values—imposed or otherwise—implies a rejection of anything posing a threat to one's subjectivity (Groves & Newman, 1983). Science, religion, law, or societal demands of reason, prudence, and the like are each forces diminishing human freedom and the subjective sense that one is free from structuring influences. As Bergmann noted, "The idea of being totally unbounded, of yielding to no authority whatever (not even that of reason), of acting without any encumbrances—that image seems close to the root-experience of freedom" (1977, p. 18). And while, as Sartre (1956) offered, many may flee this experience in the face of its anguish, there is some level at which the "root-experience" of freedom, at least for some persons, is an experienced need. It is a need to experience that "I" am the originator, beyond any structuring or determining influences, of my choices.

In this respect, we might understand the "ethic of the unethical" to be an "underground ethic," as the choice not to be ethical is perhaps best exemplified by Dostoyevsky's Underground Man (Dostoyevsky, 1960; see Barnes, 1968, pp. 3–28 on the Underground Man and the choice not to be ethical). Arguably, above all else, the Underground Man cherishes and celebrates his freedom not to be ethical: "He does not have to justify himself, he is not obliged to choose happiness or any other self-evident good. He chooses independence of all regulating value systems" (Barnes, 1968, p. 19). While his choice, one might argue, threatens other forms of freedom that he may otherwise enjoy (e.g., freedom from illness), it is the ultimate affirmation of his ontological or existential freedom—his freedom to choose. In choosing independence of all values not issuing from within himself, the Underground Man seeks release from the causal chain (Groves & Newman, 1983). He can avoid determination of choice by causal influences and, consequently, affirm through experience the ontological freedom characteristic of being human. By recognizing and embracing this freedom—despite the consequences of any choice he may make with that freedom—the Underground Man is authentic. He thus resists the demand to be inauthentic that pervades the social realm.

The Underground Man is not, to be sure, an egoist in the true sense of the concept. He is not rightfully regarded as a hedonist. Rather, his only motive for action is freedom itself: "And how do these wiseacres know that man wants a normal, virtuous choice? What has made them conceive that man must want a rationally advantageous choice? What man wants is simply *independent* choice, whatever that independence may cost and wherever it may lead" (Dostoyevsky, 1992, pp. 17–18). In this sense, freedom *is* a motive; it *is* a chosen value and, thus, an ethic by which the Underground Man lives his life. Although his choices may not be advantageous and may not lead to pleasurable consequences, the advantage and pleasure lie in the experience of freedom itself. The Underground Man *chooses* freedom as his sole value so that, with this freedom, he might retain the capacity for choice.

In his choice, the Underground Man is authentic. Like the choice to be ethical, it is a choice issuing from one's recognition and acceptance of one's own freedom. And like the choice to be ethical, "it recognizes that the decision to justify one's life derives from one's own spontaneous desire and is not imposed from the outside" (Barnes, 1968, p. 19). In avoiding conventional justifications and the values accompanying those justifications, the Underground Man chooses to justify his life through realization, reflection, and choice of his own freedom. As Barnes continues, "it is freedom itself which he chooses as the value so far beyond all others that he pits it against all possible values which might in the future result from submitting this freedom to any sort of calculated restriction, external or internal" (ibid.). Ontological freedom—the freedom to choose—is his only value. It is his only ethic.

As an ethic underlying nonnormative behavior, the "underground ethic" in no way excuses or justifies criminal and deviant activities. On the contrary, it offers that the choice to *not* conform to normative standards can be affirmative. As freely choosing human beings, of course, the existentialists above all others emphasize our responsibility for our choices. Yet the affirmation of one's freedom to choose by rejecting any and all imposed standards, norms, values, and so forth is an affirmation of one's freedom to constitute, determine, and create oneself independent of imposing and intrusive forces. Such forces can be psychological (e.g., guilt), moral (e.g., duty), religious (e.g., imposed values), social (e.g., obligatory cultural goals), and so on. In each case, self-creation is a way of life that necessitates rejection of structural influences on all levels. Alternative sexualities, homelessness, and other nonnormative engagements can be affirmative to the degree that they are chosen. This is not to suggest that one's choice or choices cannot be consistent with normative standards or those imposed by determining influences, only that they are made in the absence of them (i.e., with freedom from such forces). The choice not to be ethical, then, is not necessarily a commitment to nonnormativity for the sake of nonnormativity (this, in itself, can be normative by alternative standards); rather, the choice not to be ethical is simply a commitment to the continued affirmation of one's freedom to choose.

The affirmative dynamic of freedom and choice as exemplified by the Underground Man has rarely found its way into criminological literatures. To be sure, the concept of choice itself has a storied history in criminology, spanning from Bentham and Beccaria through neoclassicists, economists of crime, and postclassical rational choice theorists. This strain of theorizing understands human beings to be free-willed, rational, choice-making beings. Within this tradition, however, choice is almost always linked to teleological (largely instrumental) motives; that is, in traditional criminological theory, the concept of choice emerges as an element of a process wherein criminals are rationally attracted to nonnormative actions for the rewards that those actions bring. Rarely, however, has this same literature on choice and nonnormativity advanced the act of choice as itself such a reward. Indeed, as the Underground Man illustrates, choice itself can be intrinsically rewarding. It is here, perhaps, where criminology could benefit from a reconsideration of the ways in which choice informs behavior and, more specifically, the commitment to, valuation of, preference for, and motivation toward criminal and deviant behavior.

The Ethic of Play: Freedom as Dissolution

In contemporary Western societies, the idea of play stands in contrast to that of work, the latter often being routine and rational and the former enabling the sensual, creative, emotional, and spontaneous impulses of human nature. In some sense, play is a psychological and spiritual necessity. Play represents an escape, a temporary dissolution of the rational self, a moment of freedom from the oppressive encumbrances of order, regularity, and rule. Play is an event whose purpose is the event; an experience whose goal is the experience.

Play embodies and enables freedom from the second of our three perspectives—that of the act itself. Less concerned with self-constitution and self-determination, and less concerned with consequences, the freedom embodied in and enabled by play is the freedom experienced in the nonnormative act itself. The "ethic of play" is an ethic entailing commitment to and valuation of experiential freedom, not so much in choice as in human activity. Like the "underground ethic," the "ethic of play" embodies and enables freedom from that which is perceived as constraining, limiting, and structuring. It does not resist such forces, however, so much as it dissolves them in moments of freedom. The forces of constraint might be understood as "boundaries" that serve as limitations to the experience of freedom or, on a conscious level, to the experience of the sensual, emotional, visceral pleasure that accompanies playful events. In the context of criminal and deviant behavior, the "ethic of play" encourages us to attend to the "immediate, experiential dynamics of deviance and criminality" (Ferrell, Milovanovic, & Lyng, 2001, p. 178). It is within the immediate, experiential dynamics of nonnormative behaviors that is contained the possibility of the dissolution of such boundaries—however ephemeral the resulting freedom may be.

In *Being and Nothingness*, Sartre (1956, p. 581) proposes that play, "which has freedom for its foundation and its goal, deserves a special study which . . . belongs . . . to an *Ethics.*" Of especial importance is the relationship between freedom and play. Namely, "play" is coincidental to the experience of freedom in that it is within play or "playful" behavior that one experiences and realizes freedom. Sartre contrasted play to the behavior of the "serious man," for whom the "spirit of seriousness" is an attempt to give oneself a consistent, inert existence akin to that of a rock (Bell, 1989). The "spirit of seriousness" characterizes she or he who is always concerned with consequences, who "at bottom is hidden from himself the consciousness of his freedom; he is in bad faith . . . everything is a consequence for him, and there is never any beginning" (Sartre, 1956, p. 580). Play is that state within which human beings are fully cognizant of their freedom and enjoy their freedom. "What is play," Sartre offers, "if not an activity of which man is the first origin, for which man himself sets the rules . . . as soon as man apprehends himself as free and wishes to use his freedom . . . then his activity is play" (1956, pp. 580–581). It is at play where freedom is both experienced and disclosed. Play is "a rapture with the spirit of seriousness . . . passage to the festive side. The festival in effect is liberation from the spirit of seriousness" (Sartre quoted in Bell, 1989, p. 113).

Play can then be understood as constitutive of those behaviors wherein freedom is both the foundation and goal (Bell, 1989). At play, freedom is not so much a means but an end in itself. Human beings play with their freedom and simultaneously play to experience their freedom. Play is not instrumental; it is not undertaken in light of some external reward. Rather, play is itself the reward; play is itself the commitment and motivation. The experience of freedom—however ephemeral—is itself experientially rewarding and itself a motivation for human activity, including forms of deviance and criminality. By recognizing nonnormative events as "play," we acknowledge that certain forms and occasions of deviant and criminal activity are largely sensual, emotional, creative, and spontaneous behaviors where the goal is the activity itself. Contrary to much criminological tradition that seeks intricate explanations for nonnormativity that often include a variety of instrumental motives, treating crime and deviance as "play" regards such activity as largely divorced from any external, independent goal. Deviance is not a means to some identifiable end but, rather, *is itself* the end.

The notion of crime and deviance as "play" has surfaced intermittently throughout the history of criminological discourse. Matza and Sykes, for example, offered an implicit link between criminal behavior and an ethic of play in proposing that delinquent values are "closely akin to those embodied in the leisure activities of the dominant society" (1961, p. 712). What makes deviance attractive is the experience of excitement and thrill standing over and against the "mundane and routine patterns of behavior" that characterize the workaday world (ibid.). In this respect, much criminal behavior is demonstrably nonutilitarian; that is, much criminality expresses less concern with the attainment of material ends than with the sensual, emotional, and visceral pleasures embodied by the playful acts themselves. Albert Cohen (1955), as well, had suggested that vandalism was often a means of play more than a pursuit of material ends.

More recently, Riemer (1981) employs a similar logic in regarding some forms of crime and deviance as "pleasure of the moment" activities. Vandalism, various forms of sexual deviance, drug use, shoplifting, auto theft, and other deviant and criminal activities can oftentimes be understood without reference to intricate incentive-based explanations. Rather, in many cases, the essential consideration is the inherent pleasure that such behaviors entail. The material gains of shoplifting, auto theft, or burglary, for example, may be a secondary consideration to the "playfulness" with which these events are undertaken. They are events "grounded in the emotional and the visceral, the immediacy of excitement" that they bring (Ferrell, Milovanovic, & Lyng, 2001).

Perhaps the most celebrated analysis along these lines is that by Jack Katz (1988). In attending to the phenomenological dimension of crime, Katz poignantly noted that instrumental (i.e., rational) motives are often secondary to the sensual and emotional "attractions" of the act itself (O'Malley & Mugford, 1994). Crime is understood as enabling "transcendence," whereby one "plays with" thresholds in experiencing the self in all its subjectivity (ibid.). Within moments of nonnormativity, the actor loses awareness of boundaries—boundaries become dissolved in moments of freedom. Such boundaries can consist, on the ontological level, as demarcations of the known from the unknown, real from unreal, conscious from unconscious, and so forth. O'Malley and Mugford implicate, in particular, the divisions "central to modern culture," including that "between body and mind, emotion and reason, chaos and order" (1994, p. 195). This boundary crossing or boundary dissolution provides the seductive appeal of criminal and deviant activities.

During the activity itself, the actor is free in the sense of her or his immunity from constraining forces, be they ontological, moral, psychological, financial, or otherwise (Halleck, 1967). As well, such behaviors often call for the agent to employ talents, faculties, abilities, and so forth that may receive little attention elsewhere (ibid.). To this degree, nonnormative behaviors can be experienced as self-realizing, self-actualizing, and self-determining (O'Malley & Mugford, 1994). Lyng exemplifies the latter in describing the experiential element of "edgework" as "the direct antithesis of that under conditions of alienation and reification" (1990, p. 878; see also 1993, 1998). When "behavior is not coerced by the normative or structural constraints of their social environment" (ibid.), people experience a sense of self-actualization, a sense of authorship, and a corresponding sense of freedom.

The necessary adoption of "play" and "transcendence" as ethical prescriptions was also a theme running throughout German Romantic philosophy, as well as that of Nietzsche. Campbell suggests in reference to the Romantic spirit that self "requires expression through release and the overthrow of constraints, necessarily imposing as a duty the pursuit of exciting, pleasurable and stimulating experiences" (1983, p. 287). "Duty" is an especially interesting choice of terms, implying a deontological pre- scription for an ethics of play. In addition to its motivational dimension, playful deviance and criminality may be commitments and valuations. More directly, crime and deviance can be motivated by a commitment to and valuation of momentary transgressions that carry the "pleasur- able" experience of freedom. Problematically, normative behaviors and events carrying the experience or realization of freedom are not equally available to all. Consequently, we should expect to find criminal and deviant alternatives to normative experiences in cases where the experi- encing agent is largely or, to some subjective extent, generally "cut off" from normative possibilities. The "ethics of play" assumes sociological import in this context, whether in reference to the modernization and mechanization of social life, pervasive social inequalities, or simply the plethora of moral forces serving as mechanisms of formal and informal social control. In any case, the *possibility* of "play" as a normative event and, consequently, the experience of freedom through such events is dangerously limited by forces largely beyond the control of the individ- ual actor. Nonnormative engagements become attractive and seductive alternatives where normative possibilities are constrained.

The Ethic of Transformation: Unfreedom and the Praxis of Liberation

The third and final ethic deriving from the commitment to and valua- tion of freedom can be described as an ethic of transformation. The ethic of transformation reflects the embodiment and enablement of freedom in relation to the third of the three perspectives outlined above—the results of the act. Freedom appears as something enabled through or by way of nonnormativity. In distinction from both the "underground ethic" and the "ethic of play," emphasis is placed less on the embodiment and enablement of freedom in either choice or the act itself. Rather, the ethic of transformation encourages us to conceive of freedom as something to be attained by way of nonnormativity. In other words, criminal and deviant behavior can be a means to an end, wherein the end is freedom (or, at least, freedom as subjectively experienced). While the "end" in question is not the "common good" of utilitarianism, the ethic of transformation resembles traditional teleological or consequentialist ethical formulations. Concern for choice and action become secondary considerations to desired consequences.

Dostoyevsky's Underground Man was previously described as representing a dramatic exemplar of ontological freedom and choice as they inform ethics. Crime and deviance, however, cannot in the majority of cases be understood strictly within the context of the dramatic ideal of existential freedom that was discussed as the ultimate value for the Underground Man. Of significance are the *conditions* under which the choice of nonnormativity constitutes an attractive choice. The "ethic of transformation" appeals to circumstances under which one might choose nonnormativity. In its consideration of such circumstances, the ethic of transformation begs a related concern for the conditions under which one might experience freedom as *challenged.* The choice of freedom as a guiding value becomes understood, in many cases, as a reflection of the experience of freedom as *potential* more than as reality (Groves & Newman, 1983). In the face of certain spiritual and/or material conditions, "freedom can be reduced to no more than a suppressed potentiality" (Kruks, 1990, p. 98). In other words, it becomes necessary to choose freedom as a value—to exercise the choice to be unethical or the choice of nonnormativity—if and when one's subjective experience is that of the absence, constraint, and/or limitation of freedom. Simply put, the experience of unfreedom can lead one to resolve such constraints or limitations by valuing freedom as something to be attained—whether normatively or otherwise.

The sense in which freedom can be constrained or limited is the sense in which freedom is positive, "effective" (Kruks, 1990), "practical" (Groves & Newman, 1983), or alternatively called "power" (Beauvoir, 1991). Positive freedom refers to a condition of liberation from impeding social and cultural forces (Blackburn, 1994, p. 146) and a corresponding capacity to act upon the world according to the desires of one's will (i.e., rational, free choice). Yet positive freedom exists as a matter of degree; that is, it is conditional, contingent upon external forces or circumstances (i.e., one's situation). The experienced negativity of certain social and cultural conditions is an experienced limitation on positive freedom—on power—more than ontological freedom. The two senses of freedom (ontological, positive) should be understood as interrelated and, perhaps, interdependent in that deprivations of power impinge upon the experience of ontological freedom. Though choice is ultimately retained in the ontological sense, the experienced availability of choices is subject to limitation (e.g., Arp, 2001). In *The Second Sex* (1989), for example, Simone de Beauvoir draws upon this distinction in suggesting that women, in the face of patriarchal oppression, retain ontological freedom while being deprived of positive freedom or power. Notwithstanding the oppressed status of women in both historical and contemporary cultural contexts, women theoretically retain their essential or ontological freedom. Experientially, however, the limited nature of positive freedom is problematic. The relative absence of positive freedom (i.e., freedom from restraint, autonomy) substantially limits the degree to which freedom can be meaningfully experienced and linked to an autonomous, self-determined personal, social, and cultural existence.

Power (effective, practical, positive freedom), then, becomes essentially wedded to human activity in its relationship to freedom. While ontological freedom may, theoretically, be absolute and unconstrained, freedom is most often experienced as limited by natural and social boundaries. In this sense, the experience of unfreedom is best understood as inclusive of limitations on the transition from choice to *action*. Action might be regarded as ontological freedom realizing itself. That is to say, ontological freedom is affirmed in experience only through action whereby one's choice is realized in practice (Groves & Newman, 1983). It is power that "is an expansion of the field of possible actions which are open to existential [ontological] freedom; it consists of the removal of limitations to the projects men may choose from" (p. 29).

In this respect, power is linked to human motivation. Exercising positive freedom or power is an exercise in affirming the existence and availability of choice. Activity directed toward the attainment of positive freedom, in turn, represents an exercise in the "opening up" of available choices, thereby creating possibilities for choice and the experience of freedom that were previously unavailable. In the context of human motivation, the realization of power can then be understood as transformative in that it exposes theretofore unavailable possibilities for the experience of freedom. The transformative nature of power is one of becoming free, rather than being free. In its link to nonnormativity, the realization of power through transformative activity might be regarded as an exercise in praxis—in purposeful activity whereby such activity is directed toward the liberation of the self from forces perceived to be restrictive. For Aristotle, praxis was simply human goal-directed activity. For Sartre, praxis refers to moments of activity that are purposive, meaningful, in short, "any meaningful or purposeful activity" (Novac, 1966, p. xvii). At the most basic level, the "meaningfulness" of praxis lies in its negation of negation (Craib, 1976, p. 108). Praxis is most essentially an attempt to negate or overcome the negativities (i.e., restraints, barriers) of human experience. Overcoming experienced negativities is, in itself, an affirmative experience. In this respect, praxis can be understood as an affirmation of human freedom through the negation or overcoming of experienced constraints encountered within social and cultural existence.

In an important sense, negativity is absence, lack, or, rather, the subjective experience of absence or lack. In the context of human freedom, it is freedom, choice, or possibility itself that is experienced as absent or lacking. As an exercise in overcoming experienced lack or attaining, in experience, that which is absent, praxis consists in endeavors or activities that carry transformative potential. This, in turn, is where praxis becomes revolutionary in the sense that Marx used the term. Praxis is powerful in that it allows human consciousness to participate in the construction of its own experience. Praxis is an instrument whereby human activity offers the possibility of effecting meaningful change *en route* to realizing that which is experienced as absent or from which human beings experience a sense of alienation. Praxis, in short, is teleological, characterized as purposive action on the world, and revolutionary in that it holds transformative potential. Returning to the ethic of transformation, we might conceptualize such an ethic as one that values and is committed to purposive activities that carry transformative potential. Transformative, in this respect, refers to the overcoming of the experienced lack of freedom, choice, and possibility. Crucially, *becoming free* can be accomplished either through social transformation or personal transformation. In the absence of possibilities for social transformation, nonnormative or criminal activities might be understood as personal transformative endeavors.

The ethic of transformation in the context of criminal and deviant activities closely parallels Marx's criminal. Marx's criminal is one engaged in such a "struggle of the isolated individual against prevailing conditions" (Marx & Engels, 1976, p. 367). While criminal and deviant behaviors are not always conscious forms of *political* rebellion, they are often forms of rebellion or resistance nonetheless (e.g., Taylor, Walton, & Young, 1973; Groves & Newman, 1983). Nonnormative behaviors might be understood as adaptations to circumstances that are perceived as intolerable in light of the constraints they impose on individual (positive) freedom. Criminal and deviant activities might then be understood as situated forms of resistance or situated praxis. The transformation toward the realization of positive freedom that is understood as a characteristic feature of some forms and instances of crime and deviance assume that form in such instances only in light of the absence of experienced alternatives. Crime and deviance become choices where choice comes upon experienced limits.

The notion of crime as adaptation has a storied history in criminology. Perhaps most notably, Merton (1938) offered that crime is a form of innovative adaptation to the coupling of desires and imposed limitations. In a more humanistic tone, Halleck (1967) offered that crime is an adaptation to oppression or, more accurately, an adaptation to the subjectively experienced helplessness which results from oppression. While oppression can be subjective in its origin (e.g., guilt), it is more importantly objective in its origin. The objective origins of oppression include such things as social climate (e.g., racism), social conditions (e.g., poverty), and parental control. In short, objective oppression is rooted in one's social and cultural location. Though one needn't be impoverished, for example, to subjectively experience oppression, what the oppressed have in common is being "cut off from having a future, for it is the future that . . . gives meaning to . . . present existence" (Arp, 2001, p. 116). The oppressed individual is she or he who is "robbed of many possibilities for action" (ibid., 117) and, in this regard, lacks power and, through the absence of power, lacks the experience of ontological freedom. Criminal and deviant engagements, in turn, can be attractive forms of adaptation to such conditions. While Halleck (1967) acknowledges others (e.g., activism, conformity, mental illness), crime is likely to be chosen as a form of adaptation when opportunities or possibilities for other forms are blocked (e.g., one for whom activism is a situational impossibility).

Criminal and deviant behaviors, then, can be affirmative choices where choice is limited by social and cultural circumstances.

Summary

Notwithstanding recent efforts to juxtapose traditional ethical concepts and arguments alongside concerns and controversies arising within the field of criminology, scholars of the latter have rarely attempted to use the philosophy of ethics to examine the phenomenon of crime itself; that is, while ethics and criminology are increasingly wedded in textbooks, courses, seminars, and scholarly analyses, criminologists have yet to effectively integrate the philosophy of ethics into the theoretical study of crime. My intent in this chapter was to explore the possibility of an ethics of crime; that is, the possibility that many forms and instances of nonnormative behavior might be better understood with reference to some underlying "ethic" or conceptual foundation that relies upon ethical theory. The resulting ethics of nonnormativity is not an "ethics" in the conventional sense. It is not virtue-based, deontological, nor purely utilitarian in its theoretical foundations. Rather, the somewhat unconventional examination of crime in ethical terms seems to require an equally unconventional approach to ethics itself. In this light, I have offered that such an exploration might benefit from attention to one human commitment, value, preference, and motivation: that of freedom. An ethics of freedom, in turn, arguably gives rise to an ethics of crime and deviance that has freedom as its foundation and its goal.

Accordingly, I have attempted to lay out a suggestive framework wherein deviant and criminal behaviors represent embodiments of or attempts to embody the commitment to, valuation of, preference for, and/or motivation toward freedom (consciously or otherwise). The foundational premise of this framework is that freedom itself can be and often is a commitment, value, preference, and motivation guiding human behavior and, further, that deviant and criminal behaviors often reflect, either through choice or action, the commitment to, valuation of, preference for, and motivation toward freedom.

Both conceptually and experientially, however, freedom is complex and multifaceted. At least some of this complexity might be addressed by accounting for different types, experiences, and conceptualizations of freedom. Through the framework outlined in this chapter I have attempted to confront, however provisionally, some of this complexity by offering a threefold characterization of freedom, wherein each of three perspectives from which to understand human behavior offers a different conceptual starting point and experiential basis for human freedom, thereby giving rise to three interrelated ethics of nonnormativity. Accordingly, the commitment to, valuation of, preference for, and motivation toward freedom might emerge in the experience of choice (existential ethic of freedom), the act itself (phenomenological ethic of freedom), and/or the consequences of the act (teleological ethic of freedom). In the context of an ethics of crime and deviance, an ethic of freedom might manifest in the choice to be criminal or deviant, the experience of the criminal or deviant act, or the consequences that criminal and deviant acts bring. My intent in this chapter, however, was not to outline *the* ethics of crime and deviance; rather, it was to demonstrate the value or potential value of ethics for understanding—though not necessarily explaining—crime and deviance.

References

Anderson, T. (1979). *The foundation and structure of Sartrean ethics.* Lawrence: Regents Press of Kansas.

Arp, K. (2001). *The bonds of freedom: Simone de Beauvoir's existentialist ethics.* Chicago: Open Court.

Balaban, O., & Erev, A. (1995). *The bounds of freedom: About Eastern and Western approaches to freedom.* New York: Peter Lang.

Barnes, H. (1968). *An existentialist ethics.* New York: Alfred A. Knopf.

Beauvoir, S. (1989). *The second sex.* New York: Vintage Books.

———. (1991). *The ethics of ambiguity.* New York: Carol Publishing Group.

Beccaria, C. (1953). *An essay on crimes and punishments.* Stanford, CA: Stanford University Press.

Bell, L. (1989). *Sartre's ethics of authenticity.* Tuscaloosa: University of Alabama Press.

Bentham, J. (1970). *An introduction to the principles of morals and legislation.* London: Athlone Press.

Bergmann, F. (1977). *On being free.* Notre Dame: University of Notre Dame Press.

Blackburn, S. (1994). *The Oxford dictionary of philosophy.* New York: Oxford University Press.

Campbell, C. (1983). Romanticism and the consumer ethic: Intimations of a Weber-style thesis. *Sociological Analysis, 44,* 279–296.

Cohen, A. (1955). *Delinquent boys: The culture of the gang.* Glencoe, IL: Free Press.

Craib, I. (1976). *Existentialism and sociology.* Cambridge: Cambridge University Press.

Crowell, S. (2003). Kantianism and phenomenology. In E. Wyschogrod & G. McKenny (eds.), *The ethical.* Malden, MA: Blackwell.

Detmer, D. (1988). *Freedom as value: A critique of the ethical theory of Jean-Paul Sartre.* LaSalle, IL: Open Court.

Dostoyevsky, F. (1960). *Notes from the underground.* R. Matlaw (trans.). New York: Dutton and Co.

———. (1992). *Notes from the underground.* New York: Dover.

Ferrell, J., Milovanovic, D., & Lyng, S. (2001). Edgework, media practices, and the elongation of meaning: A theoretical ethnography of the Bridge Day event. *Theoretical Criminology, 5*(2), 177–202.

Foucault, M. (1997). *Ethics: Subjectivity and truth.* P. Rabinow (ed.). New York: New Press.

Groves, B., & Newman, G. (1983). Marx, Sartre, and the resurrection of choice in theoretical criminology. *Israel Studies in Criminology, 6,* 173–192. Reprinted in G. Newman, M. Lynch, & D. Galaty (eds.), *Discovering criminology: From W. Byron Groves.* New York: Harrow and Heston, 1993.

Halleck, S. (1967). *Psychiatry and the dilemmas of crime.* New York: Harper and Row.

Kant, I. (1784 [1983]). An answer to the question: What is enlightenment? In *Perpetual peace and other essays.* T. Humphrey (trans.). Indianapolis: Hackett.

Katz, J. (1988). *Seductions of crime: Moral and sensual attractions in doing evil.* New York: Basic Books.

King, M. L., Jr. (1963). *Letter from a Birmingham jail.* New York: Harper Collins.

Kruks, S. (1990). *Situation and human existence.* London: Unwin Hyman.

Lacey, H., & Schwartz, B. (1996). The formation and transformation of values. In W. O'Donohue & R. Kitchener (eds.), *The philosophy of psychology.* Thousand Oaks: Sage.

Lyng, S. (1990). Edgework: A social psychological analysis of voluntary risk taking. *American Journal of Sociology, 95* (4), 876–921.

———. (1993). Dysfunctional risk taking: Criminal behavior as edgework. In N. Bell & R. Bell (eds.), *Adolescent risk taking.* Newbury Park, CA: Sage.

———. (1998). Dangerous methods: Risk taking and the research process. In J. Ferrell & M. Hamm (eds.), *Ethnography at the edge.* Boston: Northeastern University Press.

Marx, K., & Engels, F. (1976). *The German ideology.* New York: International Publishers.

Matza, D. (1964). *Delinquency and drift.* New York: John Wiley.

Matza, D., & Sykes, G. (1961). Juvenile delinquency and subterranean values. *American Sociological Review, 26*(5), 712–719.

Merton, R. (1938). Social structure and anomie. *American Sociological Review, 3,* 672–682.

Novac, G. (1966). *Existentialism and human existence*. London: Unwin Hyman.

Nussbaum, M. (1994). *The therapy of desire: theory and practice in Hellenistic ethics*. Princeton, NJ: Princeton University Press.

O'Malley, P., & Mugford, S. (1994). Crime, excitement, and modernity. In G. Barak (ed.), *Varieties of criminology: Readings from a dynamic discipline* (pp. 189–211). Westport, CT: Praeger.

Pollock, J. (1994). *Ethics in crime and justice: Dilemmas and decisions* (2nd ed.). Belmont, CA: Wadsworth.

Riemer, J. W. (1981). Deviance as fun. *Adolescence, 16*, 39–43.

Sartre, J. (1943). *L'etre et le néant*. Paris: Gallimard.

———. (1956). *Being and nothingness*. H. Barnes (trans.). New York: Pocket Books.

———. (1957). *Existentialism and human emotions*. New York: Wisdom Library.

———. (1973). *Existentialism and humanism*. London: Eyre Methuen.

Solomon, R. (1987). *From Hegel to existentialism*. New York: Oxford University Press.

Taylor, L., Walton, P., & Young, J. (1973). *The new criminology*. London: Routledge.

SIX

Ethics of Edgework: Spinoza, Nietzsche, and Deleuze

DRAGAN MILOVANOVIC

Edgeworkers provide the opportunity for engaging in expanded ethical discussion in justice studies. Edgework deals with non-materialistic expressions of motivation and how they account for or otherwise explain crime. Several forms of motivation along these lines include adrenalin rushes, visceral excitements, sneaky thrills, and emotional highs. Deleuze's synthesis of the ethics of Nietzsche and Spinoza—for Nietzsche, an ethic of activity, for Spinoza, an ethic of joyfulness—has provided innovative concepts for an understanding of those who engage in edgework activity. This chapter, accordingly, will first spell out a Deleuzian informed ethic. Second, we will apply this to nonnormative activity of the edgeworker, particularly in light of Chris Williams's three "ethics of freedom" (see chapter 5 of this volume).

The importance of this exercise is in developing a conceptual framework that privileges difference, collective development, change, and ongoing metamorphosis. Edgeworkers provide an instance where dualisms are transcended.[1] We witness a reunification of body-mind, the loci from which lines of flight are reenergized. These can be studied for how they put into nonlinear resonance what we have termed COREL sets (historically contingent, relatively autonomous configurations of coupled iterative loops). We are also sensitive to the emergences of both positive and negative outcomes illuminated by a genealogical analysis (schizoanalysis) that is ever vigilant to possible negative emergent forms. This study stresses an ethics of difference, individuation, and productive collective development. The edgeworker contributes insight into how these may materialize.

Deleuzian Synthesis on Ethics and Situating the Phenomenon of Edgework

A Deleuzian ethics is based on Spinoza's initial question concerning "what a body can do."[2] Become active, become joyful, following Nietzsche and Spinoza, is the guiding principle in developing an answer. This can be first conceptualized as the relation between the will to power and forces (table 6.1) and then reconceptualized in Deleuzian discourse as the relation between positive and negative forms of deterritorialization (table 6.2). We would like to show how edgework can be situated within these spaces. We will then move onto an engagement with Williams's "three ethics of freedom."

Nietzsche's Will to Power and Forces: Toward a Critical Ethics

In developing an ethics of edgework, we may briefly examine Deleuze's (1983) rendition of Nietzsche's will to power and forces. In this schematization, forces and the will to power are qualities that may have, respectively, active or reactive, and affirmative and negative developments. Ranging both, we can develop a four-way typology in constructing "ideal types" (see table 6.1). Genealogical analysis, sensitive to nuance, is necessary to provide concrete historical understanding of the specific configurations in existence.[3]

The first dimension concerns forces. Nietzsche's ontology assumes dynamic forces existing. The universe is composed of "dynamic quanta" in relation to other dynamic quanta (Nietzsche, 1994, para. 635; Hardt,

Table 6.1. Nietzsche: Will to Power and Forces

| | | Forces | |
		Active	Reactive
Will to Power	Affirmative	Affirmative-active: affirming; becoming; becoming-other; eternal return; boundary transcendance	Affirmative-reactive: overcoming; mechanical and utilitarian accommodations; boundaries maintained
	Negative	Negative-active: self-destruction; completed nihilism; active destruction; transmutation	Negative-reactive: nihilism; will to nothingness; ressentiment; bad conscience; ascetic ideal

1993, pp. 91–95; see also Patton, 2000, pp. 51–52). These remain in tension, what chaos theorists refer to as far-from-equilibrium conditions. Forces are defined in terms of differences, qualitative and quantitative. They both can affect and be affected by other forces. They exist in "mutual 'relations of tension'" (Deleuze, 1983, p. 40, 50). As Patton tells us, "'force' is equivalent to 'power' in its primary sense of capacity to do or to be certain things" (2000, p. 52). Not only are there quantitative differences, there are also qualitative differences referred to as either active or reactive. Active forces are dominant and superior; reactive, dominated and inferior. The difference in force in any instance can be defined as "hierarchy" (ibid., pp. 40, 59–61). Reactive force is about adaptability, accommodation, utility, and means-ends calculation. Reactive force "limits active forces, imposes limitations, and partial restrictions on it" (ibid, p. 56). Reactive force denies differences. An active force, on the other hand, has the power of transformation; it "asserts itself, it affirms its difference and makes its difference an object of enjoyment and affirmation" (ibid.). Active forces affirm difference.[4]

The second dimension is will to power. Not to be confused with the will to dominate and to seek power over others, will to power is what relates various forces (Deleuze, 1983, p. 7, 62; Patton, 2000, p. 61) in producing their quality. According to Nietzsche, "a living thing seeks above all to discharge its strength—life itself is will to power; self-preservation is only one of the indirect and most frequent results" (1966, p. 21). It is not only the determinant in relating forces, but is in turn determined by relating forces (Deleuze, 1983, p. 62). The will to power can be either affirmative or negative. In the negative, we have self-destructive forces;

in the affirmative, forces that allow the body to go to its limits, including its own transmutation into something new. Negative will to power "separates active force from what it can do" (ibid., p. 57). The triumph of a negative will to power can produce the will to nothingness. Which force is at play is conditioned by the form of the will to power, affirmative or negative. It "determines the character and the outcome of the relations between forces" (Deleuze 1983, p. 50, cited in Patton, 2000, p. 52). "Will to power is what wills" (Deleuze, ibid.).

Given these two dimensions, we can create a typology (see table 6.1). Affirmative-active forces characterize becoming, a becoming-other, and ongoing metamorphosis. Affirmative-reactive forces characterize accommodations that are utilitarian and mechanical (Deleuze, 1983, p. 41). That is, given a reactive force, an affirmative will works within some limits, some boundaries to produce the most efficient and productive result. Deleuze (ibid., pp. 66–67) provides the example of the onset of an illness (reactive force). One may respond affirmatively or negatively: negatively by resigning oneself to adaptation; affirmatively by exploring new ways of being and becoming. Consider incarcerated inmates: some adapt by resignation and despair, some by finding a niche within which to overcome the pains of imprisonment (i.e., jailhouse lawyers), some align themselves with gangs, and some liken the prison to the womb where they feel they can develop themselves outside of the responsibilities of the free world (Duncan, 1996).

Negative-reactive forces are characterized by a will to nothingness: for Nietzsche, ressentiment, bad conscience, and the ascetic ideal. It is nihilism and the denial of difference, a becoming-reactive of forces. Various present-day manifestations include political correctness, hate politics, revenge politics, reversal of hierarchies, and exorcism (constructing the evil in the other and attacking the other based on this construction).

For negative-active forces, there is an active destruction of reactive forces (will to nothingness), a self-destruction, which leads to a transmutation into an affirmatively active state (Deleuze, 1983, 174–177; see also Hardt, 1993, p. 51). It is a rebirth, a turning point, an epiphany that is characterized by an affirmative will to power and active forces, an affirmative becoming-active. It is the basis of change, mutation, and metamorphosis. It is an overcoming of nihilism itself.

To reconceptualize by the use of dynamic systems theory (chaos theory): at the singularity (turning point), previous symmetries (relative equilibrium) give way to bifurcations that culminate into further cascades as one's core values undergo transition (i.e., conversion). We may, following Delanda's exposition on Deleuze, refer to this as "symmetry breaking cascades" (2002, pp. 19–20, 135). Indeed, a point attractor, reflective of a person's state in equilibrium conditions, may become destabilized and undergo transition to a periodic, and subsequently to a torus, and possibly even a strange attractor. This is but one example of Deleuze's notion of a line of flight.

Nietzsche's ethics privileges one ideal type, devaluates two for their limitations placed on metamorphic potentials, and places the third in a potentially transitional role toward affirmatively active forces. "Crime," in this view, can range from the "ethical,"[5] a will to nothingness, a will to self-destruction, or at times, a transitional stage to a new self-awareness. We may find similar ranges with edgework activity.

Given the two determining dimensions, it is genealogical analysis that examines the possible nuances. Genealogy both interprets and evaluates (Deleuze, 1983, p. 6; see also Patton, 2000, p. 59, 63). Thus Deleuze's ethics includes the possibility of an evaluation of forces (see table 6.1). According to Deleuze, "Forces can only be judged if one takes into account in the first place their active or reactive quality, in the second the affinity of this quality for the corresponding pole of the will to power (affirmative or negative) and in the third place the nuance of quality that the force presents at the particular moment of its development, in relation to its affinity" (1983, p. 61). Evaluation is mindful of the "eternal return" by which affirmative-active forces predominate. A negatively reactive force does not "return"; it can, however, become intertwined with negative-active forces and produce a transmutation.

Nuance and genealogical analysis can be brought to bear on the study of the edgeworker. Elsewhere (Milovanovic, 2003, 2004), we have created a five-dimensional topological space within which we can situate the various forms of edgework. These would be minimal determinants in any bona fide understanding of the edgeworker. These dimensions (or continua) include structural factors (historical, political, economic contingencies), legal versus illegal; in control versus out of control; greater versus lesser emotional intensities; *jouissance* of the body versus phallic *jouissance*. Thus, we can situate various forms of edgework: packaged, workplace, extreme sports, "sneaky thrills," "badass," "righteous slaughter," transcendental experiences. The specific form of edgework is partly determined by structural opportunities, definitions of legality, degree of control exerted in an activity, degree of emotional intensity experienced, and the form of *jouissance* at play.

Within this topological space, the notion of forces and will to power can be integrated. That is, Nietzschean ontology and epistemology provide the grounds for situating the subject (the edgeworker) within the flow of forces and how these forces find coordination in a specific form of edgework. Some forms of edgework, for example, can be characterized more as affirmative-reactive, some affirmative-active. Consider, for example, Katz's (1988) "righteous slaughterer." He must summon up some higher ethical principle (i.e., safeguarding conventional values) before his release of rage toward the other. This action can be seen in terms of affirmative-reactive dynamics. Others, on the other hand, may participate in extreme sports such as skydiving, free-style climbing, or hang gliding and attain incredible degrees of elation in the sense of accomplishment in exerting exceptional skills when faced with immanent danger (Lyng, 1990). This could be characterized more as affirmative-active edgework. We shall return to further development of this idea in relation to Williams's "three ethics of freedom" in the last section of this chapter. At this point, we suggest that an affirmative will to power and active forces can underlie some forms of edgeworker activity. Of course, other forms of edgework based on reactive forces may be unethical in a Nietzschean and Deleuzian sense, in terms of the limitations placed on others. We need to be vigilant against negative will to power and reactive forces. Central to this understanding, then, is a Deleuzian ethics. We shall return to a further conceptualization of a constitutively based operational definition of ethics below.

Deleuze's ethics is based on the actualization of an affirmative will to power and active forces. Values, therefore, can be judged in terms of how well they contribute to this becoming-active. "Active force goes to the limit of what it can do, even to the point of its own destruction and transmutation into something else" (Deleuze, 1983, pp. 174–176; see also Patton, 2000, p. 61; Hardt, 1993, p. 51). Genealogical analysis, therefore, judges and critically evaluates prevalent forces and the form of will to power. Typological constructions, such as in table 6.1 and table 6.2, are only sensitizing conceptual schemas; it is "nuance" that indicates unique configurations of will to power and forces in historical conditions and political economies.

Deleuze's ethics, based on Spinoza (become joyful!) and Nietzsche (become active!), lead to a first-order ethical mandate: "investigate what affects we are capable of, discover what our body can do" (Hardt, 1993, p. 93). Deleuzian ethics is about affirmation via becoming joyful and active. We must, in short, seek, create, engage, and sustain projects in becoming active, becoming joyful. Central to much of edgeworker activity is this passion, this ethic of joy and activity. We shall see below in our engagement with Williams's "ethics of freedom" how this becoming can be situated.

Let us now turn to a furtherance of Deleuze's ethics, exemplified in his analysis of deterritorialization.

Deleuze's Deterritorialization and Ethics

Deleuze reformulates insights from Nietzsche and Spinoza with his concept of deterritorialization. Deterritorialization could be conceived as the centerpiece of a Deleuzian ethics (Patton, 2000, p. 136). Deterritorialization can be seen in a positive and negative form. It also can be understood as operating within two strata, the absolute (molecular) or relative (molar) levels. By ranging the two, we can identify, once again, four ideal types (see table 6.2).

Deterritorialization is the process by which relatively stabilized forces are destabilized and reconstituted. The body could be conceived as crisscrossed by various forces that attain a degree of stability. The totality of these stabilized forces constitutes a particular body ("diagrams of power," according to Deleuze and Guattari, 1987).[6] Positive deterritorialization can be characterized by new arrangements that contribute maximally to "lines of flight" that mobilize active forces and an affirmative will to power. These lines of flight emerge from relatively stabilized configurations of forces, the center of which contain an abstract machine[7] of change, mutation, and transformation. For Deleuze, becoming-other is one positive form within which this appears. Generally, becoming-minoritarian characterizes the positive forms.

Deterritorialization may also appear in negative forms. Thus mobilized are reactive force and negative will to power. Here, the loci of forces contain lines of destruction. The abstract machine is one of "capture," which reduces what the body can do. One finds this analysis evident in Foucault's (1977) notion of the disciplinary mechanisms. Thus, in Deleuzian ethics, deterritorialization may be "both the line of maximal creative potential and the line of greatest danger, offering at once the possibility of the greatest joy and that of the most extreme anguish" (Patton, 2000, p. 66).

Table 6.2. Deleuze: Deterritorialization

		Deterritorialization	
		Negative	Positive
Level	Absolute (molecular)	Conjugation; capture; striated space; equilibrium; homeostasis; being; linear development; lines of destruction; abstract machine of capture	Connection; smooth space; becoming; lines of flight; rhizomatic; far-from-equilibrium; nonlinear development; abstract machines of change, mutation, and metamorphosis
	Relative (molar)	Conjugation; closed; axiomatic; discourse of master/university; structural functionalism; bureaucracy; point and limit attractors; equivalence principle; state form; freedom from/to; class, gender, and work organization under capitalism; overcoding; Oedipus	Connection; orderly disorder; dissipative structures; discourse of analyst; tori and strange attractors; singularities; difference principle; war-machine; nomad; minoritarianism becoming-other; critical freedom; emergents; dynamic coding; symmetry-breaking cascades

Deterritorialization may appear at two "levels" or strata. The absolute (or molecular) level can be seen as the more unconscious strata where quanta of forces are constantly interacting, producing latent or subterranean effects. It is the sphere of the "virtual" where qualitative multiplicities emerge, dissipate, and remerge. It is "unformed matter on the plane of consistency" (Deleuze & Guattari, 1987, pp. 55–57). Deleuze's ontology does not assume essences but rather dynamic multiplicities that remain in tension.

On the relative (or molar) level are the institutional, everyday structures. It includes class, gender, and race constructions as well as forms of organization of work, the particular state form, and notions of the subject (i.e., the Enlightenment construction of the individual, the juridic subject).

Let us briefly situate possible outcomes (see table 6.2) ranging negative and positive deterritorialization by the two strata. This has been suggested by Deleuze and Guattari: "there are thus at least four forms of D that confront and combine, and must be distinguished from one another following concrete rules" (1987, pp. 508–510). Positive deterritorialization is characterized by "connection"; whereas negative forms are characterized by "conjugation" (or conjunction). Connection, for Deleuze, exists where various assemblages (collectivities)[8] remain relatively autonomous, always subject to dissipation and reconstruction. These remain open, sensitive to perturbation, and yet offer relative stabilities. Conjugation, on the other hand, stands for more rigid assemblages that resist change; they often have appearances of "essences" and are routinely reified as so. Core logics of a political economy, such as the equivalent form of capitalism, conceptualized as "axioms" by Deleuze, find themselves conjugated in various unities that remain impervious to change. We are now ready to specify four ideal types.

Positive deterritorialization at the molecular level is characterized by "smooth space" (a nonlinearized, noncategorical space; here, quanta of forces remain in far-from-equilibrium conditions); a plethora of abstract machines of change, mutation, and metamorphosis; lines of flight that mobilize active forces; rhizomatic (nonlinear) movements; becoming (rather than being; continuous change and metamorphosis); and critical freedom that encourages self-change. A centerpiece of positive deterritorialization is an ethic of minoritarianism (constant critique of given molar conjugations) and an ongoing challenge and undermining ("war machine") of static molar assemblages.

Positive deterritorialization underscores a Deleuzian ethic. As Patton suggests, it is an ethic of freedom. It contrasts with "positive" and "negative" freedom (freedom to, freedom from) insomuch as it is the person herself or himself who undergoes change in values, altering interests, and desires (2000, pp. 83–84). It does not assume the person as a given (as in philosophies of liberation focused on freedom from/to) and then investigates whether she or he has positive or negative freedom.

Positive deterritorialization at the molar level is characterized by how given molecular lines of flight are incorporated in materially expressive form that remains in far-from-equilibrium conditions. Here dissipative structures as opposed to rigid bureaucracies are ubiquitous.[9] Here, too, we find abstract machines of change, mutation, and metamorphosis as well as abundant positive lines of flight ubiquitously present. We see an affinity with chaos conceptions of orderly disorder; sensitivity to initial conditions (iterations produce disproportional, nonlinear effects); tori and strange attractors (reflecting free will *and* determinism, or orderly disorder); plethora of singularities that are nonlinear loci of change and mutation; the privileging of the difference principle (consider Marx's notion of justice relying on differentials in "need" and "abilities"); and assemblages that are relatively autonomous that approximate our concept of COREL sets (historically contingent, relatively autonomous configurations of coupled iterative loops; see Henry & Milovanovic, 1996). To borrow from Delanda (2002), positive deterritorialization allows for a plethora of symmetry-breaking cascades; even very small perturbations, with iteration, can produce disproportional effects culminating in the unexpected.

Here too would be the prevalence of critical discourses that encourage the construction of novel master signifiers with which new notions of the subject and alternative narrative constructions could emerge (discourse of the analyst; Lacan, 1991). Thus, examples of these actualizations would be the generation of new thought, insights, or epiphanies; creative subversive practices (transpraxis); new inventions; new understandings of the subject and social organization; a radical decision by higher courts empowering disenfranchised groups (see also Patton, 2000, p. 110; Deleuze & Guattari, 1987, pp. 420–423);[10] in short, actualizations that propagate smooth spaces within which mutation, change, and metamorphosis is ubiquitous. The "war machine" stands opposed to state forms of capture. The war machine—not meant so much as in the military model but more in the sense of active resistance to the striation of spaces and mechanisms of capture—assures continuous far-from-equilibrium conditions and emergent structures that incorporate positive lines of flight.

Here, we also embrace activist principles that privilege contingent and provisional universalities. Notions of ethics are emergent. They arise within historical moments. Some attain verbalizations into dominant ideology; some remain latent, often subverting dominant logics.

Negative deterritorialization at the molecular level is characterized by striated space (categorized, linearized, axiomized space that provides background relevancies in Euclidean geometric spaces); homeostasis (e.g., stasis); being (accommodation to given conditions); linear development (inputs and outputs are proportional; Newtonian physics); abstract machines of capture (lines of flight are channeled into striated spaces from where control is maximized); rigid axiomatics (core logics of a political economy become major premises for further deductive, syllogistic reasoning); and conjugations (assemblages remain in more rigid form).

Negative deterritorialization at the molar level is characterized by the actualization of absolute deterritorialization. Thus we witness closed systems (structural functionalist principles); discourse of the master and university (Lacan's specifying how desire is encoded in dominant signifiers and how subjects are captured within dominant discourse; see Lacan, 1977, 1991; see also Milovanovic, 2003); point and limit attractors (social phenomena—identities, institutions, structures, ideologies, etc.—tend to gravitate toward restricted and relatively predictable spaces); state forms (as a machine of capture, creates homogeneous and categorical striated spaces); an ubiquitous equivalence principle (common measures apply to otherwise heterogeneous entities; in law, the juridic subject, formal equality, syllogisms, analogical reasoning); orderly assemblages (various social entities are brought within static relation); and normativity (centripetal forces sustain normativity; disciplinary mechanisms encourage conformity).[11] We also include the oedipalization of the social formation to which Deleuze and Guattari devote a major manuscript in criticism, *Anti-Oedipus* (1983). It is by this process that desire becomes connected with "lack" and subsequently solidified in capitalist axiomatics.

At the molar level, negative deterritorialization is actualized in rigid forms. For example, the capitalist mode of production transcended previously more rigid forms of social organization, freeing lines of flight only to subject them to the mechanisms of capture by way of the axiomatics. Flows, matter, energy, quanta of forces are brought within the purview of capitalist axiomatics channeling appropriate expressions of desire (e.g., flows are overcoded and intimately connected with core axiomatics). The legal apparatus contributes to the formation of conjugated axioms in the form of "rationalizing legal analysis" (see Unger, 1996).[12] For Unger, "the cost of our search for immanent order within governmental law . . . [is] the immunization of the basic institutions of society, defined in law, against effective criticism, challenge, and revision" (1996, p. 184). Negative deterritorialization at the molar level, then, tends to the ossification of structures and to their reification even while decisively contributing to an ideology of "formal equality" in law that sustains legitimacy.

A final caveat. Even though Deleuze suggests two "levels" or strata, they are not as distinctively separated as we make them to be. In fact, the molar level already incorporates the molecular level. Deterritorialization and reterritorialization find themselves in feedback loops, the most productive being on the side of positive deterritorialization (here with abundant lines of flight and abstract machines of change, mutation, and metamorphosis).

Edgework, Nuance, and Ethical Turns

The edgeworker, more often than not, can be situated on the positive deterritorialization side of table 6.2. Research awaits a further understanding of various forms of edgework in connection with the four ideal types.

This will take place by being sensitive to nuance and by an incorporation of a genealogical analysis. Some preliminary remarks follow. First, we witness the centrality of a smooth space in much of these activities. In many ways, the edgeworker personifies a war machine and Deleuze's notion of the "nomad," in her or his action directly or indirectly criticizing or resisting dominant forms of capture. O'Malley and Mugford (1994) suggest this in arguing that the edgeworker reacts to emerging postmodernity with its attendant hyperreality, commodification, and clock time, as well as to the historical ascendancy of privileging the rational, logical, orderly side of being human over the emotional, sensual, disorderly. The edgeworker momentarily reconstitutes the two sides of subjectivity (body-mind).

Second, we can make a distinction between positive and negative forms of deterritorialization in edgework activity. Deleuzian ethics (1983) includes the possibility of evaluation by way of genealogical analysis.[13] Positive forms include the increased development of lines of flight of change, mutation, and metamorphosis as new insights, epiphanies, and critical freedoms are discovered. Negative forms of deterritorialization include investment in and actualizations of harms of reductions and repression (Henry & Milovanovic, 1996). The "excessive investor" in energy to diminish others of their positive forms of deterritorialization exists in some forms of edgework and must be clearly distinguished from the more positive forms.

Third, a tension, or dialectic, exists in much of edgeworker activity: on the one hand, the edgeworker finds secrecy in her or his activity from some larger group to be integral to the experience or event of engaging boundaries; on the other, some edgeworkers publicly or privately yearn for greater societal understanding and seek decriminalizing of their activity. For the latter, the movement toward mechanisms of state capture by way of regulation can quickly bring them within the domain of negative deterritorialization at the absolute and molar levels.

Fourth, edgework poses the potential for transmutation. In deterritorialization and in mobilizing negative-active forces, some form of edgework may witness a self-destruction of negatively reactive forces and a transmutation into affirmative-active forces (i.e., the computer hacker turned conventional as a crime fighter; the graffiti writer turned acceptable artist; the joyrider turned professional race-car driver). But we can never be certain of these results. In other words, mediating the final actualization are such interventions as co-optation, channeling, mainstreaming, regulation, and the full force of "disciplinary mechanisms" (Foucault, 1977).

Fifth, some forms of edgework may remain in the negative-reactive mode, such as in Katz's "righteous slaughter"; some may remain in a negative-reactive mode momentarily and become transmuted into the affirmative-active forces (by way of intertwining with negative-active forces) as in the case where some epiphany produces a radical change in the subject (i.e., critical freedom); some may remain in an affirmative-reactive state whereby conventional institutions are sustained *because of* their activity, such as in the case of boundaries being further legitimized by way of symbolic criminal-justice processing (the computer hacker who now has a probation sentence whereby she or he must serve some public institution with lectures on desisting from this activity). In short, edgework cannot be fitted neatly into a positive ethic. Genealogical analysis will contribute to an understanding of any particular form.

Deleuze, Ethics, Edgework, and Constitutive Criminology

Given Deleuze's ethics, one may ask whether we may further an operationalization that is sensitive to nuance and evaluation in defining the "good" and the "bad." We suggest three components to this more integrative evaluation. Elsewhere (Milovanovic & Henry, 2001), we have suggested a constitutive definition of harm that is more interpersonal in scope. An ethics could be situated within this space. We also include a second component that incorporates a more affirmative notion of individual ethics of Deleuze in his notion of an affirmative will to power and active forces. And we need to also make room for a greater range of critical freedom.

The first component deals with a further evaluation of the good and the bad. Our constitutive definition defines harm as "the expression of some agency's energy to make a difference to others and it is the exclusion of those others who in the instant are rendered powerless to maintain or express their humanity" (Henry & Milovanovic, 1996, p. 116). A "criminal" then, is an "excessive investor" in energy who denies another her or his ability to make a difference. The other is rendered a nonperson. Accordingly, we may have "harms of reduction" (a person is reduced from a position she or he has) and "harms of repression" (a person has limits, barriers, or other restrictions placed on the ability to attain a position she or he desires). The exercise of harms of reduction and repression ultimately are connected to given power differentials in hierarchical relations. Whether an act is a harm also hinges on perception of loss, whether the person is free to object to power impositions, whether they are free to resist, and whether the resistance actually prevents a reduction (Milovanovic & Henry, 2001, p. 167). In short, "change must be co-produced through a process of conscious active participation by all of those affected by it, such that those affected are able to define their own future, and particularly their own level of risk, and not have this imposed by others" (ibid.).

The second component in a constitutively oriented notion of ethics would be in accord with Nietzsche's prioritizing an affirmative will to power and active forces, and Deleuze's prioritizing a positive deterritorialization, but qualified in consideration of a reciprocating interpersonal dynamic such as we find in our first point defining harm and excessive investors in energy to do harm to the other. In other words, we can look at our constitutive definition of harm from the front side and ask how to create conditions where excessive investors in harm to others are minimized. Deleuze's ethics suggests what needs prioritizing.

The third component would be in accord with privileging critical freedom. The question concerns historically contingent, relatively autonomous configurations of coupled iterative loops that would be most ideal in encouraging the ubiquitous development of abstract machines of change, mutation, and metamorphosis such that the subject is continuously in process. Here we are interested in emerging singularities that may become symmetry-breaking bifurcations culminating in symmetry-breaking cascades.

Edgework provides us real-world cases-in-point for momentary expressions of affirmative will to power, active forces, and deterritorialization, especially in view of a constitutive definition of harm and possible developments of critical freedom. Thus, focusing on certain forms of crime that can be characterized as excitement driven (Cohen 1955; Duncan, 1996; Halleck, 1967; Katz, 1988; Miller, 1958; Reimer, 1981; Stanley, 1996), we can begin to develop an understanding of the will to power, active forces, and deterritorialization at play. Conventional criminology, which focuses on the category "crime," misses entirely an opportunity to understand the yearning for reconstructing a bridge between the rational, logical, and orderly and the emotional, sensual, and disorderly. The tensions in the mind-body dualism, resolved by Renaissance thought in the privileging of the mind over the body, needs to be brought back into accord.[14] If

Campbell (1983, 1987), Elias (1982), and O'Malley and Mugford (1994) are correct—and their arguments are certainly persuasive—that, historically speaking, we have foregone an opportunity to privilege the emotional, sensual, and disorderly, or at the minimum, neglected to bring it into balance with the rational, logical, and orderly, we nevertheless remain with a challenge of overcoming that which has been erected. Deleuzian ethics, resting on a nonessentialist ontology, strikes at this yearning to express repressed active forces.

The edgeworker seems necessarily implicated in inevitably approaching existing, historically defined boundaries, and in doing so, finding expression for emotions, feelings, adrenaline rush, and the sensual; in short, experimentation in what the body can do. O'Malley and Mugford's (1994) call for a phenomenology of pleasure in historically situated structures is a materialization of a call for a Deleuzian ethics. Of course, pursuit of "pleasure" connected with the will to power, forces, and deterritorialization may have "bad" and "good" expression as our constitutive definition of harm indicates. But we must be open to imaginary play, utopian thinking, experimentalism, and the protection of the imaginary domain as Cornell (1995, 1998) and Unger (1996) suggest. To not do so is to encourage the spontaneous development of "wild zones" (Stanley, 1996):[15] ungovernable, deregulated, nomadic, disruptive, disorderly spaces where forces and will to power will make their own accommodations—which might not be so bad after all is said and done. Some accommodations with molar institutions do take place. Take, for example, the yearly event Bridge Day at Fayetteville, West Virginia, where BASE jumpers from around the world congregate to do one of the few legal BASE jumps (Ferrell, Milovanovic, & Lyng, 2001). Here a "tame zone" has been created where creative expressions of BASE jumping have reached new levels of originality.

But with order reestablished, one wonders about the intensity of emotions in governed places? Wild zones, as Stanley tells us, are "sites of intersubjective negotiation of social identities," and it is "the instability of these events-spaces which can be affirmatively utilized in a process of reconfiguration in the determination of desire and identity" (1996, p. 154).

To return to our beginning point of three components of a more constitutively based ethics and the possibility of "evaluation" by way of a genealogical analysis, it seems that on the first, wild zones can be conceivably evaluated by way of constitutively defined harm, or lack thereof;

on the second, evaluation could consider the specific historically situated nuances in the expression of will to power, active forces, and deterritorialization; and on the third, evaluation could be brought to bear on critical freedom. Hacking, wilding, and raving, for example, can each be evaluated accordingly. This notion of "evaluation" is counter to much of the early thrust of nihilistic forms of postmodern analysis, which argued for relativism and "antifoundationalism."

Williams's Three Ethics of Freedom, Deleuze, and Edgeworkers

Patton has described Deleuze's work as "an ethics of freedom" (2000, p. 83). Williams (see chapter 5, this volume) has undertaken an ethical understanding of crime and deviance. We would like to engage Williams's three ethics of freedom in light of Deleuzian thought and particularly with an application to the edgeworker.

Williams specifies three ethics of freedom: underground ethic, ethic of play, and ethics of transformation. He undertakes an original exercise in bringing ethics into the analysis of deviance. "Ethics," he tells us, "is a way of knowing, seeing, living, and experiencing human existence and the relationships that human beings maintain with themselves, others, and their world. . . . Being ethical reflects a commitment to certain ways of being and ways of relating, a valuing of certain forms of experience, a preference for certain things over and above others, and an underlying motivation to pursue these commitments, values, and preferences." This would be in accord with a Deleuzian definition of ethics. We have previously seen how one's actions can be evaluated in terms of will to power and positive forces. We have also seen how we may evaluate deterritorialization in terms of ethics. In both cases, nuance and genealogical analysis is what allows an understanding in a particular action.

We add to Williams's preliminary remarks that conceptualizing freedom in terms of the traditional freedom from and freedom to (positive and negative freedom) could be extended to a critical freedom implicit in a Deleuzian ethics (see Patton, 2000). The differentiating factor here is that ethical principles need to include the component of self-critique, evaluation, and change so that values and interests themselves may be reevaluated. The subject himself or herself could be understood as having the potential to transform his or her desires, interests, and values. We have previously delved into the Nietzschean notion of transmutation.

Deleuze's integration would suggest that deterritorialization dynamics apply to notions of the self. At the molar level, positive deterritorialization stands for the capacity for the self to reevaluate, change, and metamorphize into a new self.

Let us see how these three ethics apply to forms of edgework. The "underground ethic" would be more consistent with the reactive-negative dynamics of Nietzsche. In other words, choice is exercised against forms of domination. Here, presupposed is some limitation or boundary that becomes the basis of resistance; in this resistance, freedom is exercised (one recalls Goffman's book *Asylum*, in which he tells us the self is born in the cracks, in the ability to resist powers of domination). Williams points out an example of the "Underground Man" in Dostoevsky's novel. Some forms of edgework have affinities with this. Sneaky thrills (Katz, 1988), for example, assume some normative order against which one secretly transgresses. The thrill is in transgressing without discovery. Similarly, for the righteous slaughterer, assumed is a dominant system of values that are not being challenged. "The impassioned killers . . . were upholding the respective social statuses of husband, mother, wife, father, property owner, virile male, deserving poor/self-improving welfare mother, and responsible debtor" (ibid., p. 19). In Deleuze's schema, the underground ethic, without more, can be situated more on the side of negative deterritorialization insomuch as traditional normative orders are maintained, advertently or inadvertently. At best, we have affirmative-reactive forces at play.

The second ethic, "ethic of play," would approximate an internecine activity located between affirmative-active forces and affirmative-reactive forces, on the one hand, and between negative and positive deterritorialization on the other. Much edgework falls within this space. It is a space oscillating between smooth and striated. In other words, boundaries, limits, and edges are assumed, and the edgeworker negotiates these boundaries in indicating a freedom ethic. This is apparent in the work of Cohen (1955), Ferrell, Milovanovic, and Lyng (2001), Halleck (1967), Katz (1988), Lyng (1990), Matza (1969), Matza and Sykes (1961), Miller (1958), and Reimer (1981). Take, for example, Stanley's analysis of computer hacking, raving, and joyriding. "These activities involve the active participation of the individual in the shaping of desires, fantasies, pleasures and identities within established boundaries of meaning but inverting and appropriating these boundaries" (1996, p. 165).

The third ethic, an "ethic of transformation," would be consistent with affirmatively active forces and positive deterritorialization. It might arise from transmutations from an ethic of play (some epiphany produces a reevaluation of one's values, interests, desires), or from an underground ethic that works its way into an ethic of play and subsequently onto an ethic of transformation. It may also transmute from the underground ethic into the transformative ethic. Thus in Deleuzian ethics, initially reactive-negative forces can undergo a change into negative-active and by a transmutation become affirmatively active. Here, lines of flight would generate a plethora of original ideas, thoughts, inventions, new forms of resistance, and so forth.

Much edgework activity remains within the internecine space characterized by affirmative-active and affirmative-reactive forces. To become an ethic of transformation, this state itself has to be transcended. A transmutation is a necessary condition for this process. In other words, understanding the edgeworker also provides an opportunity for understanding how this process proceeds.

The ethic of transformation has affinities with critical freedom. A person may undergo a death and rebirth (e.g., a near-death experience and new realizations of the meaning of life; a detoxification program and a subsequent commitment to transform debilitating family and community conditions; delinquency during teenage years and subsequent work in a child care agency, social work organization, or attaining a professorial position or becoming an activist in Gramsci's "organic intellectual" form; a hacker turned employee of a health care organization plagued by viruses transcends his previous notion of self; Malcolm X's early engagement in petty thievery transformed during prison experience into a leader of dispossessed African Americans, etc.). An underground ethic has the potential to provide the grounds for a transmutation; but more is needed. An ethic of play comes close to the realization of an alternative space, a smooth space within which lines of flight are rhizomatic, open, and dynamic. Smooth space is often found as we approach or even cross the boundary; approaching it or crossing it, however, may be too challenging to the integrity of self to be maintained for long. Under the circumstance, one may quickly retreat to the security of the normative order.

The challenge, of course, is to grasp the moment. Perhaps this state (an ethics of transformation) also has the potential to undergo a complete deterritorialization leading to schizophrenia as Deleuze and Guattari suggest in *Anti-Oedipus*. It would then seem that what is perhaps desirable is an ethics of transformation that maintains a dialectic with the past, present, and future. A "nonmolarizing socius" (Massumi, 1992, p. 89; see also Patton's critique, 2000, pp. 82–83) as well as nonmolarizing identities would seem unlikely desired ends in political practice. A Deleuzian ethic would counter any suggestion for the desirability of a preannounced end state with the posited idea of the "person yet to come." We cannot in advance know this person. We can only advocate affirmative-active forces and positive deterritorialization. Thus becoming-minoritarian, becoming-other is an ongoing process without end states. The ethic of transformation suggests this form of ethic. We, too, must always be vigilant as to the positive or negative outcomes.

Conclusion

We have undergone a rhizomatic journey. Applying a Deleuzian ethics in edgework experiences promises to open creative, imaginary inquiries. We have no endpoint to suggest. We can only be one with Deleuze's ethical mandate drawn from Spinoza and Nietzsche: "Be active! Be joyful!"

Notes

1. See Grosz (1994); Milovanovic (2003, chapter 9; 2004).

2. Contrary to post-Enlightenment thought privileging the rational, logical, and orderly over the emotional, unpredictable, intensive, and disorderly, postmodern thought attempts to bridge the dualism of body-mind. Deleuze's epistemology and ontology is in this direction.

3. In an earlier explication (Milovanovic, 2003, chapter 9), I developed a five-dimensional conceptualization that specified key interacting determinants that together provided possible nuances in the emergence of various forms of edgework.

4. Deleuze (1983, p. 42; see also Patton's discussion, 2000, p. 50) notes Nietzsche's criticism of Darwinism insomuch as Darwinism privileges the reactive forces of adaptation and homeostasis, whereas for Nietzsche, privileged are active forces of transformations and metamorphosis.

5. For example, in the U.S context, the "necessity defense" is recognized in certain transgressions; consider also Hobbsbawm's (1969) discussion of the bandit or mass rebellion against tyrannies.

6. One recalls from Foucault's *Discipline and Punish* how a microphysics of power reconstitutes them via the disciplinary mechanism into bodies of docility and utility.

7. An abstract machine is a particular arrangement that initiates lines of flight. These can be likened to solitons that traverse COREL sets, setting them into resonance with effect. Two main ones are identified by Deleuze: abstract machines of capture and abstract machines of change, mutation, and metamorphosis.

8. At the molar level, assemblages are "extensive . . . divisible, unifiable, totalisable." At the molecular level, assemblages are "intensive . . . not unifiable or totalisable . . . that do not divide without changing in nature" (Patton, 2000, p. 42).

9. For some provocative insights on new forms of social organization ("super-liberalism") and new forms of legal institutions that are in accord with Deleuze's notions of positive deterritorialization at the molar level, see Unger (1987, 1996). Unger (1987), for example, recommends the development of institutional structures that remain always susceptible to critique and change in societal conditions, an idea that resonates with dynamic systems theory's (chaos theory) notion of far-from-equilibrium conditions. He (1996) also suggests an alternative to "rationalizing legal analysis" in his idea of making legal analysis more focused on envisioning alternative institutional structures and encouraging experimentalism in democratic society. In both treatises, Unger, using different language than Deleuze, is advocating creating institutional arrangements that contribute to the maximal flow of lines of flight. His is a theory of how abstract machines of change, mutation, and transformation may find multiple points of origination and how they may continue to flourish. Conventional arrangements, Unger would argue in Deleuze's language, are replete with abstract machines of capture such as the formal rational legal form.

10. In the legal sphere, consider Patton's example of how the high court of Australia ruled on native title in the *Mabo* decision (*Mabo v. Queensland*, 1992). According to Patton, "It was more a question of the opening up of a fissure within the social imaginary with respect to the colonial past and the treatment of the indigenous population. This could represent the beginning of a becoming indigenous of the social imaginary, a line of flight along which legal and social change is possible" (2000, p. 126). In the U.S. experience, consider the U.S. Supreme Court decision *Brown v. Board of Education* (1984). More recently, consider the U.S. Supreme Court decisions *Gratz v. Bollinger* and *Grutter v. Bollinger* (both delivered on June 23, 2003), on admission standards to the University of Michigan, respectively, undergraduate admissions and law school admissions. The decisions stated that an "individualized" (i.e., totality) admission standard must exist to assure "diversity" (found to be a "compelling state interest") in higher education. In each instance, we can argue that a positive deterritorialization at the molar level is being actualized. Notwithstanding the surprising court decision, students will find educational milieus encouraging a becoming-other.

11. Negative deterritorialization can be contrasted to the positive forms of deterritorialization at the molar level: "social and political assemblages are truly revolutionary only when they involve assemblages of connection rather than conjugation" (Patton, 2000, p. 107).

12. This is better known in the literature as formal rationality in law with its attendant syllogistic reasoning and deductive logic. Delanda (2002, p. 121) also argues that conventional science has been "captured" by a "deductive-nomological" approach in reasoning that follows the reasoning reified in law.

It is an exercise of mechanical, deductive applications of core axioms that act much like "essences" in deductive fashion toward some conclusion. He offers, instead, a "problematic approach" (ibid., 134–135) that focuses on posing correct problems, much in accord with Deleuze's ideas.

13. Evaluation is also conceivable in the Nietzschean schema (1994; see essay 2). Both Deleuze and Nietzsche are opposed, however, to the Enlightenment's conceptualization of potential universally objective standards for evaluation (see also Patton's concise summary, 2000, pp. 63–67).

14. Grosz's (1994) insightful analysis of the dualism being resolved by way of the Mobius strip is educative as to how to bring the two back into accord.

15. Stanley develops two examples in computer hacking, joyriding, and "raving" at disused warehouses. As he tells us, wild zones witness "affirmative transgressions" and "this zone of the out-law becomes a possible site in the socialization of non-repressed desire and alternative orders of community without-law" (1996, p. 149).

References

Campbell, D. (1983). Romanticism and the Consumer Ethic. *Sociological Analysis, 44*, 279–296.

———. (1987). *The Romantic Ethic and the Spirit of Modern Consumerism*. Oxford: Blackwell.

Cohen, A. (1955). *Delinquent Boys*. New York: Free Press.

Cornell, D. (1995). *The Imaginary Domain*. New York: Routledge.

———. (1998). *At the Heart of Freedom*. Princeton, NJ: Princeton University Press.

Delanda, M. (2002). *Intensive Science and Virtual Philosophy*. New York: Continuum.

Deleuze, G. (1983). *Nietzsche and Philosophy*. New York: Columbia University Press.

Deleuze, G., & Guattari, F. (1983). *Anti-Oedipus: Capitalism and Schizophrenia*. Minneapolis: University of Minnesota Press.

———. (1987). *A Thousand Plateaus*. Minneapolis: University of Minnesota Press.

Duncan, M. (1996). *Romantic Outlaws, Beloved Prisons: The Unconscious Meaning of Crime and Punishment*. New York: New York University Press.

Elias, N. (1982). *The Civilizing Process*. Oxford: Blackwell.

Ferrell, J., Milovanovic, D., & Lyng, S. (2001). Edgework, Media Practices, and the Elongation of Meaning. *Theoretical Criminology, 5*(2), 177–202.

Foucault, M. (1977). *Discipline and Punish*. New York: Pantheon Press.

Gratz v. Bollinger. (2003). 38 U.S. 959.

Grosz, E. (1994). *Volatile Bodies*. Bloomington: Indiana University Press.

Grutter v. Bollinger. (2003). 539 U.S. 982.

Halleck, S. (1967). *Psychiatry and the Dilemmas of Crime*. Berkeley: University of California Press.

———. (1979). *Psychiatry and the Dilemmas of Crime*. Berkeley: University of California Press.

Hardt, M. (1993). *Gilles Deleuze*. Minneapolis: University of Minnesota Press.

Henry, S., & Milovanovic, D. (1996). *Constitutive Criminology*. London: Sage.

Hobbsbawm, E. (1969). *Bandits*. London: George Weidenfield and Nicolson.

Katz, J. (1988). *Seductions of Crime*. New York: Basic Books.

Lacan, J. (1977). *Ecrits*. New York: Norton.

———. (1991). *L'Envers de la Psychoanalysis*. Paris: Seuil.

Lyng, S. (1990). Edgework. *American Journal of Sociology, 95*(4), 876–921.

Massumi, B. (1992). *A User's Guide to Capitalism and Schizophrenia*. Cambridge: MIT Press.

Matza, D. (1969). *Becoming Deviant*. Englewood Cliffs, NJ: Prentice Hall.

Matza, D., & Sykes, G. (1961). Juvenile Delinquency and Subterranean Values. *American Sociological Review, 26*, 712–719.

Miller, W. (1958). Lower Class Culture as a Generating Milieu of Gang Delinquency. *Journal of Social Issues, 14*, 5–19.

Milovanovic, D. (2003). *Critical Criminology at the Edge*. Monsey, NY: Criminal Justice Press.

———. (2004). Edgework: A Subjective and Structural Model of Negotiating Boundaries. In S. Lyng (ed.), *Edgework*. Albany: SUNY Press.

Milovanovic, D., & Henry, S. (2001). Constitutive Definition of Crime: Power and Harm. In S. Henry & M. Lanier (eds.), *What Is Crime?* New York: Rowman and Littlefield.

Nietzsche, F. (1966). *Beyond Good and Evil*. New York: Vintage Books.

———. (1994). *On the Genealogy of Morality*. New York: Cambridge University Press.

O'Malley, P., & Mugford, S. (1994). Crime, Excitement, and Modernity. In G. Barak (ed.), *Varieties of Criminology*. Westport, CT: Praeger.

Patton, P. (2000). *Deleuze and the Political*. New York: Routledge.

Reimer, J. W. (1981). Deviance as Fun. *Adolescence, 16*, 39–43.

Stanley, C. (1996). *Urban Excess and the Law*. London: Cavendish.

Sykes, G., & Matza, D. (1957). Techniques of Neutralization: A Theory of Delinquency. *American Sociological Review, 22*, 664–670.

Unger, R. (1987). *False Necessity*. New York: Cambridge University Press.

———. (1996). *What Should Legal Analysis Become?* New York: Verso.

PART FOUR

Aesthetics and Crime

The study of aesthetics addresses many provocative questions involving image, style, perception, and symbolism. These are matters that transcend the modernist scientific polarities of factual and counterfactual, form and content, reality and representation. A philosophy of crime that is steeped in the logic of aesthetics exposes, challenges, and/or displaces cultural depictions of such phenomena as beauty, truth, and justice. In this aesthetic excursion, the line between good and evil, virtue and vice, law makers and law breakers is blurred, reconfigured, and, in the extreme, obliterated.

As chapter 7 explains, the study of aesthetics is a field whose attention is directed at once toward the limits of the human imagination and the transgression of those limits as a site for the transcendent in representation. Through a brief genealogy of Kant's notion of the sublime, the chapter lays out a point from which to consider the development of modern aesthetics and the emergence of a post-structuralist perspective, a turn that the author assumes to be among the essential markers of an aesthetics of crime and criminology. The chapter then outlines an aesthetics of crime based upon Foucault's theoretical insights, arguing that, in the act of prohibition and the intentional removal of the practice of punishment from visibility, a dislocation and consequent proliferation in crime occurs. The spectacle of crime, removed in practice, is translated into an aesthetics of representation that is consequently severed from crime's actuality, resulting in an invisibility and consequent aphasia that establishes the contemporary parameters of sociocultural understandings of crime. Criminology's task remains importantly to move beyond traditional social constructionist perspectives of crime by acknowledging that its foundations rest upon this elemental crisis of representation. The chapter concludes with a case study of these various theoretical points in cultural practice.

Chapter 8 furthers this philosophical inquiry by examining the aesthetics of cultural criminology. As the author notes, efforts to comprehend the nature of crime and its control have typically relied upon favored ways of modernist thinking, invoking the false dichotomies of form versus substance, and the corresponding hierarchy of presumed rational scientific inquiry. This investigatory model presumes that surfaces must be stripped away so as to reveal the deeper structure of meaning that lies beneath them.

However, over the past decade, the emerging subfield of cultural criminology has offered a considerable departure from conventional interpretive sociology and theoretical analysis. At its core, this heterodox orientation problematizes crime and crime control by proposing a radical ontology. As chapter 8 explains, the philosophy of aesthetics concerns itself with representation, style, image, and perception. As theoretical critique, it asserts that illusion and reality, form and content, beauty and disfigurement co-constitute the social reality of crime. As a provocative alternative, cultural criminology coalesces the factual and the counterfactual, the authentic and the counterfeit, regarding them as part of an interwoven kaleidoscopic tapestry, a textured and layered pastiche where surfaces contribute to rather than detract from the overall meaning-making process. Indeed, these are sites of knowledge awaiting discovery, interpretation, and interrogation.

In addition, chapter 8 explains how cultural criminology represents an ontological and epistemological filter of sorts through which conventional criminology can be demystified and debunked and a counterdiscourse on crime and its control can be articulated and valorized. More fundamentally, however, the chapter delineates how cultural criminology has relied upon its own heterodox theorizing to assess criminology proper. Arguing that traditional interpretations of criminology's intellectual limitations are rooted in a flawed aesthetic, cultural criminology proposes a philosophical approach more consonant with the aesthetic imperative of representation, style, image, symbol, and perception.

The chapters in this section reveal the manner in which the sundry representations of crime are themselves problematic, limiting the horizon of meaning for aesthetic truth and criminology proper. To this end, the chapters expose the taken-for-granted iconic scenes, spatial discontinuities, and indexical images that constitute the popular discourse on crime and its control. Accordingly, the growth of criminological *verstehen* depends on how cultural manifestations of crime, criminals, and criminal behavior are interpreted and transcended both in theory and action. This is a task of deconstruction and reconstruction, one that seeks to wrestle with the philosophical foundations of crime emanating from the contemporary crisis in image, sign, and symbol.

SEVEN

The Aesthetics of Crime

MICHELLE BROWN

As a form of intellectual inquiry, any exploration of the subject of aesthetics engages fundamental aspects of human experience with an extensiveness that spans such questions as what it means to be human and express sensibilities, subjectivities, and interpretations. Consequently, in the study of art and aesthetics, we find the kinds of philosophical questions which drive human thought, a few of which include: What is being? What is meaning? What is happiness, beauty, evil, and transcendence? And certainly, not least of all, what is justice? However, the conceptualization of crime in connection to aesthetics is a relatively unarticulated and undertheorized relationship. For this reason, of course, the application of aesthetic theory to crime is a particularly fascinating one. In developing a chapter that might address this relationship, I have found it most useful to ask what an aesthetics of crime might teach us about criminology, including a discussion of criminology's limits and its possibilities.

Crime, per se, is difficult to situate within traditional frameworks of philosophy with regard to aesthetics and its location fleeting across perspectives, accounts, and applications. It is, in fact, the kind of question that most generally would not have interested, for instance, the German Idealists. However, if we consider the meanings, relations, and definitions of crime more broadly, we find that such considerations are carefully articulated in philosophies of art and representation with regard to the production of subjectivity through notions like that of the transgressive and the transcendent. This chapter marks a somewhat narrow and preliminary treatment of the topic, designed to achieve a particular sense of depth with regard to criminology in spite of an absence of breadth more generally. The order of such a treatment emerges as follows: In part 1, through a brief genealogy of Kant's notion of the sublime, I lay out a point from which to consider the development of modern aesthetics and the emergence of a poststructuralist perspective, a turn that I assume to be among the essential markers of an aesthetics of crime and criminology. In part 2, I attempt to lay out one conception of an aesthetics of crime (among an unlimited number of possibilities) based upon Foucault's implications, a model that I believe is politically cogent as well as stimulating in its potential to promote the criminologically vigilant toward that perpetual rethinking necessary to the vibrancy of the field.[1] I then take this model and point toward what I consider to be the predominant understandings of aesthetics in criminology and their relationship to the aesthetics of crime Foucault implies. Finally, I will provide a case study of these theoretical points in action. Throughout the piece, I use crime and criminality as categories of experience, events that are always and inevitably real, mediated, and ideological. I assume as well that, in social expression and engagement, criminality as a category serves as "a good place to hide things" where "it can effectively signify and create disconnections in communication across the groups, networks, states, and other relationships through which people symbolize themselves and others" but can also simultaneously "inspire new political discourses" through this very disconnectedness, by drawing attention to the obscuring of cultural communication and structural process (Parnell, 2003, p. 21).

An Introduction to Aesthetics by Way of the Sublime

Aesthetics is traditionally conceptualized with regard to art but can be understood more broadly as the world of human experience mediated by way of perceptions and representations. The aesthetic itself is an idea crucially concerned with the relationship between what is inside juxtaposed with what is outside human thought, while serving as the precise setting for articulating the contradictions found within this division. Kant, whose work marks the modernist unfolding of the aesthetic, famously surmised in *The Critique of Pure Reason* that "all the interests of my reason, speculative as well as practical, combine in the following three questions: (i) What can I know? (ii) What ought I to do? (iii) What may I hope?" (1781/1991, p. 104). For Kant, the aesthetic emerges in reference to the third question and the relationship of reason to hope as the locus for the beautiful, the sublime, and ultimately, the religious, with the role of art that of the revelation of the human condition and the implication of transcendence. The engine for such a transformation is found in Kant's notion of the sublime.

For Kant, beyond the form and unity of beauty is the sublime, an essentially otherworldly experience, beyond human comprehension, centered in a contradiction. The sublime, unlike beauty, is thus an experience dependent upon a specific formlessness, a precise inability to comprehend and articulate the experience that is occurring. However, simultaneous to this awareness is an insistent struggle by the mind directed toward processing the totality of the external event, of rendering it as something singular, something containable, regardless of its impossibility. Centered upon nature, the location of the sublime classically is found in vast, overpowering, clearly romanticized spaces, such things as oceans, storms, mountains, and chasms. These are sites for the sublime in that they convey a certain sense of the inability to articulate and comprehend the magnitude and scope of what one is witnessing. Such aspects of nature can only be experienced and never adequately described, although one's being is compelled to find a way in which to achieve such an expression and representation. This pursuit, for Kant, is, of course, an impossibility, but more importantly, it is also emblematic of the moment in which we recognize the limits of our humanity and beg the question simultaneously of what exists beyond those limits. In the end, then, the sublime is subjective, a state of mind, and, thus, a distinctly human faculty. It is a phenomenon that occurs inside us and not externally in some empirically measurable manner. But it does represent an external encounter with some thing, some object that defies the power of imagination to account fully, totally through representation, articulation, or comprehension of the thing before us. We stand confounded, speechless, awestruck, not at nature *but at our own incapacities to process what we are, in fact, witnessing.* Realization, then, is cued to anagnorisis (an awakening) and, consequently, transcendence (transformation). At the extreme ends of reality, the margins of which include crime, there is the alluring promise of serendipitous revelation. This capacity to imagine the very constraints of our own reality and the (im)possibility of going beyond them is the realm of the creative. Aesthetics emerges as the counterpart of reason.

It is a notion of aesthetics that permits us to resist our own finitude and regard the fearful without simply fearing it but also appraising it and imagining what lies beyond it, the pain of mortality thus confronted with the possibility nonetheless of something other, a terrible kind of pleasure. Thus, we may anxiously regard our own mortality and finitude through the natural fury of the storm or, more contemporarily, through other categories of vastness (for instance, Lyotard references the sublime in the face of capitalist consumer economies), without immediately fearing for our own mortality but instead be reminded of it and the possibility of a meaningful or meaningless existence. This anxiety of the sublime is potentially a productive source for moral judgment and a catalyst for action, but always from within an internal oscillation between paralysis and liberation. In this respect, the sublime, like crime, is centered upon the limits of representation, the inherent confines of a finite human sensibility in the face of infinity, out of which emerges the strange possibility of transcendence. In the face of something so powerful and immense that all our attempts to comprehend it are thwarted, in the midst of that very realization, we momentarily witness the sublime.

In a general consideration of art and aesthetics, crime, in and of itself, would not have concerned, for instance, the German Idealists, but it was not entirely disconnected from their meditations either. Take the notion of radical evil. Implicit in the poised moment of judgment summoned by the sublime, the freedom of choice unleashes the possibility of radical evil, an evil that, as Emil Fackenheim writes, "is radical only in the sense that at each moment we find we have already committed evil; and we had to be evil in order to do it. But evil is not radical in the sense that we are not now responsible. On the contrary in each empirical action, at every here and now, our whole being is at stake, and we are wholly responsible" (1996, p. 33). In considerations of criminality from this perspective, moral freedom and the limits of genius assume center stage. Kant, however, would remind us that it is precisely what the perception of this reality creates in ourselves, the realization of our uniquely human quality as moral center in such vastness, that is, in fact, sublime. Schopenhauer furthers this sense of the sublime through the Aristotelian question as to the "tragic effect": why we intentionally submit ourselves to the terrible, destructive aspects of human nature. And an early Nietzsche, who would have us live through art alone and inescapably, insists that the sublime is in fact the "artistic taming of the horrible," without which the reality that "delusion and error are conditions of human knowledge" ends only in "nausea and suicide" (1968, p. 822). For Nietzsche, "Truth is ugly. We possess art lest we perish of the truth" (ibid.).

The sublime remains for Kant and the philosophers who follow him a moment of critical reflection and an opportunity for weighing moral judgment. It is that sought-after instance where the underlying deep structure of existence may be made manifest through a reasoned intuition. But it is also an instance founded upon the confrontation of the limits of the human condition, our inevitable fallibility, and the limitlessness of the external once overpoweringly natural, now devastatingly social world. Consequently, the sublime encapsulates a particular relationship between pain and pleasure and the ability to enjoy precisely what we fear, an experience grounded in the belief of what we know must exist but whose essence we can never know. In this regard, the sublime was envisioned by Kant as a bridge between the moral and the aesthetic realm but also between science, the natural, the empirical and perception, feeling, intuition. In the face of the sublime, Kant leaves us poised for interpretation and judgment.

The postmodernist critique leaves this aspect of Kant's sublime relatively intact. For instance, Lyotard's interpretation of Kant's sublime values it primarily as a tool of reflection and critical thinking. Kant's theorizing gestures toward the manner in which conceptual thought cannot know its own limits as "It is the limit itself that understanding cannot conceive of as its object" (1994, p. 59). However, for Lyotard, the postmodern notion of the sublime is no longer a sense of the gap between human comprehension and the absolute vastness of nature but rather an unceasing failure in representation, the human ability to imagine the possibility of what can never achieve representation—with absence, thus, the key index of the sublime. In the world of Lyotard's language games as well as Baudrillard's simulacrum, the postmodern sublime is an ethical turn where we confront the human condition and its limits in a context in which the self "exists in a fabric of relations that is now more complex and mobile than ever before" and in which "the question of the social bond, insofar as it is a question, is itself a language game, the game of inquiry" (Lyotard, 1991, p. 15). The turn from a modernist to postmodernist aesthetics is marked by a movement from intrinsic properties and systematic unities of art toward art as historically contingent and culturally circumscribed: texts, narratives, languages, discourses that are inherently ideologically produced. In such a realm, the meaning of the aesthetic is unstable, shifting, and open to multiple points of interpretation, as is the category of crime.

In the move from structuralism to poststructuralism, we map an aesthetic that entails a reformulation of the appearance/reality distinction in Nietzschean fashion, where the real becomes always a representation. Patterns, narratives, and reason are left behind in search of instabilities and contradictions that bring to bear hidden, subjugated discourses. This movement also chronicles a shift from the deeply personal sense of aesthetic privileged by modernity to the superficial flatness of aesthetics as pastiche, style, and duplication. From unity to heterogeneity, from singular identity to hybridity, from master narratives to fragmented discourses, we move from a modernist story of ethics and morality to one of indeterminacy and ambiguity. Along the way, from Kant's invocation of the sublime to Nietzsche's intolerable truths from which art will save us, the genealogy of aesthetics in Western thought is centered fundamentally upon the key indices of crime: contradiction and rupture, terms that carefully and systematically prefigure the unrelenting ambivalence of the poststructuralist critique. And for Lyotard, this transformation is most intensely captured in the chasm between the act of presentation and the unpresentable, a gesture ceaselessly chronicled within the act of representation. This is the contemporary philosophical context for an aesthetics of crime, and the philosopher who will articulate this turn specifically (and consequently presents this chapter with its road map) is Michel Foucault.

A Rudimentary Outline of a Theory of Crime and Aesthetics

> What was being celebrated was the symbolic figure of an illegality kept
> within the bounds of delinquency and transformed into discourse—
> that is to say, made doubly inoffensive; the bourgeoisie had invented
> for itself a new pleasure, which it has still far from outgrown.
>
> —Michel Foucault, *Discipline and Punish*

I have chosen to employ a conceptualization of aesthetics implied by Foucault as he provides us with a point of origin and an obvious criminological beginning. The genealogical projects that make up his work with their archaeological emphasis provide ample terrain for an exploration of an account that speaks to the appearance of a particular metaphysics of crime, that "moment when the political and economic illegalities actually practiced by the bourgeoisie were to be duplicated in theoretical and aesthetic representation," where the discursive is conjoined with the birth of the prison, the production of delinquency, the establishment of the carceral society, and the contradictions these transformations embody and conceal (1995, p. 285). In short, he leaves us a conceptualization of aesthetics that permits us a better understanding of the social and the criminological—a doorway into the ambiguous spaces of crime and punishment at the ends of modernity. Thus, Foucault will serve as architect in this essay's articulation of an aesthetics of crime primarily because he supplies a logic that can serve as both a usable point of establishment and, later, counterpoint.

In *Discipline and Punish*, Foucault alludes to an "aesthetics of crime, that is to say, towards an art of the privileged classes" that appears at a critical instant in the history of punishment—that crucial moment when the impossibility of justice is revealed as due in part to a complicity between criminal justice and delinquency (p. 284). In Foucault's words, "A figure had haunted earlier times, that of the monstrous king, the source of all justice and yet besmirched with crime; another fear now appeared, that of some dark, secret understanding between those who enforced the law and those who violated it" (p. 283). Thus, justice tainted with the knowledge of its own inherent criminality, the intimation of the law's inherent violence, is the setting necessary for the emergence of what Foucault considers to be a contemporary aesthetics of crime directed by and toward the powerful. Like discipline itself, this aesthetic will rapidly become embedded in the fabric of modernity, bound up with the mapping of the carceral archipelago, extensive, repetitive, always turning in upon itself—and in doing so it will forever bring the criminologist back not to crime itself but to the representation of crime.

For Foucault, the aesthetic of crime is, first and foremost, one of the "privileged classes." As an art, it resides among those who have the power to shape discourses of criminality and will ultimately use their power to do so. Second, the appearance of this discourse is intentionally related to the disappearance of another kind of aesthetic—one that is popularly presented in interpretations of Foucault's work as the end of punishment as public spectacle. Here, in the removal of the scaffold, the sovereign fear of its potential to incite popular sentiment in the criminal's favor and mark a collective movement outside of the law is revealed in the act of erasure. This is the predominant theoretical gesture and movement that marks the history of punishment for Foucault. What I seek to argue is that implied in Foucault's vision of the disappearance of punishment as public spectacle is a crucial act of sublimation. In the act of prohibition and the intentional removal of the practice of punishment from visibility, a dislocation and consequent proliferation occurs. The spectacle of crime (whose existence is marked by punishment), removed in practice, is translated into an aesthetics and metaphysics that is invisibly severed from crime's actuality, an invisibility and consequent aphasia that marks the contemporary parameters of sociocultural understandings of crime. No longer will the people look directly toward the act of crime nor its punishment to glean the meanings of these actions. Rather, removed from the public field of history, punishment and its contingent production of delinquency will be displaced into the realm of representation and mediation. This new aesthetics of crime will reveal the transportation of meaning making about crime to the realm of the mediated and the imagined, in short, to the image. And there, turned in upon itself, crime will multiply exponentially in networks and layers of prohibition, the stuff that binds the carceral archipelago into a specific set of social relationships with a disciplinary structure. Criminality will combine ideologies, discourses, languages, events, and representations of crime into dense networks of penality, all of which will take place with, not surprisingly Foucault might add, little criminological notice.

The particular aesthetic that Foucault outlines involves the emergence of "a whole new literature of crime . . . in which crime is glorified, because it is one of the fine arts, because it can be the work only of exceptional natures, because it reveals the monstrousness of the strong and powerful, because villainy is yet another form of privilege. . . . There is a whole aesthetic rewriting of crime, which is also the appropriation of criminality in acceptable forms" (p. 68). It is crime dislocated and transposed along class lines in this particular instance as the existing axis of power. And in this transposition, there is an appropriation through representation of categories of criminality. The potentially subversive spectacles of criminality and punishment that had once marked popular movements against the sovereign now become "the grey, unheroic details of everyday crime and punishment" published in the press (p. 69).

In Foucault's words, "the split was complete; the people were robbed of its old pride in its crimes; the great murders had become the quiet game of the well behaved" (p. 69). So what is to be made of this? In the erasure of the act of punishment, at the birth of the prison, was, in fact, a new social order laid out in which the disciplinary society would displace its own fantasies of law and order, crime and punishment by way of a new aesthetics into realms, languages, and categories safely removed from the possibility of popular incitement? And in the ignoring of this displacement, in this illegitimate space of the cultural imaginary, what kinds of new crimes would emerge? In a mass-mediated world of perpetually recycled images, the question remains, as always with Foucault, at what present have we arrived?

The Power of the Image

In short, whether registered in the event of crime or in the archives of criminology, the confusion of semblance and substance marks the experience of criminality in ultramodernity. As such, it is the aestheticization of everyday life—and the place of crime in it—that needs to be addressed.

—Alison Young, *Imagining Crime*

Few theorists before or after have understood the power of the image with respect to crime and punishment like Foucault. His use of metaphors as key indices of transformations in social institutions, the history of ideas, and everyday practice are unforgettable. Take, for example, *Discipline and Punish* with its two essential icons, the symbols that typify the redistribution of the economy of punishment in modernity: the drawing and quartering of Damiens the regicide juxtaposed with the rigorously scheduled prison timetable, one brutal in the spectacle of its systematic description, the other ultimately insidious in its symbolism of the emergent disciplinary society. Across his oeuvre, Foucault's choice of images, metaphors, artifacts, and institutions is never arbitrary; rather, they are the evidence of transformation, the signs that congeal the symbolic activities of society into the hardened practice of discourse and ultimately ideology. However, between the icons that open *Discipline and Punish* exist an army of others. For the hiding of the spectacle of punishment, illustrated in the iconography above, would only serve to open up other spectacles of crime—to displace and relocate them, and, like the return of the repressed, the scale of their reappearance would be staggering.

This displacement and its potential for proliferation is intimated in Foucault's understanding of the redistributions of power and their transformation of the narrative of justice. His story of criminal justice is ultimately one of rupture and disengagement where the sentence no longer speaks at all to the crime, but rather is justified "only by this perpetual reference to something other than itself . . . a displacement, a whole field of recent objects, a whole new system of truth and a mass of roles hitherto unknown" (1995, pp. 22-23). This gesture is the essence of dislocation. Although it is tempting to read the major transformation implied in *Discipline and Punish* as a removal of punishment (and crime consequently) from the public scene, Foucault persistently reminds us that any dislocation is deceptive and illusionary on other levels. Take the outlaw, for instance. Foucault writes,

> The carceral network does not cast the unassimilable into a confused hell; there is no outside. It takes back with one hand what it comes to exclude with the other. It saves everything, including what it punishes. It is unwilling to waste even what it has decided to disqualify. In this panoptic society of which incarceration is the omnipresent armature, the delinquent is not outside the law; he is, from the very outset, in the law, at the very heart of the law. (1995, p. 301)

No binary opposition is sustainable in such a conceptualization, and transposed, marginality stands in as the center. It is here that Foucault makes his critical thesis concerning the production of delinquency: "it is not on the fringes of society and through successive exiles that criminality is born, but by means of ever more closely placed insertions, under ever more insistent surveillance, by an accumulation of disciplinary coercion" (p. 301). Thus, the birth of crime seeps relentlessly from all the crevices and corners of the carceral archipelago, albeit in a manner that is disconnected from its sources. The origin of criminality is, by necessity of the disciplinary structure in which it exists, concealed. And in that secret, across the fabric of the social foundation, at the heart of everyday practice, crime—in its semblances, logics, and images—runs rampant.

The center of crime then exists always, and in a manner specific to this act alone, upon an absent articulation. Crime is emblematic of the social rupture, that moment of transgression, where the dangerous knowledge of the boundaries of society and their potential crossings are disclosed. Crime, in this sense, is essentially related to Foucault's notion of transgression:

> an action that involves the limit, that narrow zone of a line where it displays the flash of its passage, but perhaps also its entire trajectory, even its origin; it is likely that transgression has its entire space in the line it crosses. The play of limits and transgression seems to be regulated by a simple obstinacy: transgression incessantly crosses and recrosses a line that closes up behind it in a wave of extremely short duration, and thus it is made to return once more right to the horizon of the uncrossable. But this play is considerably more complex: these elements are situated in an uncertain context, in certainties that are immediately upset so that thought is ineffectual as soon as it attempts to seize them (1998a, p. 73).

Crime and our understandings of it originate then at sites of uncertainties, indeterminacies, and contradiction. Foucault characterizes this moment elsewhere as "the discourse of the limit, of ruptured subjectivity, transgression" (1998b, p. 151). In this respect, the aesthetics of crime he invokes emerge as the language of the transgressive, that rather nondiscursive space where I attempt, as Foucault advises, to make crime speak "from the depths where its language fails, from precisely the place where words escape it, where the subject who speaks has just vanished, where the spectacle topples over before an upturned eye" (1998a, p. 77). To engage the aesthetics of crime then is to work within a paradox where crime itself as "transgression . . . is not related to the limit as black to white, the prohibited to the lawful, the outside to the inside, or as the open area of a building to its enclosed spaces. Rather, their relationship takes the form of a spiral that no simple infraction can exhaust" (1998, pp. 73–74). Instead, crime reveals itself ultimately to be, in the words of Bruno Latour, "simultaneously real, social and narrated" (1993, p. 7). Importantly, as Alison Young theorizes, "this is not to counterpose a 'real' world to a 'representational' world, or an image to a reality. My point is that nothing can remain of the dichotomy; appearance and reality are abolished to the extent that reality is an appearance and appearance is our reality" (1996, p. 20). In this confusion of "substance" and "semblance," crime becomes most accessible through its imagining. In such a setting, it is the image of crime then that is always covering the rupture of crime's own absence of boundaries, its essential indeterminacy—always attempting to suture an inherent breach that transgression necessarily imparts. Crime catches us at the limits of the social, in a space where language fails, and the horizon of articulation, of communicating its meaningfulness, is always closing behind us just as we open our mouths to speak. Who then will speak for us? Crime's image.

The Proliferation

> The breakdown of philosophical subjectivity and its dispersion in a language that dispossesses it while multiplying it within the space created by its absence is probably one of the fundamental structures of contemporary thought.
>
> —Foucault, *Aesthetics, Methods, and Epistemology*

In Foucault's aesthetics of crime, the carceral city is the site of proliferation. Here, in the dense networks of "walls, space, institution, rules, discourse" (Foucault, 1995, p. 307), a strategic redistribution of criminality and penality occurs, one that will safely secure its operations "at every level of the social body" (1995, p. 303). The representation of crime at the center of this redistribution is, at its core, an attempt to classify, regulate, define crime—and thus a project of modernity. The constitution of crime is defined in multiple as social, biological, cultural, psychological, anarchic—fleeting events of various discursive origins and accounts. And beneath the classification schemes of this formation is what Bruno Latour labels a "proliferation of the hybrids," quasi-objects that are "much more social, much more fabricated, much more collective than the 'hard' parts of nature, lost in the great gap between objects and subjects, an obscuring which results inevitably in proliferation" (1993, p. 55). In such a world, we witness how crime and criminality as a "series of substitutions, displacements and translations mobilize peoples and things on an ever-increasing scale" and of how the hybrid status of crime, due to its unacknowledged and repressed state, proliferates (1993, p. 84).

As crime's hybridity is primarily an omission, albeit a structuring one, its appearance is often characterized as spectral. As Peter Hutchings writes, in a manner reminiscent of Derrida, Foucault, and Benjamin, "The criminal is, thus, not some shadowy counterpart of the law-abiding citizen but as spectre the very form of law and the shape it seeks to control, a spectre jointly produced through the discourses of law, literature, psychiatry, aesthetics and criminology" (2001, p. 2). And so crime comes to exist primarily as disembodied, immaterial, unmarked, and yet flourishing. This paradox captures the essence of surveillance and regulation at the core of the disciplinary society, where the secret of crime is the manner in which its prohibition sustains it.

Derrida's theorization of the notion of the archive speaks clearly to this act of sublimation. For Derrida, the archival mandate is found in the declaration *"L'un se garde de l'autre"* (1996, p. 51). This mandate, when translated, contains a double gesture: "The one guards against/keeps some of the other." Here we are reminded of Foucault's "carceral network," which "takes back with one hand what it comes to exclude with the other" (1995, p. 301). From this theoretical viewpoint, the archive (as the carceral society, the machinery of crime control, and/or criminology) is at once a site of preservation (and hence, incorporation) as well as a defensive act, guarding against the very thing it seeks to process. Consequently, the archive is inevitably selective, both assertive and repressive, and the outcome is a historical record replete with gaps and structuring absences. For instance, the prison as a physical archive serves to guard against what a "normalized" society cannot process—abnormality, evil, the pathological, the illegal, and disorder—by preserving it within its walls. Yet within its containment, on another level, crimes, transgressions, and the violence of the law multiply.

Thus, the archive occurs in contradictory space, creating a place where the ambiguous essence of disciplinary and epistemological borders and boundaries are exposed. In its pursuit of cohesiveness, of "putting *into order,"* strange circumstances and questions arise related to classification. Schemes overlap. Divisions disintegrate. Arrangements shift in combination and meanings fluctuate. Categories, as fabrications, express eternal circularity, where legitimacy and credibility act as origins themselves. In such zones, notions of history, law, science, justice, and Truth are destabilized. Derrida observes that in these moments, "the limits, the borders, and the distinctions have been shaken by an earthquake from which no classificational concept and no implementation of the archive can be sheltered. Order is no longer assured" (1996, p. 11). This is the postmodernist's perspective of the modern dilemma, a criminal "convulsion"—the shudder of trauma denying the fulfillment of the processing of particular events, which, then ghostlike, haunt the archive, disappearing and reappearing, materializing as *"le mal d'archive,"* the evil of the archive.[2] Thus, in the public erasure of the spectacle of crime, the state ensures the emergence of an even more insidious criminality—the perpetual expansion of a justice apparatus and a disciplinary society.

In our inability to name the object of our designs, to catch it, classify it, both guard against and preserve it, we create a crimino-hybrid that, due to its inherently unacknowledgeable and repressed state, proliferates.

The archive serves to sustain this unifying, albeit paradoxical, impulse. Within the archive's double gesture of preservation and defense, this sort of problematic representation appears less irrational and more comprehensible as it is bound up with cultural forms of (mis)understanding, a phenomenon that demands further representation, a proliferation of attempts to classify the "subjects" (criminals, delinquents, prisoners) that incessantly disrupt schemes and categories. Thus, the "evil" of the archive is found in the perpetual *need* for more archives, more materials, more research. This mad pursuit of origins, which Derrida argues derives from the threat of a Freudian-like death drive, is a totalizing pursuit, an "archive fever," verging on "radical evil"[3] while ironically sustaining the myth of archives as totally inclusive (1996, p. 19). The archive, then, as a site of inscription, expresses a certain inevitable violence in order to fulfill its function, a reckless insistence upon expansion in order to contain disruptive individuals and identities (which proliferate in the process), like the contemporary crime control and penal system.

Within the archival mandate of *"L'un se garde de l'autre,"* an inevitable violence is done to the self and the other, to the researcher and the "object" of research as the pursuit of knowledge becomes a pursuit of classification. In short, the very act of inquiry is bound up with representational violence, as investigations place the complexities of the empirically real within the discursive fantasy of totality above a proliferation of hyperreal images of crime. This end is the reason why the archival motion contains within it the kernel of the archive's destruction—its infinite pursuit. Of course, these archives are understudied and the theories of them underdeveloped in part because of the spectral nature of their subjects, in this case, crime and the invisibility that predominates the transformation of crime's spectacle. Instead we are more likely to find ourselves asking from within the omissions of the archive, as Toni Morrison asks of blackness in American culture, "What intellectual feats had to be performed by the author or his critic to erase me from a society seething with my presence, and what effect has that performance had on the work? What are the strategies of escape from knowledge? Of willful oblivion?" (1989, p. 12). We arrive at the present, nonetheless insisting that we are criminologists and that criminology is still possible.

Criminology as the "Dwelling Place of a Ruined Object"

> But what language can arise from such an absence? And, above all,
> who is the philosopher who will now begin to speak?
>
> —Foucault, *Aesthetics, Methods, and Epistemology*

> Criminology therefore invented itself as a response to a crisis named
> as a gap in knowledge's representation of reality . . . a crisis in repre-
> sentation (by which appearances are desired as reality while their rep-
> resentational status is perpetuated).
>
> —Young, *Imagining Crime*

In criminology, the aesthetics of crime are engaged on a daily basis. The practices, the knowledges, the professions all constitute a set of aesthetics, encompassing the motivations and attractions to the field and its disciplines, the stylistic flourishes of presentation, argument, investigation, and method; the continued production of knowledge through an appreciation of particular forms of scholarly work, research, and training; the field of practice and professionalism with its contingent coordinates of judgment, pain, and punishment. As aesthetes, criminologists fashion criminality into an art that is, better yet, a science, in a manner that reflects our intellectual priorities and abilities. This notion of an aesthetics of criminology remains unstated. Instead, we focus, hesitantly, elsewhere when asked of the art, the metaphysics of crime, often looking to those intellectual working places made amenable to such pursuits.

These points first tend to originate outside the criminological field (in the study of literature and culture) and when internalized, focus specifically on crime itself (and more often deviance) as having its own sense of aesthetics, its own style or artistic form. Rarely do we examine the gap in criminological knowledge that Young identifies ("by which appearances are desired as reality while their representational status is perpetuated") in a manner reminiscent of both Foucault and Derrida, nor its centrality as the representational crisis that structures the discipline. In the process of interrogating this absence, I will first outline particular criminological tendencies that lay claim to an understanding of the intellectual place for an aesthetics of crime. By no means do I intend to imply in such a discussion an all-encompassing treatment of the field; rather, I hope to lay out the fundamental dilemmas in a criminological consideration of the aesthetics of crime and how criminology's questions represent a particular kind of archival impulse.

The Culture of Crime

Although the study of cultural practice exists at the heart of the criminological enterprise from its inception, the place in which its study has been claimed and increasingly perceived as appropriately placed is cultural criminology. Cultural criminology focuses specifically upon the meanings of crime in its everyday applications and engagements—the manner in which assumptions and understandings of crime and punishment permeate the substance of daily life. In short, its concerns are clearly grounded in the aestheticization of the everyday. Within the many definitions of culture that exist among cultural criminologists, crime and deviance are generally seen as indicative of crucial cultural contests within everyday practice concerning the nature of engagement and opposition, inscription and resistance, as well as the spaces and limits of desire, consumption, style, pleasure, performance, transgression, disorder, and, always, identity transformation. For the cultural criminologist, at stake in the production of culture is the paradox of agency (in crime's capacity to challenge and disrupt social order) within a framework of existence in which all acts are immediately appropriated, commodified, and consumed. Its predominant themes then are bound up with this paradox and concerned consequently with representation, style, and power—its center of axis: "crime as culture" and "culture as crime" (Ferrell, 1999, p. 402). Within this orientation, then, there is particular emphasis upon the process of criminalization—and the ways in which cultural forms, expressions, and engagements come to be politicized and criminalized.

At the center of cultural criminology then is careful attention to the production of deviance. For cultural criminologists, crime is first and foremost to be treated as culture, and culture is most interesting when it is practiced and produced along the social borders of crime and deviance (Ferrell, 1999; Ferrell & Hamm, 1998; Ferrell & Sanders, 1995; Ferrell & Websdale, 1999). Its primary studies focus upon the production and engagement of deviant identity at the critical margins of behavior, "at the edge" of society, and its methods of choice are similarly positioned as "trouble making" and "edgework" (Ferrell, 1996, 2001; Ferrell, Milovanovic, & Lyng, 2001; Hamm, 1993, 1997, 2002; Kane, 1998; J. Miller, 2001; Presdee, 2000). Due to its political and intellectual orientation, cultural criminology effects a significant divergence from mainstream criminology in its insistence that "the study of crime necessitates not simply the examination of individual criminals and criminal events, not even the straightforward examination of media 'coverage' of criminals and criminal events, but rather a journey into the spectacle and carnival of crime, a walk down an infinite hall of mirrors where images created and consumed by criminals, criminal subcultures, control agents, media institutions, and audiences bounce endlessly one off the other" (Ferrell, 1999, p. 397). For the cultural criminologist, the only way to truly understand the production of crime is to get up close to it in all of its manifestations—as style, as power, as image. Thus, cultural criminologists situate themselves along the borders of criminology, acting "as a sort of intellectual resistance" (Ferrell, 1999, p. 409).

Cultural criminology is, then, in large part, a subcultural approach to crime, nonetheless centered upon the mediated experience of reality, where "image serves for the members of the groups themselves as a means of marking boundaries, of articulating identity and difference" (Hebdige, 1988, p. 30), where eventually the real spirals into the represented where the "dangerous" youth, as in Hebdige's case, "aspire to the flatness and the stillness of a photograph . . . completed only through the admiring glances of a stranger" (p. 31). The informing principles for the pursuit of cultural criminology then include the notions that "form is content, that style is substance, that meaning thus resides in presentation and re-presentation" (Ferrell, 1999, p. 397). But as Ferrell presents it himself, there is "a significant split between methodologies oriented toward ethnography and field work practice, and those oriented toward media and textual analysis" (p. 399). Each, in its own way, implies a different notion of the aesthetics of crime and renders an artificial methodological dichotomy in understanding the relationships between the two, one that is assumed to mean "researchers' deep participatory immersion in criminal worlds" and the other, a "scholarly reading of the various mediated texts that circulate images of crime and crime control" (p. 400). As Ferrell points out, only a few have begun the process of connecting these worlds that are so inevitably connected in everyday life in patterns of production, display, appropriation, and regeneration, and for Ferrell, this is the inevitable future as ultimately cultural criminology finds its own categories of conceptualization blurred/collapsing with mediated texts running into the practices of daily experience.

This future will derive in large part from social constructionism with its specific interest in the manner in which the creation of symbolic realities is shaped by those in positions powerful enough to have their particular claims achieve dominance in representation (Surette, 1992). As the predominant theoretical legacy in the study of crime and culture, most anthologies in the field appeal to this theoretical perspective (Anderson & Howard, 1998; Bailey & Hale, 1998; Barak, 1994; Fishman, 1978; Fishman & Cavender, 1998; Kidd-Hewitt & Osborne, 1996; La May & Dennis, 1995; Potter & Kapeller, 1998; Sparks, 1992), and other volumes incorporate specific applications, such as the social construction of serial homicide (Jenkins, 1994), the drug war (Reinarman, 1994), the death penalty (Sarat, 1999, 2001), policing (Manning, 1998, 2001), crime talk (Best, 1999; Sasson, 1995), victims (Chermak, 1995), AIDS (Kane, 1998; Young, 2003), race, crime, and the law-and-order movement (Beckett, 1997), as well as September 11 (Chermak et al., 2003). As social constructionist perspectives, these studies are centered inevitably upon the misrepresentation of crime and the manufacturing of ideologically dominant perspectives. There is, by now, a predictable formula to these research approaches, their sites of investigation,[4] and the patterns of findings they reveal. All are centered upon myth-busting, where dominant discourse about crime is consistently exposed as inconsistent with particular crime realities and this incompatibility as a source that often exacerbates the social problems underscoring criminality. This trajectory is largely directed toward the articulation of misrepresentation, where evidence persistently points to a lack of congruity between crime realities and their mass-mediated image. A necessary phase in the study of media and cultural images, these studies still often leave an uncomfortable dichotomy between available theoretical, political, and ideological positions, one that in its predictability betrays its prearrangedness. Few studies to date can address how in fact these dichotomies and categories fail to represent the nuance of public talk and the imagining of crime, getting at this "gap in knowledge's representation of reality" (Young, 1996, p. 23). Although some have begun the deep interrogation necessary to get at a more holistic image of a mass-mediated world, filled with a variety of mediums, a cacophony of voices and perspectives whose contradictions are not easily simplified, social constructionism as a reading of dominance still awaits a fuller elaboration of a mass-mediated world in all its complexity.[5]

Given the manner in which cultural criminology is historically informed by cultural studies, symbolic interactionism, British criminology, and critical studies (Becker, 1963; Cohen, 1971, 1972; Cohen & Young, 1973; Hall, 1980; Hall et al., 1978; Hebdige, 1979; Taylor, Walton, & Young, 1973), this fascination with the construction of deviance and its location within subcultural formations is understandable and necessary; however, as with every focal point, what is included simply marks the boundaries of another exclusion. And, given that exclusion is the hallmark of the Foucauldian aesthetics of crime discussed here, we must ask, what is the nature of this omission for cultural criminology? Although cultural criminology privileges what Jeff Ferrell calls "the inevitability of the image" (1999, p. 414), its specific points of emphasis and its research settings are removed from the images of criminality that make up most mainstream representation, in part due to previous criminological omissions and also in part due to assumed relationships between mass media institutions and the mechanisms of crime control. As well, methodologically, cultural criminology broadly and its specific subset of studies that focus upon the analysis of popular culture retain much of the stigma that haunts cultural studies, as investigations that are often assumed to be solely "textual" or "discursive" and thereby, disconnected from social process (T. Miller, 2003). However, remember, for Foucault, that the appropriately selected image and/or text always is most useful in its ability to signal major transformations in discourse and consequently power. Thus, "the delinquent is not outside the law; he is, from the very outset, in the law, at the very heart of the law" (T. Miller, 2003, p. 301) where marginality stands in as the center. Not surprisingly, then, with regard to crime's image, the mainstream is precisely where the majority of crime images circulate—where the stories and narratives of criminality are reproduced, recycled, and distributed at massive rates. This is not simply to imply that beyond the periphery and margins of society, then, there is much critical work to be done—in fact, precisely at its center—but rather that a distinct and unprecedented kind of proliferation is taking place in late modernity where the images of crime circulate in a manner where no center or periphery can be easily assumed. Discourse is mobile, embedded, circulating, recycled, appropriated, and reproduced across all of social structure. Thus, the location in which crime is subsumed in its removal from the public scene of spectacle, where "the symbolic figure of an illegality kept within the bounds of delinquency and transformed into discourse" is rendered "doubly offensive" as "a new pleasure" that we have still not outgrown (Foucault, 1995, p. 284), is all-pervasive. Daily, we must ask ourselves in the ceaseless ebb, flow, and, sometimes (as in the case of the embedded iconography of the storming of Iraq) bombardment of visual culture, in this vast sensual immediacy, what experiences are occurring? What crimes are taking place? What proliferation occurs beneath such pleasures? If Foucault is correct, this is precisely the space in which discourse hardens into ideology, in which occurs "a whole aesthetic rewriting of crime, which is also the appropriation of criminality in acceptable forms" (1995, p. 68). As Stuart Hall reminds us, in such a world, "there is no escape from the politics of representation" (1993, p. 111).

The Sensuality of Crime

Jack Katz in *Seductions of Crime* engages what I consider to be in large part a particular extension of cultural criminology, a category that most probably assume to be the classical notion of aesthetics surrounding crime. In his investigation of "what it means, feels, sounds, tastes, or looks like to commit a particular crime" (1988, p. 3), Katz recuperates the vision of aesthetics as one of the immediate and the real, privileging human senses and emotions with their own phenomenology in relationship to crime. Thus, he describes his research as an "address of evil—not as judged by moral philosophy or imputed by political ideology but as lived in the everyday realities of contemporary society" (1988, p. 10). If we pursue Alison Young's definition of evil as "the lack of correspondence between appearance and being," we arrive once more at the gap in knowledge that issues the crisis of representation (1996, p. 114). In Katz's vision, there are propulsions, compulsions, and seductions in all kinds of criminality, attractions built upon visceral emotions like humiliation, vengeance, and righteousness, with seduction in the aspects of transcendence implied in the criminal performance and the outlaw status. Significantly, this image of crime has been omitted from the criminological archive as "somehow in the psychological and sociological disciplines, the lived mysticism and magic in the foreground of criminal experience became unseeable, while the abstractions hypothesized by 'empirical theory' as the determining background causes, especially those conveniently quantified by state agencies, became the stuff of 'scientific' thought and 'rigorous' method" (1988, p. 312). Katz offers us a perspective of crime's aesthetics as that kind of sensory knowledge that develops on the borders of human experience. He evokes transcendence in a manner reminiscent of Kant's sublime, and he describes the manner in which the power of the criminal experience is inherently structured through the potential unleashing of violent transgression for inapparent reasons.[6] In his chapter on righteous slaughter, Katz outlines these dimensions:

> But distinctive to righteous slaughter is an objective that makes such attentions obscenely mundane: the project of transcending one's existential future. After humiliation makes one painfully aware that what has just now happened cannot be reconciled with a respectable vision of oneself in any imaginable, concrete future, rage rises to block out concern for what will be, "then." These criminal slayings are the results of leaps into blind faith. Impassioned slayings are both morally familiar moves typically taken on familiar grounds and acts that make no sense unless they attempt to go beyond the familiar, to produce an irreversible, unprecedented transformation. Ultimately, the open character of sacrificial violence is due not to failings of evidence or to features of interaction, but to the phenomenological fact that its final seduction is the unknown (1988, 43).

In these spaces, Katz insists that the meanings of crime are as complex as the definitions of beauty where some force, some quality that is generally unnameable renders interpretation as ultimately dependent upon subjective understandings of the sheer visceralness of the act.

Another critical point Katz alludes to is found in his insistence that criminal acts and the actors who commit them compose a point of moral fascination, of seduction, for not simply these actors but for those who track them across culture as well, those who invoke the fantasy of crime vicariously to break the mundane experience of everyday life. Katz brings us full circle to the image when he describes how notions of the sacrificial order are acted out on a popular scale through particularly influential "fictions." Thus, "the image that it is socially isolated, cold-blooded men who commit 'senseless' murders may be an artificial reflection of the relationship of authors to the social means of producing their books" (1988, p. 309). Here, Katz alludes to a point he never fully makes, one that pushes well beyond his focused critique of "sentimental materialism," and that is that the seduction of crime is a social phenomena in which all are complicit through their own adrenalin-rushed fantasies of representation, provoking seduction and repulsion in a perspective that attaches crime to "primordial evil." Here again, we come up against the "symbolic figure of an illegality kept within the bounds of delinquency and transformed into discourse . . . a new pleasure, which it has still far from outgrown" (Foucault, 1995, p. 284).

At the criminological end, the aesthetics of crime most often implied by criminology is found in the assumption that it is a peculiar form of aesthetics that organizes subcultures of crime and deviance. This is well documented in the celebration of deviance behind notions of "crime as culture." From "making trouble" to "edgework" to "the adrenaline rush" to the "thrill of defiance," the seduction of crime, in its culmination, its imagination, its scientific analysis, is premised upon a particular account of the primacy of pleasure found in the excitement and thrill of transgression—and the strategic disruption to social order such acts seductively promise. Behind this seduction lurks another: the promise of resolution, recuperation, appropriation—and thus, new limits and boundaries to be violated. Thus, cultural criminology's own research agenda and its preoccupation with power inevitably merges with this aesthetics of criminology, whose own pleasures are openly admitted as bound up with the transgressive. Otherwise, and worse, within what is more widely considered to be mainstream criminology, the notion of an aesthetics of crime is largely treated as that ignoble "soft" part of science that Latour refers to as "religion, consumption, popular culture and politics—while the 'hard' list is made of all the sciences they naively believe in at the time" (1993, p. 53). In short, it is treated as omission and gap.

Yet, as Foucault's notion of aesthetics implies, there is always left behind "a trace, a reminder, a scar arising from the very impossibility of bringing off such a separation" (Latour, 1993, p. 61). And criminology, as a primary participant in such exclusionary practices, in part by the sheer manner in which researchers are socialized to ask questions, caught up in the disciplinary society, overlooks the proliferation of criminality as an experience that crosses all levels of human experience. As Stallybrass and White remind us in *The Politics and Poetics of Transgression*, the omission and point of exile that bind us will ultimately produce potentially even larger fantastical threats: "The point is that the *exclusion* necessary to the formation of social identity at level one is simultaneously a *production* at the level of the Imaginary, and a production, what is more, of a complex hybrid fantasy emerging out of the very attempt to demarcate boundaries, to unite and purify the social collectivity" (1986, p. 193). In Durkheimian fashion, this production, although the engine for the production of social solidarity, much like the production of the archive, it too contains the source of its own destruction in the possibility of creating peculiar forms of divisive intolerance, potentially ending in the escalation of social violence and cultural schism. Alison Young takes this notion a step further in her work, asking what happens when the criminal, who was always seen as originating in the same community as the law abiding, is placed outside, beyond the pale of the law in his or her origin? What then? Young brings us back to that moment when crime and punishment as public spectacle is erased and the criminal is repositioned, reproduced, and replicated. As Foucault writes of this moment, now "we are standing on the edge of an abyss that had long been invisible" (1998b, p. 149). And there, in our irresistible urge and "desire to bring to light, to incorporate into language, to make public," what remains in the dark depths of our extensive Enlightenment (Latour, 1993, p. 142)?

The Fantasy of the Criminal Hybrid: A Concluding Application

Imagination . . . is always doubled: in including one vision, it rules out another. All our understandings of crime exist in a tense relation with these *other* stories, sights, voices which are now *beyond* the narrative, the frame, the listening ear.

—Young, *Imagining Crime*

We can agree, I think, that invisible things are not necessarily "not-there"; that a void may be empty, but is not a vacuum. In addition, certain absences are so stressed, so ornate, so planned, they call attention to themselves; arrest us with intentionality and purpose, like neighborhoods that are defined by the population held away from them.

—Toni Morrison, "Unspeakable Things Unspoken"

Don't look for the functions social practices fulfill, look for the contradictions they embody!

—Anthony Giddens, *Central Problems in Social Theory*

A central argument of this chapter is that there are often many criminologies at work in culture, some more popular, usable, and susceptible to practice than others, regardless of their reliability. A peculiar confluence of factors often preclude these explanations and accounts from serious scientific consideration, including the convergence of these realms that tend to disrupt fundamental boundaries between the private and the public as well as the real and the imagined, exposing reality and experience as inseparable from image and appearance. In this confusion, we locate the aesthetics of crime. As Alison Young asserts, "confusion results from responses to crime which have faith in criminology as a representational structure which holds the reality of crime. But criminology exists in its own image, as an image, and therefore is an institution of simulation" (1996, p. 21). In Young's account, this confusion of the "substance" of reality with the "semblance" of representation in any consideration of crime and punishment is precisely the center of confusion and trauma in criminological accounts. It is this unarticulated relationship that (1) makes the experience of crime in public life a crucial center of investigation—a site from which to assess the role of simulation in the experiences and production of everyday life—and (2) exposes the epistemological gap opened by crime's existence, like the crisis of Young's crimino-legal tradition, as, again, "a crisis in representation (by which appearances are desired as reality while their representational status is perpetuated)" (1996, p. 23).

In modernity, the crime scene is the point that all wish to see (the myth of criminology contained in a vision where technology and knowledge will "work" ultimately to provide a "total" view of crime); the site of punishment that which must be rendered invisible. This is also why particularly heinous crimes and punishments (child murders, serial killings, and state executions) are essential points of reference within the popular imagery of crime and punishment, indicative of the kind of event "that exceeds the limits of representation and as such represents the border of what can be imagined" (Young, 1996, p. 137). These kinds of cases and events are what Young calls "occasions of extremity" that both "demand" and "forbid" interpretation and critical examination (1996, p. 212). Thus, crisis, rupture, and trauma are the dramatic centers of popular visions of crime and punishment. Young argues that the imagery of popular culture and media serve to suture these ruptures in a grafting of the incomprehensible with the reaffirmation (albeit troubling) of social order and acceptable hierarchies, a suture that is "fragmented but continuous" (1996, p. 143). The hallmark of contemporary imagery is contained in how difficult this suture is to maintain.

Popular culture is one of the centers where crime and its attendant absence of coherence, its privileging of uncertainty, and its swirling engagement of shifting identities can be denied through imposed resolution/recuperation (the safe, easy narrative), sustained through playful inversions (where we are lost in the funhouse), and/or stressful, spectacular reenactments. This is the space where the maps of modernity are broken up and renavigated in a complex, often conflicting environment of images, motives, and moralities. That there is a very real interplay between these imagined worlds and the reality of crime is only beginning to be acknowledged, in part because mapping this interrelationship is so very difficult. The cultural imaginary is not subject to simple cause-and-effect models and is a nebulous, playful arena where vicarious identities and moralities are picked up and later discarded, but with consistent patterns and attractions to particular disguises. These tendencies then gradually harden into ideology and convention, habit and value, proper narratives of punishment. Below I offer an example (see also chapter 1 and the discussion of Aileen Wuornos for related comments).

The Silence of the Lambs (1991)

By his cunning, his tricks, his sharp-wittedness, the criminal represented in this literature has made himself impervious to suspicion; and the struggle between two pure minds—the murderer and the detective—will constitute the essential form of the confrontation. We are far removed indeed from those accounts of the life and misdeeds of the criminal in which he admits his crimes, and which recounted in detail the tortures of his execution: we have moved from the exposition of the facts or the confession to the slow process of discovery; from the execution to the investigation, from the physical confrontation to the intellectual struggle between criminal and investigator. (Foucault, 1998a, p. 69)

Director: Jonathan Demme
Writer: Thomas Harris (novel); Ted Tally (screenplay)
Orion Pictures (118 minutes, rated R)
Budget: $22 million
U.S. box office gross: $130,727 million

CAST
Clarice Starling: *Jodie Foster*
Dr. Hannibal Lecter: *Anthony Hopkins*
Jack Crawford: *Scott Glenn*
Dr. Frederick Chilton: *Anthony Heald*
James "Buffalo Bill" Gumb: *Ted Levine*

Tagline
Dr. Hannibal Lecter. Brilliant. Cunning. Psychotic. In his mind lies the clue to a ruthless killer.—Clarice Starling, FBI. Brilliant. Vulnerable. Alone. She must trust him to stop the killer.

The serial killer film is a genre that extends back to the very beginnings of film history and is a category that is particularly instrumental in the innovation of narrative film conventions. It is still difficult to assess the cultural impact and industry effects of such films as Fritz Lang's *M* (1931) and Alfred Hitchcock's *Psycho* (1960) and so forth. *The Silence of the Lambs* falls squarely within these tendencies but is particularly emblematic for a contemporary assessment of the imagery and aesthetics of crime for a number of reasons. First, it achieved a level of unprecedented critical and popular acclaim, issuing a series of narratives that continue into the present (*Hannibal*, 2001; *Red Dragon*, 2002; as well as a recuperation of Michael Mann's *Manhunter*, 1986). It is only the third movie and the first crime thriller in Hollywood history to win all five major Academy Awards (best picture, director, actor, actress, and screenplay). Its success ushered in an ongoing wave of films directed at similar themes and concerns by way of a central relationship between a killer and a law enforcement agent. In its aftermath, the film was considered instrumental in boosting criminal justice college enrollments and FBI recruitments. It also garnered a serious amount of public criticism and debate concerning its engagement of sexuality—with a wide degree of diversity in its reception, depending upon the identity politics of its audience. In intellectual circles, the film has inspired a vast critical reaction in articles, books, and commentary that still continues (Staiger, 2000). Finally, Thomas Harris, the author of the Hannibal Lecter series, is widely treated as instrumental in ushering in a new form of conventional crime fiction centered upon the serial killer (Simpson, 2000).

I include the film as a primary example of a specific enactment of the aesthetics of crime, one that emerged as a major point of cultural fascination, its own site of cultural proliferation. But also, the film is particularly usable because it permits us to read the nature of this fascination and its motivation. Ultimately, *Silence* reveals to us the manner in which the representation of crime serves as an essential cultural resource for late modern anxieties and insecurities centered upon debates about identity, often centered upon axes of social identification that are only indirectly linked to contemporary conditions of crime and punishment. *The Silence of the Lambs* is precisely the kind of film that teaches us how to read crime as a narrative, centered upon the scene of the crime and the consequent development of the killer's psychological profile, but it also teaches us how to read the social writ large upon the body of crime—in its connection to specific cultural fears, vulnerabilities, and potentialities.

In this respect, as a robust literature insists, serial killer thrillers are never really about the overt instances of crime, violence, or punishment.

They are never about the literal occurrence of serial killing (the rarest kind of criminal behavior in the United States). They are films centrally concerned with the nature and trauma of identity transformation, particularly the blurring of safe, easy binary oppositions (good/evil, male/female, truth/lies, etc.), which persistently overlap within these texts in a troubling disruption of social order and conventional boundaries. The serial killer, as the quintessential transgressor, violates all boundaries while simultaneously presenting himself as rational, familiar, and within, rather than without, society and social production. As such, he (the conventions center upon males) is simultaneously pathologized as a singular focal point for free-floating, ontological fears and anxieties, simplistically resolved generally as an evil beyond human comprehension, so intractable as to have only one solution: eradication. But as Hannibal Lecter so clearly demonstrates, this elimination is always temporary, never total. The killer is always looming in the cultural imaginary, waiting to be pulled from prison, waiting to be invoked—as is the essential nature of the repressed.

Within such tendencies, the central enigma is always the self—the essential site for playing out the uncertainty of the human condition. At the center of *The Silence of the Lambs* is a total preoccupation with shifting notions of self-identity. This problematic is most overtly contained in the shape-shifting figure of the primary villain—James "Buffalo Bill" Gumb, who skins his victims in order to fulfill his desire of gender transformation through the construction of a full body mask made from the pieces of his female victims. This wish is symbolically communicated in various aspects of the crime and the villain's character: the systematic interconnecting of victims' bodies as materials for a dress (a gender prop itself); the insertion of insect cocoons into the throats of the victims joined by Gumb's fascination with raising moths (symbolizing a desire for transformation); the conventional insistence upon the role of a dominant mother in Gumb's pathology. Thus, the film persistently codes polymorphous sexuality as perverse while simultaneously, as we will see, insisting upon the inevitable reality of such an intermingling.

The essential performance at the center of this dilemma, the identity whose transformation is the film's most obsessive form of preoccupation, is carefully situated as backstage behavior. Clarice Starling, female, petite, working class, orphaned, socially isolated (by career, family, etc.), and alone, perpetually sexualized with intermittent breaks of agency and assertion, is the primary identity struggle undergirding the film's structure. The narrative exigesis is directed really at a developing series of situations from which to assess Starling's own gendered identity. This is apparent in the frequent binary oppositions the film builds for Clarice, with father figure/lover counterpoints alternating between her father, FBI director Jack Crawford, Jame Gumb, and, of course, Hannibal Lecter—pairings that Lecter is always careful to comment upon, culminating in the film's central voyeuristic tension. As a film that is centered upon the gaze and the politics of desire at the heart of looking, Clarice is consistently (and usually very overtly) configured as the object of the gaze, often squirming uncomfortably within that positioning, attempting to gently and subtly maneuver within the deeply masculine terrain of criminal and criminal justice perspectives. In the introductory sequences of the film, we see Starling—small, distinct, female—emerge from an elevator at Quantico from a crowd of towering male agents in training. This kind of scene is replicated a number of times from within the gendered space of the FBI academy. Lecter serves as the primary articulation of this visually gendered relationship: "We begin by coveting what we see every day. Don't you feel eyes moving over your body, Clarice? I hardly see how you couldn't. And don't your eyes move over the things you want?" In fact, the film's anagnorisis is structured entirely through Clarice's awareness and manipulation of this lesson in gender, exemplified in the film's climax as Starling must lash blindly at a male (who wants to be female) killer equipped with night vision goggles.

The film ultimately serves as a primer in the gendered organization of the gaze, encouraging a particular kind of arrangement specifically designed to position the audience as profiler. We are carefully taught how to read the scene of the crime and the psychological concomitants of this scene as cued to gender perversity. It is only through particular kinds of gendered orders that we are able to decode such a world into a meaningful framework and "solve" the crime—a solution that, in keeping with a Foucauldian sense of aesthetics, sets appropriate boundaries and prescriptions for gendered identity roles. In this way, the dense imagery of gore—the torn bodies and gaping wounds—are projections of mutilated selves, broken down, disorganized, no longer coherent under traditional frames of understanding. As Janet Staiger asserts, *The Silence of the Lambs* is an unusually porous, open text where no single, unified reading is possible. Rather, the text and its actors are caught up in deep discursive formations that are contradictory and heterogenous. In this way, the film could be read simultaneously as (1) deeply homophobic,

(2) an empowering image of women successfully maneuvering within patriarchal frameworks, and (3) engineering irresponsible associations between homosexuality, sexual perverseness, and violence. The film is an effective hybridization and grafting of incompatible terms and ambivalent desires in the social life of crime and punishment, which lends it a good deal of cultural usage, mapped through the conduits of concern.

Beyond its major configurations, *Silence* is particularly important within the objectives of this project as it is a narrative that provides a particular kind of ideological closure, a resolution that is acutely apparent as a temporary suture that will not last—but nevertheless is the kind of conclusion that superficially legitimates and affirms a trajectory toward incapacitation—it is, as with most popular mainstream representations, a discourse of appropriation. The serial killer remains essential to questions of crime control that focus upon the role of violence in American culture. There is no end of social dialogue, true crime literature, media coverage, popular culture, and moral panics and crusades directed at the singular, fascinating figure of the serial killer, evidence not simply of struggles to comprehend and stop violence, but also of fundamental concerns about the changing nature of the self, desire, and identity in late modernity. Perhaps nowhere is this more evident than in the gesture toward futility that the serial killer himself frames—anxieties, uncertainties, traumatic histories so large and intractable that empty, meaningless gestures of violence are all that is left. But, as *The Silence of the Lambs* so clearly demonstrates through the perpetual resurgence of Hannibal Lecter, the ways in which we tell ourselves these stories undercuts this interpretation. As futile as a future of meaningless recuperation may be, we never tire of telling ourselves these stories repeatedly—a proliferation in its own right. The tale of the serial killer is then our own circular law-and-order story, caught up in the aesthetics of crime, where boundaries are transgressed in order to be reaffirmed, in order to be transgressed again.

In the end, *The Silence of the Lambs* expresses within its own structure the formula of aesthetics implied by Foucault. There is first a rupture in knowledge made manifest by particular revelations concerning the nature, possibilities, and associations of crime and punishment. This knowledge in *Silence* is bound up with shifting gender orientations, an emergent understanding of identity's fluidity and its construction, and (as always with Foucault) transformations in notions of the self, all converging together in the midst of a sociopolitical scene that is not entirely ready to process such information. This knowledge must, in turn, be displaced, caught, killed in order to be rendered safe and unthreatening to the existing social order—hidden under the guise of crime in the bodies of more or less dangerous serial killers and their victims. In such an erasure, there is, of course, a vast proliferation. The unmarked and unarticulated flourishes beneath ground in the persistent return of the repressed as a re-presentation, an image that can safely be appropriated, packaged, and resolved—but with an ending open enough to guarantee crime's resurgence. What the aesthetics of crime reveal, then, is a cycle of disappearances that promise endless reappearances, a proliferation that maps our own cultural attractions and fascinations with crime and the social ruptures we desire—"a new pleasure" that we have still not outgrown.

Notes

1. It is true that Foucault offers only one perspective into an aesthetics of crime and that perspective privileges power. The critiques of Foucault that have been proffered can easily be transposed here, and I submit that all of these concerns are worth consideration. Thus, this application has its limits, but that is in part precisely why I pursued a Foucauldian account, as a discussion of aesthetics is one in which few limits exist. Second, in a discussion that privileges the image of crime, I by no means intend to deny crime's reality nor its violence; on the contrary, through a discussion of the extensions of crime throughout the social fabric and its vast, mass-mediated production through law, criminal justice, criminology, and state power, I intend to initiate a discussion on the possible limits of criminality in a late modern setting whose structure provokes proliferation.

2. Baudrillard writes similarly, "For ethnology to live, its object must die. But the latter revenges itself by dying for having been 'discovered,' and defies by its death the science that wants to take hold of it" (1983, p. 13).

3. The Jewish Holocaust is Derrida's example.

4. Social constructionist perspectives in criminology tend to focus predominantly upon a particular type of media, the news, for understandable reasons. Most assume news to be a particularly influential form of media due to its status as the legitimate source for factual current events. It is a primary site in which crime is foregrounded due to industry necessities—thus, the old adage: "if it bleeds, it leads." Finally, the news is archived in a manner that is highly accessible and easily breaks down into manageable components for study. The feel, experience, and fantasies of crime that take place elsewhere popularly are in dire need of alternative forms of intellectual investigation.

5. For an interesting survey of how some of this work has begun, see Chermak, 2002; Garland, 2001; Girling, Loader, & Sparks, 1999; Sasson, 1995; Scheingold, 1984.

6. This violence is often complexly grounded in primary points in the social axis related to race, class, and gender. For instance, Edgar Allen Poe writes in "The Philosophy of Composition," "the death . . . of a beautiful woman is, unquestionably, the most poetical topic in the world" (1846) (found at http://www.volny.cz/helpforenglish/lit_poe_composition.html).

References

Anderson, S. E., & Howard, G. J. (1998). *Interrogating Popular Culture: Deviance, Justice, and Social Order.* Guilderland, NY: Harrow & Heston.

Bailey, F. Y., & Hale, D. C. (Eds.). (1998). *Popular Culture, Crime, and Justice.* Belmont, CA: West/Wadsworth.

Barack, G. (Ed.). (1994). *Media, Process, and the Social Construction of Crime: Studies in Newsmaking Criminology.* New York: Garland.

Baudrillard, J. (1983). *Simulations.* New York: Semiotext(e).

Becker, H. S. (1963). *Outsiders: Studies in the Sociology of Deviance.* New York: Free Press.

Beckett, K. (1997). *Making Crime Pay: Law and Order in Contemporary American Politics.* New York: Oxford University Press.

Best, J. (1999). *Random Violence: How We Talk about New Crimes and New Victims.* Berkeley: University of California Press.

Chermak, S. (1995). *Victims in the News: Crime and the American News Media.* Boulder, CO: Westview.

———. (2002). *Searching for a Demon: The Media Construction of the Militia Movement.* Boston: Northeastern Press.

Chermak, S., Bailey, F., & Brown, M. (Eds.). (2003). *Media Representations of September 11.* Westport, CT: Praeger.

Cohen, S. (Ed.). (1971). *Images of Deviance.* Hammondsworth, UK: Penguin.

Cohen, S. (1972). *Folk Devils and Moral Panics.* London: Macgibbon and Kee.

Cohen, S., & Young, J. (Eds.). (1973). *The Manufacture of News: Deviance, Social Problems, and the Mass Media.* London: Constable.

Derrida, J. (1996). *Archive Fever: A Freudian Impression* (trans. Eric Prenowitz). Chicago: University of Chicago Press.

Fackenheim, E. (1996). *The God Within: Kant, Schelling, and Historicity.* Toronto: University of Toronto Press.

Ferrell, J. (1996). *Crimes of Style: Urban Graffiti and the Politics of Criminality.* Boston: Northeastern University Press.

———. (1999). Cultural Criminology. *Annual Review of Sociology,* 25: 395–418.

———. (2001). *Tearing Down the Streets: Adventures in Urban Anarchy.* New York: Palgrave.

Ferrell, J., & Hamm, M. S. (1998). *Ethnography at the Edge: Crime, Deviance, and Field Research.* Boston: Northeastern University Press.

Ferrell, J., Milovanovic, D., & Lyng, S. (2001). Edgework, Media Practices, and the Elongation of Meaning: A Theoretical Ethnography of the Bridge Day Event. *Theoretical Criminology,* 5(2), 177–202.

Ferrell, J., & Sanders, C. (1995). *Cultural Criminology*. Boston: Northeastern University Press.

Ferrell, J., & Websdale, N. (1999). *Making Trouble: Cultural Constructions of Crime, Deviance, and Control*. New York: Aldine de Gruyter.

Fishman, M. (1978). Crime Waves as Ideology. *Social Problems, 25,* 531–543.

Fishman, M., & Cavender, G. (Eds.). (1998). *Entertaining Crime: Television Reality Programs*. Hawthorne, NY: Aldine de Gruyter.

Foucault, M. (1995). *Discipline and Punish: The Birth of the Prison* (2nd ed.). New York: Vintage Books.

———. (1998a). A Preface to Transgression. In James D. Faubion (ed.) & Paul Rabinow (series ed.), *Aesthetics, Methods, and Epistemology* (vol. 2, *Essential Works of Foucault, 1954–1984)* (pp. 69–87). New York: New Press.

———. (1998b). The Thought of the Outside. In James D. Faubion (ed.) & Paul Rabinow (series ed.), *Aesthetics, Methods, and Epistemology* (vol. 2, *Essential Works of Foucault, 1954–1984).* (pp. 147–169). New York: New Press.

Garland, D. (2001). *The Culture of Control*. Chicago: University of Chicago Press.

Giddens, A. (1979). *Central Problems in Social Theory*. Berkeley: University of California Press.

Girling, E., Loader, I., & Sparks, R. (1999). *Crime and Social Change in Middle England: Questions of Order in an English Town*. New York: Routledge.

Hall, S. (1980). Encoding/Decoding. In *Culture, Media, Language*. London: Hutchinson.

———. (1993). What Is This "Black" in Black Popular Culture? *Social Justice, 20,* 104–114.

Hall, S., Critcher, C., Jefferson, T., & Roberts, B. (1978). *Policing the Crisis: Mugging, the State, and Law and Order*. London: Macmillan.

Hamm, M. S. (1993). *American Skinheads: The Criminology and Control of Hate Crime*. Westport, CT: Praeger.

———. (1997). *Apocalypse in Oklahoma: Waco and Ruby Ridge Revenged*. Boston: Northeastern University Press.

———. (2002). *In Bad Company: America's Terrorist Underground*. Boston: Northeastern University Press.

Hebdige, D. (1979). *Subculture: The Meaning of Style*. London: Methuen.

———. (1988). *Hiding in the Light: On Images and Things*. New York: Routledge.

Hutchings, P. J. (2001). *The Criminal Spectre in Law, Literature, and Aesthetics: Incriminating Subjects*. New York: Routledge.

Jenkins, P. (1994). *Using Murder: The Social Construction of Serial Homicide*. Hawthorne, NY: Aldine de Gruyter.

Kane, S. (1998). *AIDS Alibis: Sex, Drugs, and Crime in the Americas*. Philadelphia: Temple University Press.

Kant, I. (1781; reprint 1991). Transcendental Doctrine of Method. Chapter 2, section 2 in *Critique of Pure Reason*. Cambridge: Cambridge University Press.

Katz, J. (1988). *Seductions of Crime: Moral and Sensual Attractions in Doing Evil.* New York: Basic Books.

Kidd-Hewitt, D., & Osborne, R. (Eds.). (1996). *Crime and the Media: The Post-Modern Spectacle.* London: Pluto.

La May, C. L., & Dennis, E. E. (1995). *The Culture of Crime.* New Brunswick, NJ: Transaction Publishers.

Latour, B. (1993). *We Have Never Been Modern.* Cambridge: Harvard University Press.

Lyotard, J.-F. (1991). *The Postmodern Condition: A Report on Knowledge.* Minneapolis: University of Minnesota Press.

———. (1994). *Lessons on the Analytic of the Sublime* (trans. Elizabeth Rottenberg). Stanford, CA: Stanford University Press.

Manning, P. K. (1998). Media Loops. In *Popular Culture, Crime, and Justice.* Belmont, CA: West/Wadsworth.

———. (2001). Theorizing Policing: The Drama and Myth of Crime Control in the NYPD. *Theoretical Criminology, 5*(3) 315–344.

Miller, J. (2001). *One of the Guys: Girls, Gangs, and Gender.* New York: Oxford University Press.

Miller, T. (2003). "What It Is and What It Isn't: Cultural Studies Meets Graduate Student Labor." In A. Sarat & J. Simon (eds.), *Cultural Analysis, Cultural Studies, and the Law* (p. 73–104). Durham, NC: Duke University Press.

Morrison, T. (1989). Unspeakable Things Unspoken. *Michigan Quarterly Review,* 1–34.

Nietzsche, F. (1968). *The Will to Power.* New York: Random House.

Parnell, P. C. (2003). Introduction: Crime's Power. In P. C. Parnell & S. C. Kane (eds.), *Crime's Power: Anthropologists and the Ethnography of Crime* (pp. 1–32). New York: Palgrave Macmillan.

Potter, G. W., & Kappeler, V. E. (Eds.). (1998). *Constructing Crime: Perspectives on Making News and Social Problems.* Prospect Heights, IL: Waveland.

Presdee, M. (2000). *Cultural Criminology and the Carnival of Crime.* New York: Routledge.

Reinarman, C. (1994). The Social Construction of Drug Scares. In P. A. Adler & P. Adler (eds.), *Constructions of Deviance: Social Power, Context and Interaction* (p. 92-103). Belmont, CA: Wadsworth.

Sarat, A. (1999). *The Killing State: Capital Punishment in Law, Politics, and Culture.* New York: Oxford University Press.

———. (2001). *When the State Kills: Capital Punishment and the American Condition.* Princeton: Princeton University Press.

Sasson, T. (1995). *Crime Talk: How Citizens Construct a Social Problem.* Hawthorne, NY: Aldinede Gruyter.

Scheingold, S. (1984). *Politics of Law and Order: Street Crime and Public Policy.* New York: Longman.

Simpson, P. L. (2000). *Psycho Paths: Tracking the Serial Killer through Contem-*

porary *American Film and Fiction.* Carbondale: Southern Illinois University Press.

Sparks, R. (1992). *Television and the Drama of Crime: Moral Tales and the Place of Crime in Public Life.* Philadelphia: Open University Press.

Staiger, J. (2000). *Perverse Spectators: The Practices of Film Reception.* New York: New York University Press.

Stallybrass, P., & White, A. (1986). *The Politics and Poetics of Transgression.* London: Metheun.

Surette, R. (1992). *Media, Crime, and Criminal Justice: Images and Realities.* Pacific Grove, CA: Brooks/Cole Publishing.

Taylor, I., Walton, P., & Young, J. (1973). *The New Criminology: For a Theory of Social Deviance.* London: Routledge and Kegan Paul.

Young, A. (1996). *Imagining Crime.* Thousand Oaks: Sage.

———. (2003). "Into the Blue": The Image Written on Law. In A. Sarat & J. Simon (eds.), *Cultural Analysis, Cultural Studies, and the Law: Moving Beyond Legal Realism* (pp. 327–351). Durham, NC: Duke University Press.

EIGHT

The Aesthetics of Cultural Criminology

JEFF FERRELL

Attempts to understand the nature of crime
and crime control have often relied on the
old social scientific dualism of form versus
content, and on the associated hierarchy
of investigation whereby surfaces must be
stripped away so as to reveal the meaningful core of content. Emerging perspectives
in the fields of social theory, cultural studies, sociology, and criminology over the
past half century—and specifically in the
field of cultural criminology over the past
decade or so—have proposed a radically different ontology of crime and crime control.
Founded in philosophic orientations sometimes categorized under the heading of
aesthetics—that is, orientations concerned
with image, style, and perception—this
ontology proposes that image and symbolism, beauty and disfigurement in fact shape
the reality of crime and crime control.
From this alternative ontology, form, and

content exist not as a duality but as an interwoven whole—and surfaces stand not as impediments to deeper analysis but as deeply meaningful texts themselves worthy of critical interrogation.

Working from within this alternative ontology, cultural criminology has emerged over the past decade as a corrective of sorts to conventional criminology, a counterdiscourse on crime and crime control. Cultural criminology investigates criminal and delinquent subcultures as aesthetic communities, held together by fine threads of symbolism and style. It explores the aesthetic foundations of crime control and legal authority and considers the essential role of stylized media dynamics in constructing the contemporary reality of crime and crime control. In turn, it focuses on stylized meaning as a medium—perhaps the essential medium—through which criminals, crime control agents, and others contest the everyday politics of crime and justice. As importantly, cultural criminology aims this alternative analysis at the enterprise of criminology itself, finding criminology's intellectual limitations displayed in its flawed aesthetic, and offering instead a cultural criminology more attuned to the seductive power of aesthetic imperatives.

Ugly Criminology

Over the past decade or so, criminology has drifted into a subtle shift in emphasis. The conventional categories are certainly still there—criminality, policing, punishment—but the angle of approach has altered. Increasingly, studies of criminality examine not just criminals, criminal actions, and criminal careers but the mediated construction of criminal identities and the cultural dissemination of fears and perceptions regarding criminals and crime. Attempts to account for the dynamics of policing or punishment often account also for the interplay of policing and carceral institutions with the various institutions of the mass media. Even those concerned primarily with criminal justice policy recognize that stylized images of policing and corrections, circulating through the channels of contemporary culture, shape public perceptions and support for public policy. Phrases like "media constructions of" and "images of" seem now to be common—and commonly acceptable—prefixes to the conventional categories of criminological inquiry.

This is of course an entirely reasonable response to a world of crime and crime control suffused with imagery and representation. Members of illicit subcultures appropriate conventional images and symbols, converting them into subterranean signals of marginality and defiance; circulate these remade representations within their own self-invented subcultural media of communication; they then watch as their subversive images and symbols are reappropriated by news reporters and corporate marketers. Within this looping dynamic, some criminals emerge as overnight cultural icons, some as instant folk devils—and many as both. "Reality TV" shows like *C.O.P.S.* sell seductively unreal images of everyday policing and yet emerge as real tools of everyday police publicity campaigns and police recruiting; television crime dramas and action films likewise offer manufactured images of violence, transgression, and control that, for many viewers, become real reference points in their understandings of crime and criminal justice. As "crime" increasingly functions as a code word for deeper social concerns, issues of ethnicity, social class, gender, and age emerge—and are masked—in public debates over crime control. All the while, public spaces are policed in the interest of public perception, public memorials to crime victims proliferate, and controversies over the death penalty or the legal rights of gays and lesbians explode as public spectacles. In this world, the most essential of issues—criminality, safety, justice—circulate as images, and as reflections of other images. In this world, the dualism of form and content falls apart; the ontological center that sets "real" crime and crime control apart from "unreal" representations of them cannot hold.[1]

In this sense, criminology's subtle shift constitutes an engagement with this world and a tacit acknowledgment of image and perception as fundamental dimensions of contemporary crime and crime control. And yet this shift is not enough. Unless coupled with a concomitant reexamination of philosophical underpinnings, this disciplinary drift into the realms of imagery and aesthetics seems likely to generate more confusion than clarification. Put bluntly, the unthinking importation of traditional social scientific assumptions—among them the dualistic hierarchy of content over form—into a criminology of image and style seems sure to produce mostly ugly distortions of these very issues. A change in substantive focus certainly begins the process of introducing criminology into the aesthetic and representational dynamics of the new century—but only a change in philosophical foundations can consolidate this substantive migration.

Evidence of this need for philosophical reappraisal abounds. Much of criminology's recent movement into the analysis of image and representation, for example, has relied on the methodological framework offered by

content analysis—a framework built around a quantitative and purport-
edly objective analysis of a document's content. Certainly content analysis
can function as a useful tool for suggesting certain patterns in mediated
texts; used as a free-standing method of textual inquiry, though, it misses
more than it reveals. Numeric summaries of discrete textual categories
miss the larger aesthetic within which a text takes shape and miss the
structural patterns of order and juxtaposition that enliven a text's flow of
meaning. Methodological mythologies of objectivity and quantification in
turn reproduce the old notion that we can somehow free content from its
hiding place behind the false facade of stylized presentation; in this way,
they deny the sensual and aesthetic experiences by which texts come to
have meaning for their audiences. Moreover, content analysis seems often
to be used with the intent of proving the degree of divergence between
the "real" nature of crime and justice phenomena and "biased" textual
representations of them. Ignoring the essentially symbolic construction
of these phenomena in the first place, this application of content analysis of course reproduces existing fallacies of form as distinct from, and
subordinate to, content. It likewise ignores the multiplicity of audiences,
audience interpretations, and public responses that will continue to con-
found the real and the representational as a crime issue runs its course.

The failure of old philosophical foundations is equally evident in
criminology's exclusion—and inclusion—of images themselves. In an
approach that is revealing in its irony, criminological analysis increasingly acknowledges the importance of newspaper photographs, television
and film crime scenes, political imagery (as with the infamously threatening mug shot of Willie Horton circulated during the 1988 presidential
campaign),[2] and public crime/victimization displays in defining crime
and crime control policy—but without including the images under consideration. As such, this analysis produces work that is inevitably distorted in its translation from one medium to another; as a graffiti artist
once reminded me while I was writing a book about the aesthetic and
visual complexities of non-gang hip hop graffiti, "Writing about art is
like dancing about architecture."[3] This limitation is of course as much a
matter of structural constraint as personal scholarly choice, with criminological journals and book publishers seldom willing to find a place (or
a budget) for image reproduction. Yet these structural limits themselves
reflect not just stingy budgets but philosophical and scholarly assumptions. They perpetuate the tyranny of the written word in conventional

social science and the notion that written analysis can somehow penetrate the obfuscation (and opaqueness) offered by the image.[4]

Even the inclusion of images can reflect these same suppositions. Relegated to the status of illustration, an image here and there may enliven conventional scholarly analysis, but it hardly addresses the dualistic philosophical hierarchy that defines it, a priori, as no more than illustrative. Worse, the gratuitous inclusion of images as illustration can in fact undermine critical analysis and aesthetic appreciation. Particularly egregious examples, redolent in their own irony, can be found on the covers of criminological textbooks devoted to the analysis of juvenile delinquency. One features as its cover an aesthetically stunning wall of multicolored hip hop graffiti murals and tags—and no mention whatsoever of hip hop graffiti in the table of contents, text, glossary, or index (Bartollas, 2000). Another presents on its cover what appears to be an image of early (circa 1970s/1980s) hip hop graffiti—but it is difficult to know since, again, hip hop graffiti doesn't appear in the table of contents, text, or index (Jensen & Rojak, 1992). A third offers a cover apparently composed of nonspecific, computer-generated graffiti-style markings; inside is a short section dealing only with gang graffiti, and a glossary entry that defines "graffiti" as "the distinctive language/symbolism of street gangs" (Bynum & Thompson, 1996, pp. 288–290, 473). In the first two cases, the use of this cover imagery tacitly acknowledges the aesthetic power of hip hop graffiti to startle and engage while at the same time omits from discussion this very form of graffiti—the most publicly visible and aesthetically meaningful form of juvenile delinquency to emerge in last thirty years or so (Ferrell, 1996). In the third case, the visually befuddled cover belies the text's claim that "an understanding of graffiti is very important to law enforcement officers" (Bynum & Thompson, 1996, p. 288)—and the definition of graffiti exclusively in terms of street gang activity perpetuates, rather than dispels, the misguided public conflation of gang graffiti and non-gang hip hop graffiti.[5]

Absent philosophical sophistication, theoretical attempts to penetrate the aesthetics of crime and criminality foster the same sorts of misunderstanding. Perhaps the most prominent—and politically significant—of these is Wilson and Kelling's "broken windows" theory (or more accurately, pseudo-theory) of crime causation. Used as the scholarly reference point for a range of reactionary and punitive public policing strategies since its emergence in the 1980s, "broken windows" is essentially an aesthetic analysis of crime's etiology. According to this perspective, broken windows and other public displays of neglect and petty criminality function as symbolic invitations to further criminality, in that they "signal that no one cares," or perhaps "seem to signal that 'no one cares.'" Likewise, "such otherwise harmless displays as subway graffiti" communicate to subway riders "the 'inescapable knowledge that the environment . . . is uncontrolled and uncontrollable'" (Wilson & Kelling, 1982/2003, pp. 402–404). In such cases, Wilson and Kelling (see also D. Miller, 2001) argue, "residents will think that crime . . . is on the rise" (p. 404), potential criminals will perceive these signs of inattention as encouragements to accelerated misbehavior, and a downward spiral of disorder will be set in motion. Claiming in this way to directly engage issues of image, public display, knowledge, and perception, the theory of "broken windows" stands or falls on its aesthetic analysis.

It falls. A useful justification for the conservative clampdown on "quality of life" crimes and marginalized urban population, the theory is decidedly less useful as an aesthetic of crime. Imagining the contours of symbolism and perception rather than investigating them, the theory constructs a series of abstract, one-dimensional meanings that it arbitrarily assigns to dislocated images and idealized audiences. In fact, as any city dweller knows, the symbolic texture of the urban landscape is far more complex. To the extent that "broken windows" do in fact function as symbols, for example, they may symbolize any manner of activities to any number of audiences, depending on situational and historical context: community resistance to absentee ownership, a long-standing personal grudge, the failure of local code enforcement, or the illicit accommodation of the homeless. Likewise, depending on particularities of content and context, gang graffiti may symbolize a neighborhood's intergenerational history, suggest changing patterns of ethnic occupation, or even enforce a degree of community self-policing. A proliferation of hip hop graffiti in place of gang graffiti (a distinction ignored by Wilson and Kelling) may likewise suggest a *decline* in juvenile violence—that is, it may lead some neighborhood residents to understand that crime is on the decline—and in fact may display an informal, less-violent social order now negotiated through the very symbols that Wilson and Kelling so tellingly misrepresent (Sanchez-Tranquilino, 1995; Ferrell, 1996; Phillips, 1999).

Only an attentive aesthetic analysis can help us decide among these possibilities of meaning; the sort of arrogant, aesthetically uninformed readings that authors like Wilson and Kelling invent from afar only obfuscate what they claim to explain. An attentive aesthetics of crime and crime control acknowledges that symbols operate within, and embody, particular social and cultural contexts of meaning; situated in this way, they exist as something more—and more complex—than imagined evidence for some exterior political agenda. As before, a useful aesthetics of crime and crime control can therefore only develop from a philosophic reorientation toward image and representation—a reorientation that engages symbolic meaning with some degree of honesty and sophistication, that promotes human immersion in the symbolic environment under study, that acknowledges the essentially symbolic construction of all windows and all worlds, broken or not.

Toward an Aesthetic of Crime and Crime Control

Decades ago, the writer James Agee and the documentary photographer Walker Evans suggested this phenomenological reorientation in their elegantly attentive study of Southern sharecroppers' lives, characterizing their joint work as "an independent inquiry into certain normal predicaments of human divinity," a work in which "the immediate instruments are two: the motionless camera, and the printed word. The governing instrument—which is also one of the centers of the subject—is individual, anti-authoritative human consciousness. . . . The photographs are not illustrative. They, and the text, are coequal, mutually independent, and fully collaborative" (Agee & Evans, 1960, pp. xiv–xv). A brilliant writer, driven by a potent mix of "self-lacerating anger" and humanistic compassion, Agee in this study went about creating a new sort of phenomenological writing as he endeavored to "live inside the subject" (Evans, 1960, p. ix, xi) and so to undertake work that was as much "an effort in human actuality" (Agee & Evans, 1960, p. xv) as it was an exercise in reporting. For his part, Evans produced images designed to mirror this profound commitment to the subject of study. Situated firmly in the tradition of politically engaged documentary photography, Evans's work paralleled that of documentary photographers like Robert Capa and W. Eugene Smith, who once described his own work as "photographic penetration deriving from study and awareness and participation" (in R. Miller, 1997, p. 150). Together, Agee and Evans created a deeply detailed aesthetic representation of a marginalized group generally thought unworthy of such attention, and in their intertwined written and photographic accounts they created an aesthetic understanding attuned to the texture of their subjects' everyday lives.

By the 1970s, the groundbreaking work of the Birmingham School and the National Deviancy Conference in Great Britain was shaping a culturally informed "new criminology" (Taylor, Walton, & Young, 1973) that aimed a similar reorientation directly at issues of deviance, crime, marginality, and resistance. Drawing on the work of Antonio Gramsci and other neo-Marxist theorists, the new criminologists sought to reveal the cultural and ideological dimensions of social class, to demonstrate that "a social individual, born into a particular set of institutions and relations, is at the same moment born into a particular configuration of meanings, which give her access to and locate her within 'a culture'" (Clarke et al., 1976, p. 11). Arguing in this context that "much of working class culture has . . . taken shape around the sphere of leisure" (Clarke, 1976, p. 176), the new criminologists undertook to analyze the leisure aesthetics of working-class and youth cultures—that is, the styles, fashions, and symbolic practices that by turns encoded, resisted, and disrupted the economic, legal, and political structures of society.

This new sort of critical analysis, though, required new sorts of intellectual and aesthetic orientations. Dick Hebdige (1979, pp. 17–18), for example, drew from an eclectic range of literary writers, cultural theorists, and critical commentators—Jean Genet, Raymond Williams, Roland Barthes, Louis Althusser—to construct an analysis that could "discern the hidden messages inscribed in code on the glossy surfaces of style" and thus demonstrate that "the challenge to hegemony which subcultures represent . . . is expressed obliquely, in style." Others likewise now emphasized the need to account for "the specificity of each style" (Clarke, 1976, p. 179); the importance of carefully "reading" or "decoding" distinct symbolic practices; and the necessity of beginning not with abstract notions of social class or legal hegemony but with the situated aesthetics of marginal subcultures. As Murdock and McCron argued,

> Subcultural studies start by taking distinctive subcultural styles and the groups that are involved in them, and then working backwards to uncover their class base. The result is an elegant and eminently plausible account of the homologous relation between subcultural styles and structural situations. If this procedure is reversed however, and the analysis starts from the class location rather than from the cultural response, a serious

problem presents itself, as it soon becomes apparent that the same structural location can generate and sustain a variety of responses and modes
of accommodation. (1976, p. 205)

Within British cultural studies and the new criminology, an aesthetic
sensibility—and a new range of intellectual perspectives geared to precise aesthetic analysis—had become the essential tools of social and
cultural critique.

And yet for this very reason, the new criminology was animated by
the same creative tension that ran through the work of Agee and Evans
and other progressive documentarians: the tension between wide-ranging
analysis and critique on the one hand, and attentiveness to the aesthetic
particulars of the subject matter on the other. At times this tension surfaced as a sense of theoretical discomfort, a reluctance to overtheorize
the aesthetics of subculture and style lest such theorizing obscure the
very subject of study; in an echo of Agee and Evans's phenomenology,
Hebdige (1988, p. 12) at one point noted his "obdurate English preference
for the particular, for the thing itself," and his hope that particularity
would ultimately override theory. More to the point, this tension gave
rise to a type of grounded theory (Glaser & Strauss, 1967)—that is, an
aesthetic analysis driven, as much as possible, by the dynamics of the
subcultures and styles under study. The new criminologists argued, for
example, that precisely because post–World War II youth subcultures and
their styles had come to occupy such "a pivotal position in the history
and consciousness of the period," their symbolic and stylistic practices
demanded aesthetic attention by critical theorists (Clarke et al., 1976,
p. 10). In the United States as well as Great Britain, researchers of all
sorts began to confirm this, discovering time and again that drug users,
juvenile offenders, working-class school kids, zoot-suiters, punks, and
rude boys all found in subcultural style both their own collective identity and their ongoing entanglement with legal and political authorities
(Ferrell, 1995/2004). In this sense, the aesthetic orientation of the new
criminology was meant to bridge the gap between researcher and subject
of study; it was not imposed as a theoretical construct so much as it was
offered up as a subcultural practice, as a model of identity and meaning
grounded in the everyday lives of those under study.

Today, as criminology stumbles once again into new realms of image
and representation, some scholars seem still to be heeding Agee and
Evans's mandate to create works in which text and image are "coequal,

mutually independent, and fully collaborative" and to be hearing once again Tony Jefferson's call for developing an attentive "'grammar' for decoding cultural symbols" (1976, p. 86). In so doing, these scholars continue earlier efforts to transcend the old dualism of form and content; moving beyond textbook covers, content analysis, and "broken windows," their work continues to reinvent the philosophical and aesthetic foundations of criminology. Camilo José Vergara's *The New American Ghetto* (1995), for example, incorporates hundreds of photographic images selected from the over 9,000 images he shot and archived over an 18-year period in various urban settings. Attempting to overcome the "rigid aesthetic conventions" that have at times governed the practice of photojournalism, Vergara structures his own images into "pictorial networks" that capture intersecting dimensions of urban space. Offering "thematic categories and arguments [that] originated *in the images* and my experiences of the places visited" (1995, pp. xiv–xv; emphasis added), Vergara also presents in-series photographs that document the evolution of urban neighborhoods over a period of years. In this way, he develops a visual grammar by which to document and analyze social and spatial change, embedding what social scientists would inelegantly call "longitudinal analysis" in the very images and their juxtaposition, and offering a vivid social ecology of crime, marginalization, decay, and redevelopment.

East Side Stories: Gang Life in East LA, a collaboration between photographer Joseph Rodriguez and writers Ruben Martinez and Louis Rodriguez (1998), undertakes a similar social ecology, this one more directly criminological. Intending, as Martinez notes, to represent gang life in its cultural and ecological complexity, unafraid to expose contradictions in gang life that defy easy categorization, the book intermingles disturbing images of guns, gun dealers, blood, and drugs with reassuring images of family life, affection, rehabilitation, and education—and sometimes in the same photograph. In so doing, it creates a striking, uncertain criminology of gang life that undermines both the gang stereotypes generated by media and political institutions and the prefabricated gang images offered by criminological textbooks. In its intermingling of text, interview, and photograph, it likewise affirms the sort of aesthetic analysis first developed within British cultural studies and the new criminology. Featured in many of the book's photographs, Daniel "Chivo" Cortez substantiates his photographic representations as he recalls his days gangbanging: "I used to be really particular about my clothes. . . . I used to iron my clothes for hours to look good, to impress and intimidate. I'd wear my gang-affiliated wear—my white T-shirt, Ben Davis, and Nikes—so people would know, 'Hey, there's trouble walking down the street right there.' They'd know I was from somewhere" (in Rodriguez, Martinez, & Rodriguez, 1998, p. 167). Concluding the book, Louis Rodriguez offers an historical context for Chivo's recollections that echoes the context sketched by the new criminology a quarter century before. "The pachucos were the epitome of rebellious youth," says Rodriguez. "One thing about the pachucos is they did things that most kids hadn't done before, what a lot of kids do now: they had strange clothing, a new way of talking, in Spanish or English, they tattooed themselves all over. They had a walk, you know, they had a style" (Rodriguez, Martinez, & Rodriguez, 1998, p. 176).

Louis Kontos, David Brotherton, and Luis Barrios (2003) further refine this sort of aesthetically rich criminology in their edited book, *Gangs and Society: Alternative Perspectives.* The perspectives provided by the book are alternative indeed; contributors explore elements of political activism and resistance that intertwine with gang life, and the editors devote an entire section of the book to photographic representations of gangs. Most importantly for an emerging criminological aesthetic, the very politics of image production are explored in Richard Rodriguez's essay "On the Subject of Gang Photography" (2003, p. 280). Investigating the production of gang photography within the conflicting realms of ethnography, self-representation, media circulation, and policing, Rodriguez draws on the work of Walter Benjamin, Roland Barthes, Pierre Bourdie, and the British new criminologists in exploring the political practices embedded in representations of gangs. He notes, for example, that "photographs give credence to identifying a suspected gang member on the basis of a shaved head, baggy pants, white T-shirt, body posture, and other signifiers of the gangster stance" and concludes that, if nothing else, the representation of gang life "is never an innocent practice."

Other criminologists are likewise now developing a close analysis of symbolism and style that stands in direct opposition to the sloppy abstractions of authors like Wilson and Kelling, not just because their conclusions about crime and crime control differ but because these criminologists engage a different politics of paying attention. Criminologists like Jody Miller (1995) and Stephen Lyng (Lyng & Bracey, 1995) have undertaken detailed investigations of illicit subcultural styles as the medium through which subcultural participants and outsiders conduct complex negotiations of criminality, resistance, and control, with Miller documenting the practice of policing and Lyng the dynamics of corporate appropriation. Samuel R. Delany (1999), Mike Davis (1992), Mike Presdee (2000), Barry Glassner (1999), and others have detailed the broader social and historical dynamics by which stylized symbols of fear, exclusion, and transgression come to circulate throughout contemporary social life. Regarding Wilson and Kelling's claim as to the "inescapable knowledge" of disorder that graffiti and other public displays allegedly communicate, Heitor Alvelos (2003) has recently completed an intricate longitudinal study of urban graffiti; intertwining extensive, on-the-street visual and written analysis, he reveals the complex, shifting uses of urban graffiti—including its extensive co-optation by the very forces of political and economic order that Wilson and Kelling would celebrate.

Likewise, I have attempted over the past decade to theorize the multiplicity of styles that emerge in the interplay of crime and crime control, and to document both emerging patterns of contemporary cultural resistance and the specific "aesthetics of authority" mobilized against such resistance (Ferrell 1996, 2002, 1995/2004). Like the work of Miller, Lyng, and others, this research reveals that it is not only illicit subcultures that find definition in representation and in style; legal, political, and economic authorities do as well, and so institute aggressive public campaigns to reclaim the meaning of their symbolic terrain from those who might undermine it. In addition, I have photographed and analyzed the particularities of personal and cultural symbolism embedded in roadside shrines—the informal memorials that families and friends build in honor of those lost to automotive violence. Such shrines, I've found, offer a variety of negotiable meanings; while some read them as intricate life histories, tragic commemorations, or collective reminders of automotive danger, others interpret them as dangerous distractions, even violations of legal control, to be regulated or removed (Ferrell, 2003).

Certainly many of these works can be understood within the context of a new sort of visual criminology, a visual and representational analysis emerging in parallel to the work developing within the fields of visual sociology and anthropology (Harper, 2001; Greek, 2003). More generally, this work today increasingly coalesces under the heading of *cultural criminology*—a criminology that, in building from an alternative philosophic foundation to that of conventional criminology, embraces an alternative aesthetic and political sensibility as well.

The Aesthetic Politics of Cultural Criminology

At its core, cultural criminology positions issues of symbolism, style, representation, and meaning at the center of the inquiry into crime and crime control (Ferrell, 1999; Ferrell & Sanders, 1995; Ferrell et al., 2004; Presdee, 2000). Put more broadly, cultural criminology embraces realms of negotiated representation and symbolic discourse as essential avenues for understanding the social practice of transgression and containment. In so doing, cultural criminology continues the project undertaken by the National Deviancy Conference and the Birmingham School and since advanced by various practitioners of cultural studies, field ethnography, media studies, and postmodern inquiry. It continues the attempt to salvage human imagery and symbolic interaction, indeed "culture" itself, from the epiphenomenal marginality to which various forms of Marxist materialism and sociological determinism once assigned them. Likewise, cultural criminology continues the project of recapturing a sense of situated meaning, of human engagement, long held captive within the numeric abstractions of administrative criminology and mainstream social science.

The research now gathering under the broad rubric of cultural criminology in fact reveals, time and again, that the human construction of meaning around issues of crime and crime control overwhelms, in its stylistic elegance and symbolic nuance, any reduction of human action to independent variables, data sets, or statistical summaries. Likewise, it highlights the inadequacy and inhumanity of the sorts of reductionist philosophic models that undergird "rational choice" and "behaviorist" criminological approaches (Young, 2003). In this sense the "cultural" in "cultural criminology" denotes an orientation that is essentially humanistic in its approach to transgression and control. It acknowledges the boundless ability of humans to create their own complexities of horror and beauty and acknowledges the ongoing entanglement of the two in representations of crime and justice.

Within an always contested and changing symbolic environment, then, the meaning of transgression and control, indeed the very boundaries between crime and justice, emerge out of human interaction, out of an ongoing interplay of people, symbols, and emotions real and attributed. This process in turn unfolds within and between everyday social situations and larger societal dynamics. And in an increasingly multimediated world, it is this very interplay of images and symbols large and small that must be accounted for—and contested—in order to critically understand criminality, crime control policies, and public understandings. One of the great social interactionist insights of the last century—that meaning resides not in the thing itself but in surrounding social and cultural processes—takes on even greater complexity and importance in a world where mass-produced symbols now circulate endlessly amid the situated experiences of daily life. The meanings of crime and crime control are continually renegotiated by criminals, victims, and police officers, by public officials, television programmers, and criminologists as well; in their contested human representation is their reality.

All of this of course constitutes cultural critique, a critical subversion of any authoritative claim that survey researchers or public officials might make as to the "real" meaning of crime or crime control. And, it seems to me, there is something else equally subversive lurking in this "cultural" dimension of cultural criminology. As cultural criminologists go about embracing symbolic meaning and stylized communication as essential currents of human life, they define in practice the philosophic foundations of cultural criminology itself—that is, they define it as an enterprise that must be attuned to its *own* style and symbolism as well. To put it simply, if we recognize that style matters, that aesthetics are important, that representation shapes the realities of those we study, then it seems we must recognize that these same factors shape—and should shape—the enterprise of criminology. If we embrace the essential importance of symbolic meaning in the worlds we study, shouldn't we—mustn't we—embrace its essential importance in our scholarly worlds as well?

If so, then it may well be time to abandon the philosophic foundations of social science and the old dualism of form versus content that they embody. It may be time to acknowledge the revolution that has been underway for years, to recognize the new world that has been created within the social scientific shell of the old, as a significant amount of work in criminology and other social science fields has in fact moved toward engagement with representational dynamics, symbolic discourse, and ambiguities of meaning and style. Moreover, and significantly, much of this work has begun to reflect its subject matter, has become *itself* more stylish, drifting away from dry claims of objectivity and old conventions of detached pseudo-scientific reporting, and toward more engaged, personal, and literary forms of communication. So it is with cultural criminology. Cultural criminologists have encouraged not only the study of the meanings and emotions that shape crime and control, but the engagement of the criminologist's *own* meanings and emotions in this research process (Ferrell, 1997; Presdee, 2000; Young, 2003). Likewise, cultural criminology's recent disciplinary emergence seems clearly to rest not just on the attention it pays to symbolism, style, and mediated dynamics as foci of criminological study but on its *own* stylized strategies of alternative research, image production, and writing (Kane, 1998; Presdee, 2000).

In contrast, by standards of form or function, mainstream social science increasingly seems a failed project. Over the past century or so, it has certainly not become "science" in any conventional sense of experimental rigor or explanatory scope (neither have the natural sciences, by the way)—and, worse, the greater the effort in making social science "scientific," the more systematic has been the dehumanization of research subjects and the heartlessly numeric abstraction of human experience (Feyerabend, 1975). Confronting this failure, grasping for the illusion of scientific control, some criminologists and other social scientists have turned to hyperspecialization and linguistic obfuscation, apparently on the notion that their work has got to be good looking if it is so hard to see. As a "cultural" perspective on such an enterprise would predict, of course, this sad pseudoscientific trajectory has fostered a set of symbolic codes, a social science culture, that at the same time embodies and perpetuates the problem: passive third-person writing, interruptive in-text referencing, big tables, long equations, and a general tyranny of the calculated number and the turgidly written word over the idea and the image. If style matters, then conventional criminology and the social scientific paradigm on which it rests are in trouble; their aesthetic is ugly, inhuman, boring—and revealing.

In response to this aesthetic, and to the university Institutional Review Boards (IRBs) that increasingly police it, Howard Becker (in Shea, 2000, p. 32) now claims that he no longer engages in the sort of criminological field research through which he helped define contemporary criminology, and which now falls under the heavy hand of university IRBs. Now, he says, he just does "conceptual art" in one social situation or another. And why not conceptual art instead of social science? After all, the "science" in "social science" has long functioned more as anxious metaphor than accomplished reality. Rationality has hardly displaced emotion in the practice of human inquiry, long-standing protestations of "neutrality" and "objectivity" notwithstanding; little of our work goes forward under closely controlled conditions despite the best efforts of IRB boards and other bureaucratic overseers; and the statistical residues and objectivist protestations pulled up over naked self-interest hardly cover the obscenities of aggressive careerism and intellectual pimping. Yet like other metaphors—the "war on drugs" or the "war on terrorism," for instance—the metaphor of "social science" has long organized particular meanings and behaviors, and has set the tone for a particularly inappropriate approach to human life. So, along with "conceptual art," what else might serve as a better metaphor than "social science," a better foundation, for making sense of this new cultural criminology—if by "better" we mean more honest, more liberating, more tolerant and inventive, and more useful in critically engaging with contemporary cultural worlds of crime and crime control?

We might think of cultural criminology as music—jazz, especially. As I noted in my book *Tearing Down the Streets* (Ferrell, 2002), the Nazis loathed jazz, finding in its syncopated rhythms the diseased "art of the subhuman." As I also noted there, the Communists hated it too. In the late 1950s, Robert F. Williams organized armed black resistance to the Klan in the American Deep South, and in 1961 made his escape to Cuba. There Williams started a radio station—Radio Free Dixie—with a signal powerful enough to slither back into the dark heart of Dixie. But before long Williams was in trouble with the Communist authorities, too, this time for his station's traditional jazz and "new jazz" programming, which the Communists, in a chilling echo of the Nazis, labeled "degenerate" (Tyson, 1999; Presdee, 2000, p. 116).[6]

That a musical form could so offend two of the more ruthless organizations of totalitarian control suggests something of its subversive power, and of its human value. Good jazz—good music—accomplishes just what good criminology might; it produces transcendent moments of aesthetic excitement, moments in which technical virtuosity explodes into improvisational insight. In so doing, it engages both its producers and its audience in an emergent, collective process that carries their emotions and their intellects beyond taken-for-granted structures of understanding and control. Perhaps this is why the unregulated humanity of jazz and other innovative musical forms so bothers those invested in domination and control. And perhaps this is why some cultural criminologists embrace music not only as an appropriate subject of criminological study but as a wellspring of lyrical analysis and model for rhythmic writing (Ferrell, 2003; Hamm & Ferrell, 1998; Marx, 1995; Tunnell, 1995). Joe Strummer, Billy Bragg, Bruce Springsteen, Sinead O'Connor, Steve Earle, Bob Dylan, Billie Holiday, Merle Haggard, Leadbelly—they sing insights into crime and control that we can only hope to emulate. And if as cultural criminologists we do strive to make music like they do, like Thelonious Monk and Rage against the Machine and Rancid, too, then maybe someday, at some academic conference session, an audience member will respond the way Dean Moriarity responded to a jazz improvisation in *On the Road*, "stand[ing] in the back, saying, 'God! Yes!' and clasping his hands in prayer and sweating" (Kerouac, 1955, p. 146).[7]

But I doubt it.

So if music is too much to expect, perhaps we could just think of cultural criminology as play. Welded into the very structure of Nazi death camp entrances, inviting arrivals into horrific efficiencies of forced labor and extermination, "Arbeit Macht Frei"—"Work Will Set You Free"— was during the 1930s and 1940s one of the modern world's most vicious lies. It still is. Academic bureaucrats and their political overseers are busy enough these days inscribing such lies into the professional lives of academics and intellectuals by way of tenure and post-tenure review procedures, increasing teaching loads, metastasizing committees, and growing demands for outside grant money; we need not inscribe them ourselves. In fact, I'd suggest we remember one of the more succinct slogans from the Situationist-inspired uprisings of Paris 1968—"Never Work"—and try never to let cultural criminology become one more intellectual drudgery. Engaged as it is with the vivid foreground and evocative symbolism of culture and crime, cultural criminology has in place one anchor outside the intellectual assembly line; our own sense of playful autonomy can provide the other.[8]

This sense of play—this refusal to push ourselves and our work toward serious social science—is essential not because cultural criminology doesn't matter but because it does; if we want to disseminate and develop cultural criminology's aesthetic insights into crime and crime control, we would do well to avoid the deathly disengagement now afflicting the efficient work of mainstream criminology. Ongoing intellectual excitement, and political engagement with the larger world, will more likely come from an approach that defines its own style in terms of music, or play, or carnival, or even the festival of the oppressed, than one defined by its insularity and arrogance. "Hectic, irreverent, transgressive and, above all, fun"—Jock Young's (n.d.) characterization of the National Deviancy Conference—aren't bad terms of engagement either.

"What is this 'black' in black popular culture?" (1993, p. 111) Stuart Hall once asked, willing to crack the very foundation of debates over black cultural dynamics. His answer was cautionary. "The moment the signifier 'black' is torn from its historical, cultural, and political embedding and lodged in a biologically constituted racial category," he warned, "we valorize, by inversion, the very ground of the racism we are trying to deconstruct." By way of clarification, he challenged his readers to consider the "diasporic traditions" out of which contemporary black social life has emerged:

> First, I ask you to note how, within the black repertoire, *style*—which mainstream cultural critics often believe to be the mere husk, the wrapping, the sugar coating on the pill—has become *itself* the subject of what is going on. Second, mark how, displaced from a logocentric world—where the direct mastery of cultural modes meant the mastery of writing . . . the people of the black diaspora have, in opposition to all that, found the deep form, the deep structure of their cultural life in music. Third, think of how these cultures have used the body—as if it were, and it often was, the only cultural capital we had. We have worked on ourselves as the canvases of representation. (Hall, 1993, p. 109)

As cultural criminology continues to develop, we can productively ask a parallel question: What is this "cultural" in cultural criminology? And as with Hall, any answer must address not just cultural criminology's subject matter but cultural criminology's own style, its own philosophic and aesthetic sensibilities, as evidence of what is indeed going on. At its best, the "cultural" within cultural criminology denotes an aesthetic manifesto about our own work as much as it does a new range of subject matter; it forms the deep structure of cultural criminology, the canvas of representation on which cultural criminology can be imagined.

While the "cultural" in cultural criminology certainly points to the cultural dynamics of crime and crime control, then, it also offers the "cultural" as a primary mode of appreciation, understanding, and communication—that is, as an alternative philosophic foundation for criminology. Simply put, if cultural criminology suggests new substantive orientations for criminology, it also suggests new ways of doing criminology itself. Mainstream criminology's inattentiveness to emotion, style, and aesthetics—or worse, its fondness for a style that is offputting, mechanistic, and ugly—has long perpetuated the false hierarchy of content over form, and along the way has managed to render even the most seductive of subject matters sterile. Under this new way of doing criminology, we might hope that the opposite holds true as well—that evocative writing, engaging images, and the ethnographic particulars of human meaning can establish homology with our subject matter and political engagement with our audiences.

Three decades ago, in *The New Criminology*, Ian Taylor, Paul Walton, and Jock Young included a proscriptive passage from the Scandinavian criminologist Nils Christie. "We have not made clear that our role as criminologists is not first and foremost to be received as useful problem-solvers, *but as problem-raisers,*" Christie argued. And so, "Let us turn our weaknesses into strength by admitting—and enjoying—that our situation has a great resemblance to that of artists and men [*sic*] of letters. We are working on a culture of deviance and social control. . . . Changing times create new situations and bring us to new crossroads. Together with other cultural workers—because these fields are central to all observers of society— . . . it is our obligation as well as pleasure to penetrate these problems" (1973, pp. 280–281, emphasis in the original). Three decades later, with cultural criminology emerging as another sort of "new criminology," the medium remains the message, and the message remains the same. Abandoning the philosophic foundations of conventional criminology, embracing instead the orientation offered by artists, writers, musicians, and other cultural workers, cultural criminology presents new possibilities for analysis and appreciation. Raising significant philosophic problems for the conventional practice of criminology, it at the same time offers a new aesthetic for critically confronting the problems of crime and crime control.

Notes

1. With apologies to W. B. Yeats, "The Second Coming," 1921.

2. This image—or more to the point, the damage done by this image—has now become iconic. The original 1988 Willie Horton campaign spot can be seen and heard at www.ammi.org (American Museum of the Moving Image). And today, 15 years after the fact, popular writers offer the following characterizations of various contemporary political scandals and dirty tricks: "The Willie Horton of Computer Crime?"; "From Willie Horton to Will and Grace?"; "Willie Horton's Ghost Comes to Santa Monica"; "Willie Horton Watch."

3. This phrase is in turn a paraphrase of "talking about music is like dancing about architecture," an aphorism variously attributed to Elvis Costello, Martin Mull, Laurie Anderson, Frank Zappa, and others.

4. In this sense the new journal *Crime, Media, Culture: An International*

Journal offers something of a breakthrough, with its inclusive incorporation of images and texts as part of criminological analysis.

5. Full disclosure in this regard: I have myself recently provided hip hop graffiti imagery for the cover of a book concerned with juvenile delinquency and youth crime (Roche et al., 2004).

6. Something more of the fascist aesthetic can be glimpsed in the following directive from Achille Starace, Fascist Party secretary under Mussolini: "For some time now, 'Saturdays' of every kind—artistic, musical, and springtime 'Saturdays', etc.—are being invented. I remind you that there is only the 'Fascist Saturday'" (in Sachs, 1987, p. 17).

7. And relatedly: "We were suddenly driving along the blue waters of the Gulf, and at the same time a momentous mad thing began on the radio; it was the Chicken Jazz'n Gumbo disk-jockey show from New Orleans, all mad jazz records, colored records, with the disk jockey saying, 'Don't worry 'bout *nothing!*'" (Kerouac, 1955, p. 116; emphasis in original).

8. "Contemporary society has banned all real play. . . . The desire to play returns to destroy the hierarchical society which has banished it" (Vaneigem, 1967/2001, p. 257).

References

Agee, J., & Evans, W. (1960). *Let Us Now Praise Famous Men.* New York: Ballantine.

Alvelos, H. (2003). The Fabrication of Authenticity: Graffiti Beyond Subculture. Ph.D. thesis, Royal College of Art, London.

Bartollas, C. (2000). *Juvenile Delinquency* (5th ed.). Boston: Allyn and Bacon.

Bynum, J. E., & Thompson, W. E. (1996). *Juvenile Delinquency* (3rd ed.). Boston: Allyn and Bacon.

Clarke, J. (1976). Style. In S. Hall & T. Jefferson (eds.), *Resistance through Rituals* (pp. 175–191). London: Hutchinson.

Clarke, J., Hall, S., Jefferson, T., & Roberts, B. (1976). Subcultures, Cultures, and Class. In S. Hall & T. Jefferson (eds.), *Resistance through Rituals* (pp. 9–74). London: Hutchinson.

Davis, M. (1992). *City of Quartz.* New York: Vintage.

Delany, S. R. (1999). *Times Square Red, Times Square Blue.* New York: New York University Press.

Evans, W. (1960). Foreword: James Agee in 1936. In Agee, J., & Evans, W. *Let Us Now Praise Famous Men.* New York: Ballantine.

Ferrell, J. (2004 [1995]). Style Matters: Criminal Identity and Social Control. In J. Ferrell, K. Hayward, W. Morrison, & M. Presdee (eds.), *Cultural Criminology Unleashed.* London: Cavendish/Glasshouse.

———. (1996). *Crimes of Style: Urban Graffiti and the Politics of Criminality.* Boston: Northeastern University Press.

———. (1997). Criminological *Verstehen:* Inside the Immediacy of Crime. *Justice Quarterly, 14*(1), 3–23.

———. (1999). Cultural Criminology. *Annual Review of Sociology, 25*, 395–418.

———. (2002). *Tearing Down the Streets: Adventures in Urban Anarchy.* New York: Palgrave/Macmillan/St. Martin's.

———. (2003). Speed Kills. *Critical Criminology, 13*(4), 185–198.

Ferrell, J., Hayward, K., Morrison, W., & Presdee, M., eds. (2004). *Cultural Criminology Unleashed.* London: Cavendish/Glasshouse.

Ferrell, J., & Sanders, C. R., eds. (1995). *Cultural Criminology.* Boston: Northeastern University Press.

Feyerabend, P. (1975). *Against Method.* London: Verso.

Glaser, B. G., & Strauss, A. L. (1967). *The Discovery of Grounded Theory.* Chicago: Aldine.

Glassner, B. (1999). *The Culture of Fear.* New York: Basic Books.

Greek, C. (2003). Visual Criminology: Using Photography as a Research Tool in Criminal Justice Settings. Paper presented at the meetings of the Academy of Criminal Justice Sciences, Boston, MA.

Hall, S. (1993). What Is This "Black" in Black Popular Culture? *Social Justice, 20*(1–2), 104–114.

Hamm, M. S., & Ferrell, J. (1998). Confessions of Danger and Humanity. In J. Ferrell & M. S. Hamm (eds.), *Ethnography at the Edge* (pp. 254–272). Boston: Northeastern University Press.

Harper, D. A. (2001). *Changing Works: Visions of a Lost Agriculture.* Chicago: University of Chicago Press.

Hebdige, D. (1979). *Subculture: The Meaning of Style.* London: Methuen.

———. (1988). *Hiding in the Light.* London: Routledge.

Jefferson, T. (1976). Cultural Response of the Teds. In S. Hall & T. Jefferson (eds.), *Resistance through Rituals* (pp. 81–86). London: Hutchinson.

Jensen, G. F., & Rojak, D. G. (1992). *Delinquency and Youth Crime* (2nd ed.). Prospect Heights, IL: Waveland.

Kane, S. (1998). *AIDS Alibis: Sex, Drugs, and Crime in the Americas.* Philadelphia: Temple University Press.

Kerouac, J. (1955). *On the Road.* New York: Signet.

Kontos, L., Brotherton, D., & Barrios, L., eds. (2003). *Gangs and Society: Alternative Perspectives.* New York: Columbia University Press.

Lyng, S., & Bracey, M. L., Jr. (1995). Squaring the One Percent: Bike Style and the Selling of Cultural Resistance. In J. Ferrell & C. R. Sanders (eds.), *Cultural Criminology* (pp. 235–276). Boston: Northeastern University Press.

Marx, G. (1995). Electric Eye in the Sky. In J. Ferrell & C. R. Sanders (eds.), *Cultural Criminology* (pp. 106–141). Boston: Northeastern University Press.

Miller, D. W. (2001, February 9). Poking Holes in the Theory of "Broken Windows." *Chronicle of Higher Education, 47*(22), pp. A14–A16.

Miller, J. (1995). Struggles Over the Symbolic: Gang Style and the Meaning of Social Control. In J. Ferrell & C. R. Sanders (eds.), *Cultural Criminology* (pp. 213–234). Boston: Northeastern University Press.

Miller, R. (1997). *Magnum: Fifty Years at the Front Line of History.* New York: Grove Press.

Murdock, G., & McCron, R. (1976). Consciousness of Class and Consciousness of Generation. In S. Hall & T. Jefferson (eds.), *Resistance through Rituals* (pp. 192–207). London: Hutchinson.

Phillips, S. A. (1999). *Wallbangin': Graffiti and Gangs in L.A.* Chicago: University of Chicago Press.

Presdee, M. (2000). *Cultural Criminology and the Carnival of Crime.* London: Routledge.

Roche, J., Tucker, S., Thomson, R., & Flynn, R. (2004). *Youth in Society* (2nd ed.). London: Sage.

Rodriguez, J., Martinez, R., & Rodriguez, L. (1998). *East Side Stories: Gang Life in East LA.* New York: Powerhouse.

Rodriguez, R. T. (2003). On the Subject of Gang Photography. In L. Kontos, D. Brotherton, & L. Barrios (eds.), *Gangs and Society: Alternative Perspectives* (pp. 255–282). New York: Columbia University Press.

Sachs, H. (1987). *Music in Fascist Italy.* New York: W. W. Norton.

Sanchez-Tranquilino, M. (1995). Space, Power, and Youth Culture: Mexican American Graffiti and Chicano Murals in East Los Angeles, 1972–1978. In B. J. Bright & L. Bakewell (eds.), *Looking High and Low: Art and Cultural Identity* (pp. 55–88). Tucson: University of Arizona Press.

Shea, C. (2000). Don't Talk to the Humans: The Crackdown on Social Science Research. *Lingua Franca* (September), 27–34.

Taylor, I., Walton, P., & Young, J. (1973). *The New Criminology.* New York: Harper and Row.

Tunnell, K. D. (1995). A Cultural Approach to Crime and Punishment, Bluegrass Style. In J. Ferrell & C. R. Sanders (eds.), *Cultural Criminology* (pp. 80–105). Boston: Northeastern University Press.

Tyson, T. B. (1999). *Radio Free Dixie: Robert F. Williams and the Roots of Black Power.* Chapel Hill: University of North Carolina Press.

Vaneigem, R. (2001 [1967]). *The Revolution of Everyday Life.* London: Rebel Press.

Vergara, C. J. (1995). *The New American Ghetto.* New Brunswick, NJ: Rutgers University Press.

Wilson, J. Q., & Kelling, G. L. (2003 [1982]). Broken Windows: The Police and Neighborhood Safety. Reprinted in E. McLaughlin, J. Muncie, & G. Hughes (eds.), *Criminological Perspectives: Essential Readings* (2nd ed., pp. 400–411). London: Sage.

Young, J. (n.d.). Critical Criminology in the Twenty-first Century: Critique, Irony, and the Always Unfinished. At http://www.malcolmread.co.uk/JockYoung.

———. (2003). Merton with Energy, Katz with Structure: The Sociology of Vindictiveness and the Criminology of Transgression. *Theoretical Criminology,* 7(3), 389–414.

CONTRIBUTORS

BRUCE A. ARRIGO is a professor and former chair in the Department of Criminal Justice at the University of North Carolina–Charlotte, with additional faculty appointments in the psychology department, the Public Policy Program, and the Center for Applied and Professional Ethics. He has published extensively in the areas of social and criminological theory, sociolegal studies, criminal psychology, and problems in crime and social justice. His recent books include *Psychological Jurisprudence: Critical Explorations in Law, Crime, and Society* (2004); with Stacey L. Shipley, *The Female Homicide Offender: Serial Murder and the Case of Aileen Wuornos* (2004); with Christopher R. Williams, *Theory, Justice, and Social Change: Theoretical Integrations and Critical Applications* (2004); and with Dragan Milovanovic and Robert C. Schehr, *The French Connection in Criminology: Rediscovering Crime, Law, and Social Change* (2005). Arrigo is a past recipient of the Critical Criminologist of the Year Award (2000), sponsored by the Division of Critical Criminology of the

American Society of Criminology. He is also a Fellow of the American Psychological Association through the Law-Psychology Division of the APA and a fellow of the Academy of Criminal Justice Sciences. He is the founding and current editor for the book series *Critical Perspectives in Criminology* (University of Illinois Press) and *Criminal Justice and Psychology* (Carolina Academic Press).

MICHELLE BROWN is an assistant professor in the Department of Sociology and Anthropology at Ohio University. Her research interests include the study of media, punishment, risk, and cultural theory. She recently coedited and contributed to a volume entitled *Media Representations of September 11* (2003), an anthology that examines interdisciplinary interpretive approaches to media coverage of the 2001 terrorist attacks.

LYNN S. CHANCER is a professor in the Department of Sociology and Anthropology at Fordham University. She is the author of *Sadomasochism in Everyday Life* (1992), *Reconcilable Differences: Beauty, Pornography, and the Future of Feminism* (1998), and *High Profile Crimes: When Legal Cases Become Social Causes* (2005). She is also coeditor of *Theoretical Criminology: An International Journal.*

BRUCE DICRISTINA is a professor in the Department of Criminal Justice at the University of North Dakota. His research interests center on the philosophical foundations of criminological inquiry, the sociology of crime and punishment, and classical sociological theory. He is the author of *Methods in Criminology: A Philosophical Primer* (1995).

JEFF FERRELL is a professor of criminal justice at Texas Christian University. He is the author of *Crimes of Style: Urban Graffiti and the Politics of Criminality* (1996), *Tearing Down the Streets: Adventures in Urban Anarchy* (2001/2002), and *Wreckage and Reclamation: Studies in Cultural Criminology* (forthcoming), and lead coeditor of four books: *Cultural Criminology* (1995), *Ethnography at the Edge* (1998), *Making Trouble* (1999), and *Cultural Criminology Unleashed* (2004). He is the founding and current editor of the New York University Press Book Series *Alternative Criminology,* and one of the founding and current editors of the journal *Crime, Media, Culture: An International Journal.* In 1998 he received the Critical Criminologist of the Year Award from the American Society of Criminology.

JESSIE KLEIN is an assistant professor in the Department of Sociology and Social Work at Lehman College at the City University of New York. Klein is the author of several chapters on the role of masculinity in school shootings. She is presently working on a book called *Sexuality and School Violence*.

RONNIE LIPPENS is a reader in criminology at Keele University (U.K.). He has published work on theories of justice, social justice, dependency theory and Third World studies, organizational criminology, and the postmodern turn in critical criminology. More recently, however, his research interests focus on critical legal studies, particularly on legal semiotics and legal iconography, and on the role and place of the Imaginary in the production and reproduction of (visions of) law, peace, and justice. His publications on these topics include a collection he recently edited under the title *Imaginary Boundaries of Justice* (2004).

DRAGAN MILOVANOVIC is a professor of justice studies at Northeastern Illinois University. He has published extensively in the area of postmodern criminology, law, and social justice, particularly focusing on psychoanalytic semiotics, chaos theory, edgework, and catastrophe theory. His most recent books include *Critical Criminology at the Edge* (2003) and *An Introduction to the Sociology of Law* (2003).

CHRISTOPHER R. WILLIAMS is an associate professor of criminology at the University of West Georgia. He has published in the areas of critical social and criminological theory, the sociology of mental health and illness, and the philosophy of crime and deviance. His books include, with Bruce A. Arrigo, *Law, Psychology, and Justice: Chaos Theory and the New (Dis)Order* (2002) and *Theory, Justice, and Social Change: Theoretical Integrations and Critical Applications* (2004).

INDEX

Subjects and Phrases

Names

Critical Perspectives in Criminology

Philosophy, Crime, and Criminology   *Edited by Bruce A. Arrigo and Christopher R. Williams*
Private Prisons in America: A Critical Race Perspective
Michael A. Hallett

The University of Illinois Press
is a founding member of the
Association of American University Presses.

Composed in 9.5/13 Trump Mediaeval
with Meta display
by Celia Shapland
for the University of Illinois Press
Designed by Paula Newcombe
Manufactured by Sheridan Books, Inc.

University of Illinois Press
1325 South Oak Street
Champaign, IL 61820-6903
www.press.uillinois.edu